# The
# Phenomenology
# of
# Corruption

M. A. BRATU

To Anna

This page intentionally left blank

# Table of Contents

Preface ............................................................................................ 1

1. Corruption in Legal History ........................................................ 7

    *1.1. The laws of the Fertile Crescent* ........................................... 9

    *1.2. The unwritten laws of Ancient Greece* ................................ 12

    *1.3. The science of Roman Law* .................................................. 16

    *1.4. Laws in the Dark Ages* ......................................................... 27

    *1.5. The law of the Church in the Middle Ages* ......................... 32

    *1.6. Rediscovering law in Renaissance* ..................................... 42

    *1.7. The laws of the Revolutions* ................................................ 48

    *1.8. Conclusions* .......................................................................... 58

2. Ethics and morals - antitheses for corruption ............................ 62

    *2.1. The architects of philosophy* .............................................. 64

    *2.2. The philosophers of the Church* .......................................... 73

    *2.3. Philosophers for Revolutions* .............................................. 80

    *2.4. The German idealists* ........................................................... 90

    *2.5. The British enlighteners* ...................................................... 99

    *2.6. Currents of thought in modern philosophy* ...................... 108

    *2.7. Conclusions* ........................................................................ 113

3. Defining corruption ................................................................... 117

    *3.1. Definitions in use* .............................................................. 118

    *3.2. Criticism of the definitions in use* .................................... 122

    *3.3. Definition* ........................................................................... 126

    *3.4. Characteristics* ................................................................... 126

        3.4.1. Antisocial phenomenon ............................................. 127

        3.4.2. The illegal and the immoral character ....................... 129

        3.4.3. Corrupt acts and corrupt contracts ............................ 133

3.4.3. The purpose of corruption ................................................140

3.4.4. The material object of corruption ...................................143

*3.5. Active Subjects and Passive Subjects* .................................144

*3.6. Effects* .............................................................................147

*3.7. Criminal liability* .............................................................147

*3.8. Non-criminal Liability* .....................................................149

*3.10. Nullity* ...........................................................................155

*3.11. Prescription and limitation* ............................................158

*3.12. Conclusions* ...................................................................160

4. Crimes of corruption ............................................................163

*4.1. Elements of Criminal Law Theory* ...................................166

*4.2. Crimes of Corruption against the State* ............................168

4.2.1. Case study - Aldrich Hazen Ames............................173

4.2.2. Case study - Edward Snowden .................................174

*4.3. Crimes of Corruption against Propriety*............................175

4.3.1. Case study - Bernie Madoff .....................................186

4.3.2. Case study - Enric Duran.........................................188

*4.4. Crimes of Corruption against Persons* ..............................188

4.4.1. Case study - Giovani Falcone...................................196

4.4.2. Case study - Oscar Pistorius ....................................198

*4.5. Other Forms of Crimes of Corruption* ...............................198

4.5.1. The mythical white collar crimes .............................199

4.5.2. Crimes against the environment ...............................201

4.5.3. Crimes of corruption in sports..................................203

4.5.4. Political crimes........................................................206

4.5.5. Traffic in influence..................................................208

*4.6. Defenses for crimes of corruption*.....................................210

*4.7. Conclusions* ........................................................................................212

5. Contemporary issues ...........................................................................215

    *5.1. Quantifying corruption* ...............................................................216

    *5.2. Education* ....................................................................................221

    *5.3. Corruption in the justice system* .................................................224

    *5.4. Simplify the law* ..........................................................................227

Final Conclusions .....................................................................................230

Bibliography .............................................................................................234

    *Books* ....................................................................................................234

    *Dictionaries* .........................................................................................241

    *Web Resources* .....................................................................................242

TABLE OF STATUTES ...........................................................................243

TABLE OF CASES ..................................................................................247

Abbreviations ...........................................................................................247

Index .........................................................................................................248

# Preface

The phenomenon we generally name 'corruption' became a subject of interest for the general public only in the last decade. After the end of the Cold War, with the threat of the global annihilation removed, the 90's were supposed to be a period of quiet, of dialogue and cooperation between the former communist block and the western powers. When Russia abandoned the communist doctrine and the Iron Curtin felled, it seemed that the world was entering in an age of peace and prosperity.

The Gulf War, the genocide in Rwanda, the Yugoslav Wars, are just a few human tragedies from a long list of conflicts that left tens of millions death. When we look at the history of these wars, we can clearly see that all of them could have been avoided.

The nations of the world were willing to abandon the walls, the barb wire, the minefields, and all the other artificial borders we've placed between us. But some leaders were unwilling to lose their privileges or to share the power with others in a democratic system. A doctrine of hate fueled the fires of war and otherwise normal individuals executed atrocities beyond imagination.

Somehow, we learned to hate the dictators of the world as the source of all evils, but we failed to understand a simple fact: a dictator is just a person. Behind any dictator there is a corrupt mechanism of state administrators and high ranking military officers who are enjoying undeserved benefits in exchange of their loyalty to the dictator and to the system. A dictator is just a poster boy for the corrupt system; a single person, no matter how vicious, cannot cause the death of millions. The true killer is the corrupt system behind the dictator.

Is corruption a generator of wars, perhaps the sole generator? I believe it is.

The end of the Cold War opened trading relations between the West and the former Communist Block; world became a large market, and, with few exceptions, any company was able to do businesses anywhere in the world. But the trade was unbalanced: if the West had the superior technology, the underdeveloped countries did not have much to offer, except raw natural resources.

It was not long before those natural resources begun to be exploited in a savage way, with little concern for the environment. Some of the industries were moved in underdeveloped countries which had laxer legislation on environmental issues. Industrial practices that were strictly banned in the Western world were 'exported' in other corners of the world, giving a false sense of security to the developed society.

It was a major mistake. Underdeveloped countries lacked the infrastructure necessary to deal with environmental issues, and in most cases they lack the will to address those issues since their economy is depending on the exploitation of natural resources. Industrial pollution, on the other hand, has global effects and the bill is paid by all of us; exporting the polluting industries instead of improving the manufacturing processes proved to be a bad business for the industrialized world.

Are we entitled to ask if corruption is to blame for the current state of the environment? I believe we are, and the answer is yes.

This line of reasoning may apply not only to war or to crimes against environment, but also to terrorism, drug trafficking, famine, epidemics, modern forms of slavery and all the other antisocial phenomena that are affecting our society. When we wonder why these phenomena endure, the answer is that somewhere, someone is making a profit out of them.

Corruption was taken seriously only in the last decade, when its horrible effects were beginning to show at a global level. The United Nations Convention against Corruption was adopted by the United Nations General Assembly on 31 October 2003 by Resolution 58/4. The importance of this document is undeniable; it is truly a declaration of war against corruption on several fronts.

Reading the text of the convention, one cannot help to notice that the phenomenon in question, corruption, is not defined. A search in academic books, dictionaries, encyclopedias, reveal the same problem, the absence of a clear definition for corruption. The definitions in use cover a part of the phenomenon, bribery, but unfortunately corruption is much more than that.

The first purpose of this book is to propose a clear definition for corruption. In order to understand a phenomenon, one must define the phenomenon. A clear definition is essential in the analysis of corruption, especially its causes and effects. Without a definition and a thorough analysis, the fight against corruption will fail to achieve its purpose, the eradication of corruption.

Writing a definition for corruption proved to be the easiest part of this book. The hardest effort was to reveal those facets of the phenomenon that are often neglected or misunderstood. And this is my second purpose, but perhaps the more important one. Understanding the phenomenon in question is the key to conceive and implement effective methods of eradication, which is or it should be the final objective of the fight against corruption.

In the first chapter we shall explore the history of the phenomenon. We know that corruption is old therefore we should start our search at the beginning of the human civilization.

Laws were the most important written texts in any civilization, and we are fortunate that some of them survived. The laws of a society are the most objective indicator on the phenomenon of corruption. This is why the focus will be placed on laws and not necessarily on historic accounts of the facts and acts of corruption of the past.

By examining the laws of a society we can understand those human behaviors that were considered corruption and how they were incriminated. The first positive laws emerged in the Fertile Crescent, so from there we shall start our journey in the history of the laws against corruption.

The Greek civilization secularized the laws and developed a new social model, the democracy. With the Romans, law became a science and was constantly developed until the end of the imperial period. In the Dark Ages, the law was simplified in the newly formed kingdoms, which did not have the complex state administration the Romans had.

In parallel, the Church developed its own legal system based on a moral code extracted from the Scriptures, and enforced it in ecclesiastical tribunals. Throughout the Middle Ages, the Church played a key role in the administration of the State, and had an enormous influence on the secular justice system. The role of the Church gradually diminished while the strength of the State grew, the balance of power being permanently tilted in favor of the former after the French Revolution. With an account on the Napoleonic Codes and the codification of the European law, we shall end our journey in the history of corruption.

The second chapter is dedicated to philosophy, especially morals and ethics. Here, the reader will find the relation between law, corruption and the principles of moral and ethical living. We shall recount the opinions of the most influential philosophers on corruption and its antitheses, morality and ethics.

Philosophy also influenced the laws; therefore, the second chapter comes to complete the knowledge on the phenomenon of corruption presented in the first part. Starting with the founders of philosophy, Plato and Aristotle we shall turn our attention to the philosophers of the Church, St. Augustine and St. Tomas Aquinas and the concept of sin.

The laws enacted in the revolutionary period in U.S. and France, were based on the philosophical writings of Montesquieu and Rousseau; the German legal doctrine was under the influence of Kant and Hegel. Last, the enlightenment movement is represented here by Hume and Bentham.

The chapter will end in the modern period; we shall see the modern tendencies in philosophy and we shall enter in the discussion regarding a science of ethics and morals.

Armed with the knowledge acquired in the first chapters, in the third the reader will find a new definition for corruption, one which I consider to be comprehensive and accurate.

A clear definition opens the possibility for a legal analysis of the phenomenon. But this is not a facile exercise. The laws of each country today, with few exceptions, belong to one of the two major families of legal systems, the common law or the continental law. Some key elements needed for a legal analysis are treated differently not only by the two major legal families, but even by the doctrines from the same family.

For this reason I used the laws and doctrines of four legal systems: France and Germany for the continental law family and United Kingdom and United States of America for the common law family. Thus, at least in theory, the analysis of corruption should be understandable for any reader, regardless of the legal system in which he belongs.

The forth chapter is dedicated to criminal law. The provisions of the UNCAC recommends for the member states to incriminate acts of corruptions and to address the consequences of those acts as the consequences of a criminal activity.

In this chapter we shall see that many offences that we incriminate today are also crimes of corruption and that from a criminal perspective, the phenomenon is far more complex than previously thought. Crimes that intuitively we consider to have nothing to do with corruption are

4

actually committed to obtain a profit, thus making them 'crimes of corruption'.

The last chapter is a chapter of final conclusions and reflections. Here I do not intend to reiterate what has been said before. In this chapter we shall see the issues that need to be addressed in order to make the fight against corruption more effective. I consider that there are two major problems with the way corruption is treated today.

First, there is the problem of quantifying corruption. The question 'How corrupt are we?' finds it's answer in a series of rankings elaborated by NGOs or international bodies using the methodologies developed by sociology. But corruption is an elusive phenomenon; with the help of sociologic methods we are able to quantify only a fraction of the phenomenon. Today, we simply do not know what the real dimension of corruption is.

The second major problem that needs to be addressed is education. Although is the most effective weapon against corruption, education is the most neglected. Our education on the laws is highly deficient. Our children are able make complex calculations and yet they know very little about their rights and duties as citizens.

A person aware about his rights and obligations is less likely to succumb to corruption than an ignorant on the subject. Another area where education might be helpful is the business environment; if any entrepreneur will understand how much money corruption, as a global phenomenon, is costing him, I doubt that anyone will ever be willing to pay a bribe again. Also, the general public must be educated to reject corruption and corrupt persons; here the role of the civil society is determinant in creating a culture for transparency, honesty and fairness.

In the last chapter we shall examine the justice system and the laws and see if there are any improvements that may be made in order to make them more effective in the fight against corruption.

This page intentionally left blank

*Study history, study history.*
*In history lies all the secrets of statecraft.*

Sir Winston Churchill

# 1. Corruption in Legal History

One of the most significant events in human history is the agricultural revolution that happened in the Neolithic period in several areas of the world. The small groups of hunter-gatherers discovered in areas like the Nile Delta, the Yangtze Delta and the Yellow River basin, or in the Highlands of New Guinea and Central Mexico, an abundance of food resources and a suitable climate that allowed for the development of permanent settlements.

Turning from nomadic to sedentary, these ancestors had domesticated cereals, legumes, fruits and animals thru an artificial process of selection that favored the desired characteristics in a timeline of several thousand years.

The archeological evidence of the earliest permanent settlements were discovered in the area between the rivers Nile, Tiger and Euphrates, an area referred to as the 'Fertile Crescent', and they are dated around 10,000 - 9,000 BP; continuous habitations over generations had allowed for some of this early settlements to develop in the first city-states.

Any form of organization, no matter how primitive, is based on a set of rules, of laws. Rule is proper to organization by definition. The mere presence of those early settlements implies the existence of a set of rules or customs that allowed the organization to function; caring for the young and the elders, some form of equality in the sharing food and other resources, helping other members, must have been common behavior in any incipient civilization.

Laws, in the proper sense of the term, emerged only after the society achieved a certain degree of development characterized by a language, writing and a common administration of resources.

A special category is formed by the unwritten laws. They are laws in the proper sense, but they differ from customs because they are not recorded in writing. Lycurgus, for instance, chose not to write down his

7

laws, believing that they will be better remembered and obeyed if young men would learn them by heart.

From the laws of a specific historical period, by analyzing the incrimination and the severity the sanctions, we can form a view on the levels of corruption and how this phenomenon affected the society. Drastic sanctions reveal a situation when the organization loses control on its members and becomes anarchic. Moderate laws show a successful and prosperous society where the social order is kept with little efforts.

Corruption is a phenomenon that goes against the social order, which is established and kept by laws. Among the members of the society there are always individuals deluded that they deserve a better life, a higher social status, a more pleasant existence and, since they are unable to achieve their desires within the legal frame, they are willing to take chances and acquire the wealth that can materialize their desires by dishonest means.

When we analyze those ancient civilizations, almost inevitably, we will compare them with today's standard of morality. We must keep in mind the fact that what we might consider today corrupt, immoral, illegal, in a certain point in time was legit and moral. From this perspective it may be hard to identify corruption, however, as a rule, we may consider as corruption only those conducts that posed a threat to the social order of the society we are analyzing.

A thorough historic account on every deed of corruption that transcended to us from the past would most certainly fill a library. Our purpose here is to examine the forms in which corruption manifested itself in history and how it was incriminated in different historical periods and in different forms of social organizations.

The phenomenon of corruption was recorded in clay tablets, in papyri, in stone and in parchments and it has been captured in the works of every classical author. From city-states to empires, every form of social organization have made attempts to fight it, yet, not a single legal system or organization in history was able to eradicate it.

In the following subchapters we will follow the phenomenon of corruption in time and space with the help of the laws used to oppose it. Societies, no matter how primitive, understood the danger that corruption posed to the rule of law and the social order. In this chapter we will follow mainly those laws that incriminate corruption, leaving aside those aspects that are concerning the civil laws.

The position of corruption in relation with the criminal phenomenon will be revealed and fully explained in chapter four. Some of the laws presented in the following chapter will regard criminal acts that normally are not associated with corruption, such as murder, rape or religious offences. Nevertheless, a connection between the phenomenon of corruption and any form of criminality exists, even though from a historic perspective it may be difficult to understand for now.

## 1.1. The laws of the Fertile Crescent

The primitive human settlements, after the agricultural revolution which meant a transition between pastoral lifestyle to a sedentary life, grew in size and, generation after generation, evolved in the first city-states. The oldest permanent settlements discovered until now are located in the Fertile Crescent, in the area between the rivers Tigris and Euphrates. Uruk was founded ca. 5000 BC and became the most important city of Ancient Mesopotamia. Other communities followed the model and Ur, Eridu, Lagash, Kish raised to the rank of city-state.[1]

The Sumerians are famous for inventing the wheel, architecture, mathematics and astronomy, but they were also the first who invented a state administration, a legal system and religion. Perhaps their greatest invention was writing; they developed a method to record information in clay, using simple symbols in the beginning, which developed later in the cuneiform alphabet. A staggering amount of these records was discovered until today, many of them still remain to be studied.

From the city-state of Lagash, we have the oldest code of laws, the code of Urukagina, a set of administrative laws to combat corruption, dated around 2350 BC. The original document did not survived, but some of the measures are detailed in a poem, *Praise of Urukagina*. Upon acceding to power, Urukagina removed several key officials from the state administration such as the head boatman, the livestock official, the fishery inspector, a couple of treasurers and other administrators. The document does not provide any elements in regard the actual guilt of the officials removed from power; it is possible that Urukagina removed key figures from State administration in order to strengthen his power. In any case, the most important aspect is that the ancient Sumerians were

---

[1] See Norman Yoffee, *Myths of the Archaic State* (Cambridge: Cambridge University Press, 2004), pg.54

familiar to corruption, they understood the phenomenon and they took legal measures against it.

The first sentence in the poem declaims:

> *"Since time immemorial, since life began, in those days, the head boatman appropriated boats, the livestock official appropriated asses, the livestock official appropriated sheep, and the fisheries inspector appropriated ..."*[2]

This sentence is interesting for us because it pushes the genesis of the phenomenon of corruption to *"...time immemorial, since life begun..."*

The fact that the oldest 'code of laws' discovered until now is related to the phenomenon of corruption is just a coincidence and it is not 'the oldest code', in fact Urukagina was reforming an existing system.

Another document worthy to be mentioned is the Code of Ur-Nammu,[3] king of Ur, ca. 2050 BC, which prescribes capital punishment for murder, robbery, adultery and rape, ordeal by water for sorcery, and fines for injuries, false accusations and perjury.

The most important legal document from that era is, no doubt, the Code of Hammurabi ca.1754 BC. Its object was to regulate the main aspects of daily life with laws regarding family, slavery, trade and crafts, and the function of the State. Hammurabi did not create a new legal system;[4] the principles of Hammurabi's laws are to be found in earlier contracts and in Sumerian laws.

The punishments for crimes are more severe in Hammurabi's code, compared with those in the laws of his predecessors; false accusations were punished by death, the eye for an eye principle requires the same damage to be done to the offender in cases involving bodily harm, the right of propriety is better protected.

Capital punishment was given for kidnaping, aiding a fugitive slave, looting, robbery, sheltering rebels, faulty constructions that caused the death of the owner, stealing from a temple or palace, adultery, perjury in murder trials and false accusations of murder. Fraud is punished with less severity, as well as breaches of contracts and the penalty involves the paying of the damage several fold.

---

[2] See the Jerrold S. Cooper's translation on www.humanistic texts.org/sumer.htm#Sources, accessed on 15 September 2014

[3] Martha T. Roth, *Law Collections from Mesopotamia and Asia Minor*, 2nd ed., (Georgia: Society of Biblical Literature Scholars Press, 1997), pg. 15

[4] C. H. W. Johns *Babylonian and Assyrian Laws, Contracts and Letters* (New York: Charles Scribner's Sons, 1904), pg.50

A judge guilty of errors in his verdict was supposed to pay twelve times the fine set by him in the case, to be removed from the judge's bench, and banned for life to render judgments.

From one of the letters of Hammurabi, we have a clear account on a case of bribery. He instructs Sin-iddinam to bring to him the perpetrators, *"...the money, or what was given as a bribe..."*, and the witnesses. It is notable that the king insures the integrity of the evidence, asking Sin-iddinam to *"...seal it up"*.[5]

Hammurabi's Code exerted a significant influence; Hebrew law is inspired by the Laws of Hammurabi[6] and common elements are to be found in Assyrian, Babylonian and later Persian laws. The legislators of Ancient Greece were probably influenced by Semitic laws through the trading contacts with the Phoenicians and the Persians, and Greek laws were a source of inspiration for Roman law. The circle was closed when Rome became Christian, thus making the Code of Hammurabi the ancestor of modern legal systems.

Another interesting document from Akkadia is *Warning to Monarch*[7], written on a tablet made of clay probably in the 7th century BC, that was discovered George Smith in 1873, in Iraq. The document is a form of complaint against an abusive king towards the citizens of Sippar, Nippur, and Babylon.

The anonymous writer, probably a citizen of Sippar, makes an appeal for justice to the entire pantheon of deities as supreme judges and executioners. Thus, if the king is unjust, Ea, King of Destinies, will change his fortune for worst; if he accepts bribes, Enil, Lord of the Lands will cause the destruction of his armies; if he imposes constricted labor, Marduk, Lord of Heaven and Earth, will give his lands to the enemy and so on.

The religious element is omnipresent in the laws of the Fertile Crescent. Not only in Mesopotamia but also in Egypt, the ruler claimed to be divine, a descendent from gods. The laws enacted have the consecration of the gods and therefor there are righteous, which leads to the presumption that the laws were the creation of the priesthood class. The religious elements may be found also in other documents that survived, poems, hymns, contracts and letters, documents that are not

---

[5] Ibid., pg. 326, 330
[6] David P. Wright, *Inventing God's Law* (Oxford: Oxford University Press, 2009), pg.3
[7] See the text on www.kchanson.com/ANCDOCS/meso/warning.html, accessed on 18 September 2014

fundamentally religious, yet their authors sought the power of the gods as a stamp of approval.

## 1.2. The unwritten laws of Ancient Greece

There is no greater source of frustration for the modern researcher then the issue of the ancient Greek laws. There are no primary sources on ancient Greek laws, even the Code of the city of Gortyn, Crete, often makes references to other laws with the formula "...*as is written*"[8], and the secondary sources available are not the work of jurists, but of historians like Herodotus and Plutarch or philosophers like Plato and Aristotle. Until a major archeological discovery will reveal an illuminating document, the ancient Greek laws will be a subject-matter for interpretations, disputes and contradictions.

Standing in awe in front of the monuments of Ancients Greece, we might be tempted to create a false image, an image of a perfect society, of philosophers and poets, endlessly debating moral principles. In fact ancient Greece was a violent, ruthless and utterly corrupt. Violence, social inequity, corruption, wars and injustice were the causes that spawned philosophers like Socrates, Plato, and Aristotle.

The legal systems that were developed in those times were developed out of a need, and that is to assure the survival of the society. The principle of vengeance, common among primitive societies, causes a spiral of violence that puts the entire community at risk. For this reason, ancient Greek legislators paid a special attention to murder, out the necessity to protect the community.

One aspect that is important to be mentioned is that religion played a secondary role in the construction of the Greek legal and ethical systems. The Greek Gods were not a role model for honesty or chastity, in fact they exhibited every vice known to humans.

Corruption affected the Gods of the ancient Greeks, myths and legends about murder, betrayal, rape, theft, blackmail are undisputable evidence that the phenomenon was quite common in Olympus. Thus, morals and ethics became a subject matter of interest for philosophy; Socrates was accused of not believing in the gods of the State, the works

---

[8] Michael Gagarin, *Writing Greek law*, (Cambridge: Cambridge University Press, 2008), pg. 146

of Aristotle or Plato are laic in character and Epicurus claimed that nothing should be believed without observation.

We don't see any evidence of laws enacted in the name of Zeus or Athena, none of the legislators claimed to be 'ordered' by Gods to enact such laws and nowhere can be seen any religious reverence in the justice system. This constitutes a significant advancement for legal sciences compared to the Babylonian or Egyptian justice systems where the Gods played an important role, 'endorsing' the King's decisions.

Draco, ca. 7th century BC, was an enigmatic figure even for the ancient historians; very little is known about him. Aristotle states very clearly that Draco did not invented a new constitutional system and the laws he wrote were adapted "*...to a constitution which already existed*";[9] Draco's ordinances resembles more to a Criminal or Penal Code. They remained famous for their "*...severity of the punishments*"[10] but it must be a certain degree of exaggeration, elsewhere Aristotle writes that" *...his laws were those not of a human being but of a dragon, so savage were they*".[11]

Before Draco, justice was based on the principles of self-help and vengeance,[12] which were inspired from the deeds of mythological heroes like Odysseus and Orestes or form stories about the gods. Draco's innovation was the introduction of a court of juries to settle disputes thus making the justice system accessible to ordinary men. Draco's laws instituted the death penalty for most offences; among those were probably rape, adultery, fraud, bribery, kidnaping or extortion, acts that were considered disorderly.[13]

The laws of Draco were effective only for a brief period; 60 years later they were abolished by Solon's reforms, except the prescriptions regarding murder. Another important innovation was the distinction between unintentional homicide and premeditated homicide,[14] the first form being subject to an eventual settlement between the killer and the kin of the victim, while the second form was most certainly punished by death.

---

[9] Aristotle, *Politics*, Book II 1274b15-1274b17
[10] Ibid.
[11] Aristotle, *Rhetoric*, Book III1400b17-1400b25
[12] See Edwin Carawan, *Rhetoric and the Law of Draco*, (Oxford: Clarendon Press, 1998), pg. 3
[13] The 'Gortyn Code', ca. 5th century BC from the city of Gortyn, Crete; the most complete source on the laws of that era, attests that these types of crimes were known and they were sanctioned with fines
[14] Carawan, *Rhetoric and the Law of Draco*, pg. 34

In ancient Greece, there was a social model that made a discordant note. Laconia, with the city of Sparta as capital, was transformed by Lycurgus, ca. 820 - 730 BC, in a militarized society. The story of Lycurgus was subject of controversies among the ancient historians; Herodotus and Plutarch are giving different accounts especially of his origin and early life. Regrettably, he chose not to write his laws, believing that laws should be imprinted in the hearts of the youth by good discipline.[15]

Lycurgus's reforms are probably the most effective anticorruption measures in history. He established a council of twenty-eight elders that had *"...the same authority in making important decisions as the kings"*[16], and by creating the office of the Elders and that of the Ephors *"...law became the lord and king of men, not men tyrants over the laws"*[17]. Plutarch recounts:

> *"Great inequalities existed, many poor and needy people had become a burden to the state, while wealth had got into a very few hands. Lycurgus abolished all the mass of pride, envy, crime, and luxury which flowed from those old and more terrible evils of riches and poverty, by inducing all land-owners to offer their estates for redistribution, and prevailing upon them to live on equal terms one with another, and with equal incomes, striving only to surpass each other in courage and virtue, there being henceforth no social inequalities among them except such as praise or blame can create."*[18]

Another act worthy to remember is his financial reform; he confiscated all the gold and silver coins and replaced them with coins made from worthless iron, thus eliminating also any form of luxury because trade stopped, itinerary artisans, poets, philosophers, craftsmen begun to avoid Laconia in their routes.[19] Aristotle points out that his reforms came short in one area: when he *"...wanted to bring the women under his laws, they resisted, and he gave up the attempt"*.[20]

Solon, ca. 638-558 BC, was an Athenian statesman, lawgiver, poet and philosopher. Plato describes him as *"...the wisest man in general ... and the most civilized of all the poets."*[21] Aristotle writes that Solon enacted laws *"...prohibiting an individual from possessing as much land*

---

[15] Plutarch, *Plutarch's Lives. The Translation called Dryden's*, A.H. Clough, ed. (Boston: Little Brown and Co., 1906), Lycurgus, XII
[16] Plato *Laws* III 692a
[17] Plato *Letter* VIII 354c
[18] Plutarch, *Lives*, Lycurgus, VIII
[19] Ibid.
[20] Aristotle *Politics* Book II,1269b13-1270a14
[21] Plato, *Timaeus* 21b

*as he pleased"*[22] and ended *"...the exclusiveness of the oligarchy, emancipated the people, established the ancient Athenian democracy, and harmonized the different elements of the state."*[23]

Before Solon, the law stated that a debt was guaranteed with the debtor's person who was sold or kept as a slave if he could not pay his debt, probably one of Draco's ordinances, by deductive reasoning. This led to a situation when the entire population was in debt to few; therefore Solon, perceived as impartial by both parties, was chosen to reconcile the upper class with the popular party.

In 594 BC Solon was appointed Archon and mediator and one of his first steps was the cancelation of all debts, a measure named *Seisachtheia*; apparently some of his friends got the news and they were able to profit by selling their claims and borrowing money. Solon was accused of being a part on this scheme; however, Aristotle seems to doubt that Solon was part of it, he wrote *"... is not likely to have consented to defile his hands by such a petty and palpable fraud."*[24]

Under Solon, Draco's laws became obsolete, except those regarding murder. He took measures to assure equitable representation for each tribe in public offices. People indifference towards important disputes was sanctioned with the loss of citizenship.[25]

Aristotle considers that there were three points which made Solon's Constitution the most democratic: the prohibition of loans guaranteed with the debtor's person, the right of every person to claim redress on behalf of any one to whom wrong was being done and the appeal to the jury-courts.[26]

The laws of Solon had been obliterated by disuse during the period of the tyranny, while Cleisthenes enacted new ones with the object of securing the goodwill of the masses.[27] The Athenian Constitution was subject to several drastic changes, eleven, according to Aristotle, which transformed the Athenian political system from democracy to tyranny to oligarchy and back to democracy. Over the years, new institutions were introduced and old ones were modified both in terms of people and their attributions.

---

[22] Aristotle, *Politics* Book II 1266b5-1267a1
[23] Ibid., 1273b28-1274a22
[24] Aristotle, *The Athenian Constitution*, §6
[25] Ibid., §2, §6, §7, §8
[26] Ibid., § 9
[27] Ibid., §22

Greek power, after three centuries of wars, finally and inevitably diminished while the power of Rome in the West grew constantly, following the Punic Wars. At the end of the 4th Macedonian war, in 148 BC, Greece was under total Roman control. Although the Romans were not very impressed by the civilizations they conquered (Carthage was raised to the ground), they held the Greek civilization in high esteem. The law of the Twelve Tables was modeled after the laws of Solon, and perhaps other elements of Greek law survived in the laws of the Roman Republic.

## 1.3. The science of Roman Law

When we are trying to build a historic perspective on the subject of corruption, a special attention must be paid to ancient Rome for at least two reasons. First, Roman Law is embedded in the genetic code of any modern legal system. The Roman society achieved the highest degree of sophistication in the Ancient World, comparable only to the modern society. The legal relations that the Romans created are the precursors of modern legal relations; various legal institutions of modern law, such as contracts and obligations, successions and inheritance, propriety and possession, are modeled after the Roman law.

Second, endemic corruption played a key role in the crisis of the Roman Republic and was a cause of constant decline in the imperial period, leading to the disaggregation of both the western and the eastern empires.

In search for the causes for the fall of the Roman Empire, scholars have been focused on military and economic aspects and on external factors, while the internal phenomenon of corruption as a cause for the downfall has been largely neglected.

The elaborate legal system that the Romans developed was not enough to prevent the collapse of an advanced civilization when corruption infected its institutions. Moreover, the collapse happened twice in Rome's history with the end of the Republic in 29 BC and with the fall of the Western Empire in the 6th century.

The legal analysis of Roman laws may resemble sometimes with a game of puzzle played without a board and with a set of incomplete and broken pieces. Virtually any subject of Roman law was a disputed by the ancient jurists and has been a matter of dispute among scholars ever since. My purpose here is to present the laws used by the Romans in their struggle with corruption and not to end debates or to create new ones among Romanists.

For centuries tradition held that Rome was founded in 21 April 753 BC by Romulus, 771-717 BC, who killed his twin brother Remus in a quarrel about the best place to build a new city, a tradition which was contradicted by the archeological documents.

Evidence for permanent habitations in the area can be traced back to 1000 BC. With details still a matter for dispute, we know for certain that at the time Rome was founded there were three tribes living in the area, the Latins, the Sabins and the Etruscans, a much older civilization than the former two.

Undoubtedly, the most important legal document in early Rome is the Law of the Twelve Tables (*Leges Duodecim Tabularum* or *Duodecim Tabulae*)[28] from 450 BC, a document which lay at the foundation of Roman Law. The law came into being as a consequence of the conflict between the wealthy minority, the patricians who gave the college of pontiffs, and the plebeians, who demanded written laws to avoid bias interpretations.

In 451 BC a commission of ten citizens, the decemvires, was formed and was mandated to create a legal document, similar with the Athenian Constitution. A second group wrote a set of additional two tables in 449 BC, and they were engraved in bronze to be displayed publicly. The original document did not survived; it was probably destroyed in 387 BC when the Gauls burned Rome; references to the document had survived in the works of the ancient jurists creating a foundation for modern reconstructions.

The first three tables are concerned with rules of procedures, the next two with matters of family law and tables six and seven with ownership, possession and propriety.

Table VIII is dedicated to Criminal Law and Table IX to Public Law, both of great interest to us. Offences mentioned in Table VIII are: evil incantations, articles 1 a, b and 8 b; offences against a person's integrity,

---

[28] The Latin text used in this analysis can be found in Carolus Georgius Bruns, Theodor Mommsen, Otto Gradenwitz, *Fontes Iuris Romani Antiqui,* (Tübingen, Friburgi in Brisgavia : In Libraria Academia I.C.B. Mohrii (P. Siebeck), 1909), pg. 17 – 40

articles 2-5; damages caused by animals, articles 6, 7, 9; arson, article 10; several forms of theft, articles 10-16.

Usury is considered any interest on the loan above one twelfth and it is associated with theft under article18 a, b. A patron who cheats his client will be cursed, article 21.

Article 27 states that associations can make their own laws as long they do not corrupt (*corrumpant*) the public law; Gaius notes that this provision is taken from the laws of Solon. We do not know to what extent the Latin text wrote by Gaius resembles the original but it is important to be mentioned because it uses the term *corrumpant* which was considered to be introduced for the first time by Cicero. If not the term itself, at least the concept behind it seems to go back to the very beginning of the Roman Law, four centuries before Cicero.

In Table IX article 3 it is stated that a judge or an arbiter who received bribe for a decision is punished with the death penalty. Another important principle, in article 6, declares that no one can be put to death without a conviction in a trial.

A law against bribery was proposed in 358 BC by the tribune Gaius Poetelius aiming to put an end to corrupt practices "...*of the men recently risen from the people...*",[29] known as *Lex Poetelia De Ambitu.*

Land was a very important source of income in Roman society therefore the Roman legislators passed a long list of acts stretching from the beginning of Rome to the end of the Byzantine Empire, concerning lands, propriety, possession or transfer of rights. In 367 BC the tribunes Licinius Stolo and L. Sextius proposed *Lex Licinia de Modo Agrorum* which stated that no one may possess more than 500 *jugera* of land, under a penalty of 10.000 *assess*.

One of its authors, Licinius Stolo, attempted to circumvent it by emancipating his son and transferring him 500 *jugera* of land; he was found guilty and fined. The law was effective only for a brief period, and was never imposed with full force. Moreover, *Lex Thoria Agraria* of 107 B.C. lifted the limit on possessions of lands prescribed in *Lex Licinia*; the tribunes who attempted to modify *Lex Thoria*'s effects were assassinated.[30]

---

[29] See Livy *Rome and Italy Books VI–X of The History of Rome from its Foundation,* tr. Betty Radice, (London: Penguin Books, 1982), VII.15
[30] See Ortolan, *The history of Roman law,* tr. Iltudus T. Prichard, David Nasmit (London: Butterworths, 1871), pg. 228-230

In 342 BC, the plebeian tribune Lucius Genucius passed two plebiscites known as the *Leges Genuciae* or *Lex Genucia de Feneratione* which stipulated that *"...no one should hold the same office twice within ten years, nor two offices in one year, and that it should be permissible to elect both consuls from the plebeians."*[31]

Electoral corruption (*ambitus*) was punished by several laws such as *Lex Aemilia Balbia* 182 BC, *Lex Cornelia Baebia* 181 BC, *Lex Cornelia Fulvia* 159 BC and *Lex Maria* 119 BC.

In 149 BC Lucius Calpurnius Piso Frugi (Censorinus) introduced the *Lex Calpurnia*, which establishes a court dedicated to cases of extortions performed by Roman governors.[32] It is a significant moment, because it marks the birth of the concept of assigning the judgment of certain crimes, such as high treason (*crimen maiestatis*), electoral corruption (*ambitus*) and embezzlement of public money (*peculatus*)[33], to specialized courts (*quaestio repetundarum*).[34]

*Lex Gabinia Tabellaria* 139 BC, *Lex Cassia Tabellaria* 137 BC, *Lex Papiria Tabellaria* 131 BC, *Lex Caelia Tabellaria* 107 BC were concerned with the secrecy of the vote in the election of magistrates, the trials before people, the votes approving and disapproving legislation and the vote on treason trials.

Another landmark document, preserved on eleven fragments of a bronze table, the *Tabula Bembina*, is the Acilian Law, 123-122 BC,[35] of tribune Manius Acilius concerning extortions and abuses in Roman provinces.

When Marcus Tullius Cicero, 3 January 106 BC - 7 December 43 BC, became famous, Rome was an utterly corrupt society; in fact Cicero's fulminant ascent was due to his success as a defense lawyer for Sextus Roscius against Chrysogonus in 80 BC, one of Sulla's favorites, in a murder affair and as a prosecutor of Gaius Verres, former governor of Sicily between 73 to 71 BC, accused of abuse of judicial power, extortion, robbery and embezzlement.

In the case against Verres, Cicero prepared two outstanding orations, the first, known as *"in Verrem I"* presented in the first part of the trial

---

[31] Livy, *Rome and Italy*, VII, 42
[32] See George Mousourakis *A legal history of Rome*, (2007 New York: Routledge), pg77
[33] Ibid., pg. 78
[34] Ortolan, *The history of Roman law*, pg. 236
[35] M. H. Crawford, *Roman Statutes*, (London: Institute Of Classical Studies, School Of Advanced Study, University Of London, 1996).

(*actio prima*) in 70 BC, and the second, "*in Verrem 2*", which was never presented but later published, following Verres's run into exile, after the devastating first speech.[36]

In 74 BC the Senate issued a decree, *De Corruptione Iudicis*, addressing the corruption in the judicial system; Cicero mentions it in the speech in defense of Aulus Cluentius Avitus, "*Oh, but the whole senate judged that that tribunal had been bribed.*" [37]

In 67 BC, the tribune Aulus Gabinius proposed several drastic laws against abuse of powers and corruption, so the Senate, in opposition to such measures, asked the consuls Gaius Calpurnius Piso and Marcus Acilius Glabrio to conceive a milder form of the laws; *Lex Acilia Calpurnia* demanded the exclusion from office in cases of bribery.

*Lex Tullia de Ambitu*, 63 BC, forbade for the candidates to bribe the voters with "*...gladiatorial show except in execution of a will and on a date fixed beforehand.*"[38] The *Rogatio Aufidia de Ambitu*, 61 BC, of tribune Marcus Aufidius Lurco imposed a fine of 3000 *sesterces* for candidates who bribed members of the Tribal Assembly. *Lex Pompeia de Ambitu*, 52 BC, made some changes in the components of the courts.

This avalanche of laws at the end of the Republic might be seen as an effort to combat corruption, a view that will be inaccurate. In fact, the law became a weapon used by rival factions against each other, enacted not with the objective purpose to fight corruption but with a subjective purpose to eliminate adversaries.

In 29 BC Octavius became Emperor Augustus and gradually accumulated all the power until 13 BC when he took the last public function of Pontifex Maximus. He gave all the important positions, such as consul, proconsul, tribune, and praetor to the members of his family and to his associates.[39] However, he took important steps to combat the moral corruption which was ravaging the Roman society at the end of the Republic, that were materialized in three laws, *Lex Julia de Maritandus Omnibus* 4 AD, *Lex Julia de Adulteris Coercendis* of 18 BC[40] and *Lex Papia Poppaea* 9 AD which consolidated the institution of marriage.

---

[36] Ingo Gildenhard, *Against Verres*, Cambridge: Open Book Publishers CIC Ltd., 2011
[37] Cicero. *The Orations of Marcus Tullius Cicero*, tr. C.D. Yonge, (London: G. Bell and Sons, 1913-21), Vol. 2, pg. 106
[38] M.H. Crawford, pg. 762
[39] Ortolan, pg.279
[40] M.H. Crawford, pg. 781

*Lex Julia De Ambitu,* 18 BC, was the last law against electoral corruption; from Augustus onwards it is the prerogative of the emperor to name magistrates or other public officials, therefor there are no more electoral processes that need to be regulated.[41]

The sources of law in imperial period are the statutes, the plebiscites, the *senatus consulta,* the *constitutiones principis,* the *acta magistratum,* and opinions of jurists.[42]

The freedom that the jurists enjoyed in the days of the Republic was restricted by Augustus; under the pretext of giving their opinions (*resposta*) more authority, he gave them the right to respond under the imperial sanction[43], thus he created a very effective mechanism of control and gradually, he transformed them into public officials.

From Nero onwards, a new power begins to affirm itself in the politics of Rome, the military. A long list of Emperors accede to power with the help of the legions, are appointed or assassinated by the Pretorian guard, generals become emperors only to be replaced by other generals. The imperial period is marked by civil wars and short term reigns with brief interludes of stability and attempts to put order in the affairs of the Empire.

Roman law grew constantly, and even though few new institutions and principles are introduced, the volume of legal texts became overwhelming. The process of ordering the legal knowledge begun with text books written by the jurists; one of the first works worthy to be mentioned is the Institutes of Gaius, written in 161 AD. This system allowed for interpretations on the existing laws but also created a lot of confusion, different jurists expressing different views on similar matters.

In 426, *Lex de response prudentium,* also known as the Law of Citations, establishes an order on which opinions should prevail; thus the work of Papinian, Paul, Gaius, Ulpian and Modestinus[44] gain supremacy in the legal doctrine.

Efforts to put order in the Roman law are also materialized in a process of codification; *Codex Gregorianus,* 291-294, and *Codex Hermogenianus,* 293-294, are the first collection of *constitutiones*

---

[41] Dig. XLVIII, 14

[42] Gaius, *Gai Institvtiones* I.I.2

[43] Ortolan, pg. 294

[44] W.W. Buckland, *A textbook on Roman law from Augustus to Justinian,* (Cambridge: Cambridge University Press, 1921)

*principis,* written in Diocletian's reign November 20, 284 - May 1, 305, as part of the emperor's efforts to reform the empire.

Theodosius II, January, 402 - July 28, 450, ordered the creation of a new code; between 429 and 438, *Codex Theodosianus* was compiled and, together with the previous two codes, became officially enforced in 438 in the East Roman Empire and in 439 in the Western Empire. The culmination of the tendency to codify Roman law was achieved in the reign of Justinian I 'The Great', 1 August 527 - 13/14 November 565, in the form of the *Corpus Juris Civils.*

It is very hard to find a proper word, even the adjective 'monumental' doesn't seem to do any justice, to describe the work that a group of byzantine jurists, led by Tribonianos, undertook to create the *Corpus Juris Civils,*[45] between 529 and 534.

The first part, the *Codex,* is a compilation of emperor's enactments going back to emperor Hadrian 117 - 138, the second part the *Digesta* or *Pandectae,* is a collection of the opinions of famous jurists and the third part, the *Institutiones* is a textbook designated for law students, largely based on the Institutes of Gaius. Justinian's own enactments are to be found in the fourth part, *Novellae Constitutiones.*

In Justinian's *Codex* we can find a series of emperors' enactments reflecting their efforts to control and to combat corruption. Some of these measures are directed against corruption in the justice system, for instance the bribing of the judge or of the other litigant causes the briber to lose his action [46], the decisions of a corrupt judge are void[47] and the advocates guilty of extortions shall be expelled from the profession.[48]

Other measures are directed against the corruption in the administration, fraudulently obtaining a public office for a second time is punished with deportation under the *Lex Julia* relating to political corruption[49]or if bribery and frauds are used to obtain immunity for taxation, the accountants of the municipalities guilty of such crimes are punished by fire.[50]

---

[45] The translation of the *Corpus Juris Civilis* used in this book is *The Civil Law,* Translated, edited and adapted by S. P. Scott, in seventeen volumes (Cincinnati: The Central Trust Company, 1932), from www.constitution.org/sps/spshtm
[46] Codex Justinianus 7.49.1-2
[47] CJ.7.64.7
[48] CJ.2.6.5
[49] CJ.9.10.1
[50] CJ.10.25.1

Crimes that are associated with the phenomenon of corruption such as forgery, counterfeiting or embezzlement are subjects of the Book IX of the Codex. With the Christian Emperors we can note a stricter attendance to morals; crimes of adultery and fornication or copulation with a slave are punished with the outmost severity.

The second part of the Corpus, the *Digesta* or *Pandectae*, was designed to make Roman law more understandable with the help of the jurist's opinions.

In the matter of arbitrations, Ulpian considers that the praetor should intervene when an arbiter, corrupted by bribery, refuses to give an award[51] and *"...if anyone corrupts an arbiter either with money, or by improper solicitation, or bribes the advocate of the other party, or anyone of those to whom he has entrusted his own case, he can be sued on the clause relating to fraud..."*[52]

The act of corrupting a slave was a serious crime under the Roman law. Such a crime is hard to understand by the modern lawyer; since the slaves had no official functions or any power, and corrupt acts are performed by officials or other persons in power, the concept of corrupting a slave is confusing.

The crime of corrupting a slave consisted in making him do a criminal act, either against his master or against a third party; it also meant diminishing his value by turning him into a drunkard or a gambler, or making him disobedient. The slaves were considered propriety[53] so the corruption of a slave entitles his master to a legal action, the right of property on a slave being protected just as any other real right.

This is a very interesting side of the phenomenon of corruption, which is usually associated with a person in power; it must have been a common practice to use slaves to perform a variety of criminal and immoral acts.[54]

It seems that Justinian was perfectly aware about the corruption in his State's administration. He considers corruption as *"...the beginning and the end of all wickedness"* and avarice as *"the mother of all crimes"*. General welfare can be accomplished *"...if the Governors invested with the civil administration of the provinces keep their hands clean".*[55]

---

[51] Digesta.4.8.3.(1)
[52] Dig.4.8.31
[53] David Johnston, *Roman Law in Context*, (Cambridge: Cambridge University Press, 2004)
[54] Dig.11.3
[55] Novelle.8.Pref

He understands the equation remarkably well: the one who buys the office has to borrow money thus creating a debt that is paid with interest by the people. In order to put an end to these practices he makes the accession in the office of consul, governor, judge or magistrate, gratuitous.[56]

From the founding of Rome up to the imperial period, Roman law was a secular system. The decemvires, the tribunes, the consuls were normal people, members of the community. None of them claimed to be a divine descendant or any other connection with the divine and it would have been very hard to convince the members of the community of such a thing.

None of the Roman laws made any reference to Jupiter or Minerva; Justitia, the blindfolded goddess carrying a scale was simply a décor symbol, just as it is today, she did not take any practical role in the legal process.

This doesn't mean the romans were atheists or agnostics, quite the contrary; they worshiped an impressive number of deities, they build impressive temples, sculpted magnificent statues and developed elaborate prayers, rituals and celebrations.

The pontifex, the sacerdos, the vestals, did not approve the laws in any way, nor did their functions interfere in any way with the legal process. Only with Augustus taking the title of Pontifex Maximus, the emperor becomes also the head of religion and this led to the creation of the cult for the emperor, from now on seen as divine.

With the *Corpus Iuris Civils* a link between law and religion is permanently established; Justinian claimed that the new code was created for the common good with the aid of God (*dei omnipotentis*) in the first phrase. He addresses religious matters in the beginning of each part of the Corpus, and, following a similar formula, in every introduction or preface, reminding us of the laws of the ancient Babylon, where the gods were present in the introductory text.

After the imperial administration crumbled, the Church was the only institution capable to fill in the vacuum of power[57] which meant it also attended to the legal domain.

The official texts of the Christian religion, namely the Old and the New Testaments were not enough to cover all the legal matters, so the

---

[56] N8.1
[57] Peter Stein, *Roman Law in European History*, (Cambridge: Cambridge University Press, 2004), pg. 30

24

clergy found in the *Corpus Juris Civils* an exhaustive source of legal knowledge that was perfectly acceptable form a religious perspective. Moreover, Justinian's jurists made sure that no pagan elements survived in the codes, thus depriving us from any historical evidence on the subject, but by this approach they ensured the survival of the Roman law in modern times.

Since the 2$^{nd}$ century BC, Rome was in a constant war with the Germanic tribes that lived in the northern and northeastern part of Europe. With some of these tribes, Rome established peaceful relations, materialized in trade and cultural exchange or in military alliances.

Roman emperors saw in this people a valuable human resource and granted them the status of *foederati* under the obligation to provide troops for the Roman army. This type of alliances were short lived, and, if at first Romans were the ones that were taking tribute from the people they conquered, towards the end of the empire the situation is changed completely, roman emperors are forced to buy peace or support from tribes like the Visigoths.

On August 24, 410 Rome was sacked by Alaric and in 476, Odoacer became king, thus bringing the Western Roman Empire to an end. The subtleties and intricacies of the Roman law would have been impossible to comprehend by the barbaric invaders. The Germanic languages and dialects they used lacked the vocabulary necessary to accommodate all the principles and institutions established over a thousand years.

Without a proper legal education, even with a good command of Latin language, the complicate legal system that Rome developed was hard to understand. The legal relations in the tribal societies were less complicated than those in the empire and the barbaric kings Gundobad, Alaric II and Theoderic replaced the complex legal system with simplified versions, materialized in *Lex Romana Burgundionum* (500-506), *Lex Romana Wisigothorum* or *Breviarium Alarici Regis* (506) *Lex Romana Ostrogothorum* or *Edictum Theodorici Regis* (511-515).

The only mentions about corruption in these documents refer to the corruption of virgins and this fact should not surprise. With the centralized administration vanished, even the phenomenon of corruption received a severe blow.

There were no more elections; therefore, the habit of bribing the voters disappeared together with the electoral process. Embezzlement from the public funds was not possible because there were no more public funds. Forgery of official documents was absent because there was no administration to make use of such documents.

Between 535 and 554 Justinian recaptures Italy from the Ostrogoths, so the Roman law returned to its origin in the custody of the Church.[58] From this moment onwards *Corpus Juris Civilis* becomes the main source of legal knowledge for the Western part of Europe as well as for the Eastern part.

The Church was in a privileged position; the clergy were the only people in Europe capable of understanding the language and the institutions of Roman law. The Church also had a well-established hierarchy which was more or less under papal control.

The monks created a channel of communication all over the continent, spreading the knowledge form Rome to every corner of Europe. Traveling from monastery to monastery, the monks made and distributed hand written copies of some of the books contained in the *Corpus Juris Civilis*, especially form the Digest.

In the East, Emperor Leo VI the Wise ruled the Byzantine Empire from 886 to 912. He is known for translating Justinian's Code in Greek language, a document entitled the *Basilika*. His Novels are interesting because they tend to reduce the severity of penalties for several crimes.

According to Novell 35 rape is no longer punished by death unless committed with threats of use of a deadly weapon. Under Novell 61 the collectors of public monies that overcharge tax payers are no longer punished by death but fined and deprived of office. The Novell 62 considered the previous punishments for selling public propriety to be "to harsh", the new penalty instituted is the return fourfold the value. Novell 84 lifts the ban on magistrates to purchase propriety, build houses and accept donations. Last, the novel 105 abolishes the death penalty for a magistrate convicted of plundering the Treasury.

The intentions of Emperor Leo might be commendable but the effects were contrary to the purposes of the previous punishments.

On 29 May 1453 Constantinople was conquered by the Turkish armies under Ottoman Sultan Mehmed II, event that marks the end of the Byzantine Empire and the end of the Roman Law in the East.

---

[58] Ibid., pg. 40

## 1.4. Laws in the Dark Ages

Clovis I, ca. 466 - November 27, 511, united the Frankish tribes under his rule and, adopting his wife Clotilde religion, converted to Catholicism. He commissioned a written code of laws for the Salian Franks which will remain in use, with constant amendments and revisions, for the next 300 years.

Under the Salic Law[59] we cannot find any evidence of crimes such as bribery, extortion, embezzlement, counterfeiting or forgery, crimes that are normally associated with the phenomenon of corruption.

This situation may be explained by the fact that the administrative structure of the State was almost inexistent. There cannot be any laws against electoral corruption if there were no elections held.

The public officials such as *thunginus, sagibaron, centenier,* or *graf*[60] were entitled by the king, it was one of his prerogatives, and they were acting as his agents giving account of their actions only to the king. In regard extortions from the king's subjects and embezzlements from the king's taxes or treasury, it is conceivable that these types of crimes must have existed, despite the fact that we cannot find any incriminatory laws. Upon discovery of such acts they must have been classified as treason towards the king therefore they must have been punished with the sanctions that were applied to traitors.

There aren't any laws against corrupt judges or magistrates either, and this may be explained by the fact that the king was the judge in the cases brought before him, or the judgments were a local matter outside the king's control. The power of the early kings relied on the loyalty of their vassals and they were the administrators of justice in the lands under their control; it would have required a very powerful king to challenge the judgments and the rulings of their vassals.

Another important element absent in the legislation of the first kings is the contract and the trading laws. Following the fall of the Western Roman Empire, once the military, administrative and judicial control disappeared, the international trade was also gone.

---

[59] *La Loi Salique,* see Peyre's translation on ledroitcriminelfree.fr/la_legislation_criminelle /anciens_textes/ loi_salique.htm, accessed on 1december 2014
[60] Jean Brissaud, *A History of French Public Law,* (Boston: Little, Brown &Co., 1912)

Trade became a local enterprise, subject to local regulations and customs which is the reason why we don't see any enactments of the early kings referring to contracts or trade regulations.

The little trade that might have existed in the dark ages, following the old roman trade routes must have been dependent on will of the lord of the land, which could have grant the right to free passage and free trade or impose a trading tax or confiscate the merchandise and dispose of the merchants one way or the other.

In 768 Charles I also known as Charles the Great or Charlemagne and his brother Carloman inherited the throne of France from their father Pepin and, after Carloman's death in 771, he remained the sole ruler of the Franks. During his reign, from 25 December 800 to 28 January 814, Charlemagne created a vast empire covering the territories of France, northern Italy and Germany, known as the Holy Roman Empire.

During the Carolingian Renaissance there are some notable reforms; the invention of the stirrup allowed the creation of an army based on cavalry, and a new monetary standard, the livre carolinienne, was established. Charlemagne hired Alcuin of York, *"the greatest scholar of the day"*[61] and other scholars Peter of Pisa, Paulinus of Aquileia, Rado, Abbot Fulrad, and he established a School in Aachen; he also reformed the Church, not only by advocating a pious life but by extending his control over ecclesiastical properties.

One of the most important documents he issued is the Capitulary from 802.[62] In article 5 Charles defines himself as the protector and defender of the church, the widows, the orphans and the strangers, after God and His Saints.

The form of the document is a series of articles containing obligations for clergy, public officials and laymen. Under article 10, the bishops and priests should live according to the canons and *"... bishops, abbots and abbesses, shall have bailiffs and sheriffs and judges skilled in the law, lovers of justice, peaceful and merciful..."* and *" ... on no account do we wish to have harmful or greedy prevosts or bailiffs in a monastery..."*[63] .

A prescription against corruption is to be found in article 25:

---

[61] Einhard, *Life of Charlemagne*, Translated by Samuel Epes Turner (New York: Harper & Brothers, 1880), pg. 25
[62] See full text in Ernest F. Henderson, tr. ed., *Select historical documents of the Middle Ages.* (London: Charles Bell and Sons, 1903), pg. 189
[63] Article 13

> *"That counts and centenars shall see to it that justice is done in full; ...who will not, under any pretext, induced by reward or flattery, dare to conceal thieves, robbers, or murderers, adulterers, magicians and wizards or witches, or any godless men, but will rather give them up that they may be bettered and chastised by the law..."*

A provision against extortion is prescribed in article 29:

> *"...our judges, counts, or envoys shall not have a right to extort payment of the remitted fine, on their own behalf, from those destitute persons to whom the emperor has, in his mercy, forgiven what they ought to pay by reason of his bann."*

Crimes that are explicitly mentioned in the Capitulary are murder, patricides and fratricides, perjury, rape, incest and adultery. Perjury[64] for instance is considered the most evil crime and the perpetrator must be removed from the Christian people, have his arm cut of and be deprived of his inheritance.

After Charlemagne's death in 814 he was succeeded by his son Louis the Pious and the empire was divided among his sons, a division that formed the precursor States of modern France, Germany and Italy.

In France, the Carolingian dynasty ended in 986 AD with the death of Louis V who left no legitimate heirs. Although by dynastic law he was supposed to be succeeded by his uncle, Charles of Lorraine, the clergy and the nobility chose to crown Hugo Capet as King of the Franks at Noyon in Picardy on 3 July 987 AD, the first of the Capetian dynasty which will rule France until 1792.

Between 43 AD, when the Roman Empire conquered a portion of the British Isles and established the Roman province of Britannia and 409 or 410 AD when the roman administration ended, the habitants of the area were governed by the Roman law. The Anglo-Saxons created a new legal system, mostly based on customs, which lasted from the 5th century until the Norman Conquest in the 11th century.

The early laws of England were influenced by the ecclesiastical law; for instance the laws of Alfred begin with the Ten Commandments and Exodus.[65] Crimes under the early Anglo Saxon law were plotting against the king or the lord, fighting in church, breaking the king's peace, theft, robbery, arson, and coining.[66] There are also mentions of several crimes against religion and morals, such as heathenism, witchcraft and

---

[64] Article 36
[65] See Sir Frederick Pollock and Frederic William Maitland, *The History of English Law before the Time of Edward I,* (Indianapolis: Liberty Fund, 2010), vol. 1, pg. 16
[66] Ibid., pg.49, 52, 55

adultery, unchastity or incest. The penalties, depending on the severity of the crime were death, corporal punishments, mutilation or fines.

In the Anglo-Saxon period, there is no clear line of demarcation between the secular and ecclesiastical courts. The bishop held a privileged position in the county court since he was the only one with a formal legal education.[67]

The Norman Conquest did not create a new legal system, but, undoubtedly, due to the language and cultural differences between the Norman and Saxon nobility changed the natural course of development of the English law.

A separation between Spiritual and Temporal Courts was established by an ordinance of William the Conqueror, on 1072:

> "*Wherefore I command, and by royal authority decree, that no bishop or archdeacon shall any longer hold, in the hundred court, pleas pertaining to the episcopal laws, nor shall they bring before the judgment of secular men any case which pertains to the rule of souls ...*"[68].

Perhaps King William's greatest legal innovation was the creation of the Doomsday Book, a survey of the proprieties and people of England for the purpose of establishing the taxes owed to the crown. One immediate consequence of this document was that it eliminated the arbitrary taxation and created on organized tax system.

The crime of bribing the judges and other public officials began to be sanctioned in the reigns of Richard II and Henry IV.[69] Ranulf de Glanville, died 1190, published between 1187-1189 *Tractatus de Legibus et Consuetudinibus Regni Angliae*, the first treatise on the laws of England. In Book I, chapter I, Glanville states that pleas are either Criminal or Civil.[70]

Crimes of lese majesty are killing the king, sedition, fraudulent concealment of a treasure trove, homicide, burning, robbery, rape and falsifying; the penalty is death or loss of a member. Theft and other lesser crimes are in the jurisdiction of the County Sheriffs and County Courts.

Book XIV is concerned with pleas which belong to the crown; the accused must go thru ordeal 'to purge himself' for the crime of killing the

---

[67] Ibid., pg. 46

[68] Henderson, *Select historical documents of the Middle Ages*, pg. 9

[69] James Fitzjames Stephen, *A history of Criminal Law of England*, (London : McMillan & Co. ) vol. 3, pg. 250

[70] Ranulf de Glanville. *A translation of Glanville*, John Beams, tr.,( Washington, John Byrne & Co., 1900)

king and fraudulent concealment of treasure trove. An important distinction is made between two species of homicide, the first, murder, is that type of homicide that is secretly perpetrated and simple homicide.[71] There is also a distinction between several types of falsifying; Glanville mentions false charters, false measures and false money.

King John, 24 December 1166 - 19 October 1216 in his attempt to strengthen the power of the State had powerful opponents in the person of Pope Innocent III and in a significant number of English barons. Excommunicated by the Pope on November 1209, he was able to negotiate an agreement in May 1213, the *Bulla Aurea* or the Golden Bull, by which he secured the Pope's support for the rest of his reign in exchange for conceding the kingdom of England and the kingdom of Ireland[72] to Rome's authority for a feudal service of 1,000 marks.

In his quarrel with the barons over taxation and confiscations, on 15 June 1215 he signed a peace agreement which will be remembered as one of the most important documents in English legal history, Magna Charta.[73]

The document granted *"...that the English church shall be free and shall have its rights intact and its liberties uninfringed upon"* (clause 1), the king and his bailiffs no longer can seize any land for debt (clause 9), *"To no one will we sell, to no one will we refuse or delay, right or justice."* (clause 40).

The 63 clauses charter failed to bring peace between the king and the rebel barons but it will play a significant role throughout the Middle Ages and will be a source of inspiration for later fundamental documents such as the Bill of Rights and the United States Constitution.

Henry de Bracton, ca. 1210 - ca. 1268, was one of the greatest jurists of the Middle Ages, author of *De Legibus et Consuetudinibus Angliae* or On the Laws and Customs of England. Bracton wrote that *"... it is not only necessary that the king be armed with weapons and laws but [with wisdom] ...for from a corrupt head, corruption descends to the members..."*[74]

Bracton considers as major crimes the crimes that affects the king; beside the crimes of lese-majesty he mentions forgery, counterfeiting and

---

[71] Ibid., pg.286
[72] Henderson, pg. 431
[73] Ibid pg. 137
[74] Henry de Bracton, *De Legibus et Consuetudinibus Angliae*, 4 vols., ed. G. E. Woodbine, transl. S. E. Thorne. (London: Publications of the Selden Society, 1968–77), vol. 2 pg. 306

fraudulent concealment of a treasure trove. Less serious crimes *"...since they only partly concern the king, because of the breach of his peace, and partly the private individuals against whom the wrong is committed..."*[75] are homicide, theft, robbery, wounding, rape, arson.

Punishments are *"heavy or light depending upon whether the crimes are major or minor"*[76], and the purpose of punishment is to correct the men, *"...so that those whom the fear of God cannot turn from evil may at least be restrained by a temporal penalty."*[77] The forms of punishment mentioned by Bracton are flogging, pillory, burning, beheading and loss of a limb.

The early Criminal Law in Germany was based on the principles of vengeance and self-defense.[78] There are laws against homicide or thefts that were punished with fines, or the so called *'weregildum'*; the severity of the sanctions and the diversity of criminal acts will increase with the Carolingian dynasty.[79] A statutory legal system begun to emerge in the form of *Land-frieden*[80], while the church courts created a legal system based on the Mosaic Law.

Just as in France or England there are no specific laws against corruption. The concept of treason or lèse-majesté would have covered any act against the law and such act would have been punished accordingly. The enactment of specific anticorruption laws happens only in a society with a well-established administrative and justice systems coordinated by a central ruling power.

## 1.5. The law of the Church in the Middle Ages

The fact that the *lex barbarorum* emerged almost simultaneous in several places at the beginning of the sixth century is no coincidence. The dissolution of the last vestiges of the Roman administrative and justice systems must had happened around 500, hence the need of the barbaric kings to restore order in their newly formed kingdoms.

---

[75] Ibid, vol. 2, pg. 298
[76] Ibid
[77] Ibid
[78] Carl Ludwig Von Bar, *A History of Continental Criminal Law*, tr. Thomas S. Bell, (Boston: Little Brown &Co, 1916), pg. 58
[79] Ibid, pg. 67
[80] Ibid, pg. 100

There was however an institution that survived the barbaric attacks and that was the Catholic Church. When Alaric sacked Rome he spared those who sought refuge in churches, despite the fact that he himself was an Arian Christian.

The Church was already in a missionary process to Christianize those newcomers, Clovis I was baptized in 498 at Reims by Saint Remigius, Æthelberht, the King of Kent, was converted in circa 601 by Saint Augustine of Canterbury which was sent on a mission by Pope Gregory I. By the time Charlemagne was crowned Emperor of the Romans in 800, Christianity was spread in an area from the Atlantic Ocean to the Caspian Sea and form the British Isles to the Eastern corner of Africa.

When roman administration disintegrated, the Church was a very well organized institution. It had a very well established hierarchy with the pope as its head selected from the first level of archbishops and bishops; abbots and priests formed a second level and monks and nuns a third level. Organized in a multicellular structure, the destruction of a single or even several cells did not affected the entire organism, on a contrary, it probably strengthen it. As it was said before, law is proper to organization by definition; and the Church established its own system of laws.

The Church's legal system developed on two axes; first as an internal system which had the clergy as its subject and which was exempted from secular authority and as an external system, based on the Christian moral values, which had any Christian as its subject.

The Church involvement in the administration of the State was an unavoidable event. The Church was the only institution able to provide the human resource necessary in the administration of the State. Most of the population was illiterate, including kings or nobility. Monks and priests were the only persons capable to keep records, to find and interpret legal texts, but most important, they were able to communicate in Latin, which made them natural ambassadors and translators.

The development of the Church would have been impossible without money and since the only reliable source of income was agriculture, the Church gradually accumulated proprieties that in a first phase provided for the clergy needs, then allowed for the construction of new monasteries, abbeys, churches and later cathedrals.

In the entire history no other legal system defined, protected and defended propriety better than the Roman law. The Church had every reason to recover the legal principles regarding propriety from the Roman law since it was the largest propriety owner. Secular proprieties were subject to change in regard the proprietor; they were given to loyal subjects, divided among heirs, bought and sold. The proprieties of the clergy remained in the patrimony of the Church which led to the accumulation of an impressive wealth. And when wealth accumulates, corruption appears.

The second source of income for the church was the contribution paid by the believers. It is a tradition inherited from the Mosaic Law; the word used to describe these contributions is tithes, or a tenth of the profits or fruits obtained by the members of the church.

Another significant source of income for the Church was the trade with holy merchandise; pieces and nails from the Holy Cross, bones of the Saints, beside a large variety of worship items, some of them authentic, most of them forgeries, some sold and some used as a gift to attract the benevolence of kings and nobility. Such items were believed to have miraculous powers, therefore the more venerable the relic, the higher was the market value or the influence obtained.

Even today, on some of the items, the opinions of the scientific community on their authenticity are divided, the Shroud of Turin, the Trier Robe and the Holy Lance, to nominate the most important ones. The sale of relics was prohibited by the Church since the Theodosian Code, yet the commerce with these items flourished throughout the Middle Ages, possibly with the tolerance of the clerical authorities.

The indulgences were another significant source of income. Perhaps unwillingly, the Church became a contributor for the phenomenon of corruption in the laic society, especially in the upper class. The deterrent factor from the idea of sin was annulled by the fact that forgiveness and absolution could be bought.

The legal system developed by the Christian Church embodied a number of prescriptions against human actions that are an offence to God. The word use to describe this type of actions is sin.

Sin is defined as *"a morally bad act (St. Thomas, "De malo", 7:3), an act not in accord with reason informed by the Divine law."*[81] Without entering in too many details, which we will save for the next chapter, we shall point out that the term sin is used to describe an act, murder, rape,

---

[81] O'Neil, A.C., "Sin". The Catholic Encyclopedia. (New York: Robert Appleton Company, 1912) Retrieved March 29, 2015 from http://www.newadvent.org/cathen/14004b.htm

incest, or an emotion, envy or avarice or even an opinion, atheism. These constitute 'grave matters', which according with the Christian theology are mortal sins. Venial sins are less grave sins, and they can be forgiven under some form of penitence.

Apostasy (*Perfidiœ*) is defined as the complete and voluntary abandonment of the Christian religion.[82] It is a sin under the cannon law for which the penalty is excommunication without the possibility of a pardon.

The last emperor of the Constantinian dynasty, Julian, 6 November 355 - 26 June 363, rejected Christian religion and adopted a neo-platonic philosophy. On 4 February 362 AD he issued a Tolerance Edict that granted freedom of religion and proclaimed all religions as equal before the law, a truly remarkable document. He attempted to reform the State administration and established a tribunal in Chalcedon, a suburb of Constantinople to judge the ministers of the former administration for corruption. His reforms were as short lived as his reign; he died on 26 June 363 AD from a spear wound.

Heresy is defined by St. Thomas as *"...a species of infidelity in men who, having professed the faith of Christ, corrupt its dogmas"*.[83] The difference between heresy and apostasy is that the former does not mean the rejection of the Christian faith but the adhering to a different dogma while the later means the total rejection of the Christian faith. The issue of heresy was addressed in Title 5 of Justinian's Codex and is mostly sanctioned with the loss of privileges but later on, heresy became punishable by death.

In Summa Theologica, Tomas Aquinas wrote:

> *"On their own side there is the sin, whereby they deserve not only to be separated from the Church by excommunication, but also to be severed from the world by death. For it is a much graver matter to corrupt the faith which quickens the soul, than to forge money, which supports temporal life. Wherefore if forgers of money and other evil-doers are forthwith condemned to death by the secular authority, much more reason is there for heretics, as soon as they are convicted of heresy, to be not only excommunicated but even put to death."*[84]

The concept of heresy was expanded[85] during the Spanish Inquisition (*Tribunal del Santo Oficio de la Inquisición*) and covered any act that

---

[82] Van Hove, Alphonse. "Apostasy". The Catholic Encyclopedia. (New York: Robert Appleton Company, 1907) Retrieved March 28, 2015 from http://www.newadvent.org/cathen/01624b.htm
[83] Wilhelm, Joseph. "Heresy." The Catholic Encyclopedia. (New York: Robert Appleton Company, 1910) Retrieved March 29, 2015 from http://www.newadvent.org/cathen/07256b.htm
[84] Aquinas, *Summa Theologica*, II-II.11.3

the inquisitor might see as 'heretic', including here witchcraft, blasphemy, bigamy, sodomy and freemasonry.

Blasphemy was defined by Francisco Suárez as *"any word of malediction, reproach, or contumely pronounced against God"*.[86] The punishment for blasphemy was death; however, in time, the severity of the punishment was decreased to standing at the door of the church during Mass or fines. Blasphemy was also a common law crime, Sir Blackstone wrote that *"These are offences punishable at common law by fine and imprisonment, or other infamous corporal punishment..."*[87]

Sacrilege is defined as *"the violation or injurious treatment of a sacred object"* or in a larger senses *"any transgression against the virtue of religion"*[88].

Witchcraft, sorcery, magic, fortunetelling are practices that goes back in the beginning of human history, preceding religion itself. The role of those practices was to create a form of control, illusory of course, over life's events and to provide cures and remedies for the illness of the body or the mind.

The belief in witchcraft and magic was just as strong as the belief in God. In the absence of medical knowledge numerous causes of death could have been libeled as homicidal witchcraft.[89] Virtually any unfortunate event, in the absence of a reasonable explanation, would have been seen as the work of the Devil.

The fear of witchcraft and magic was so powerful in people's mind that the last trials took place in the 19th century: the Salem witchcraft trial of 1878 in U.S., the Anna Göldi case of 1782 and the Barbara Zdunk case of 1811 in Switzerland and respectively Prussia culminating with the Helen Duncan case of 1944 in Great Britain. Penalty for witchcraft was burning at the stake in order to save the soul of the sinner, hanging, drowning.

One of the sins condemned by the Church is simony, defined as *"a deliberate intention of buying or selling for a temporal price such things*

---

[85] Michael C. Thomsett, *Heresy in the Roman Catholic church*, (Jefferson: McFarland & Company, Inc., Publishers, 2011) pg. 140

[86] Melody, J., "Blasphemy", The Catholic Encyclopedia. (New York: Robert Appleton Company). Retrieved April 4, 2015 from http://www.newadvent.org/cathen/02595a.htm

[87] William Blackstone, *Commentaries on the Laws of England*, (Philadelphia: J.B. Lippincott Co., 1893) vol. 2, pg. 325

[88] Delany, J., "Sacrilege", The Catholic Encyclopedia. (New York: Robert Appleton Company) Retrieved April 4, 2015 from http://www.newadvent.org/cathen/13321a.htm

[89] Stephen, vol. 3, pg.5

*as are spiritual or annexed unto spirituals*"[90]. Pope Benedict IX is the Pope that sold even the papacy to the priest John Gratian who became Pope Gregory VI.

Simony could have been committed also by a temporal authority; accusations of simony will often lead to conflicts between the Church and the Monarchs. In Session 43 on March 23, 1418 of the Council of Constance, Pope Martin V declared "*Many constitutions have been issued in the past against the evil of simony, but they have not been able to eradicate the disease.*" and "*Simoniacal elections ... are rendered null by the law itself and nobody acquires any rights through them.*"[91]

Usury is the practice of lending money with interest, a practice that was condemned by the Church, especially in the writings of the Fathers of the Church.[92] Pope Clement V strongly condemned the practice, but let's not forget that his ally, King Philip the Fair was in debt to the Jewish community, the Lombard bankers and to the Knights Templar. At the Tenth Session of the Fifth Lateran Council on May 4, 1515 Pope Leo X declared that "*...credit organizations, established by states and hitherto approved and confirmed by the authority of the apostolic see, do not introduce any kind of evil or provide any incentive to sin if they receive, in addition to the capital, a moderate sum for their expenses ...*"[93]. A moderate sum however will remain a matter of interpretation.

Nepotism or the practice to grant favors and high positions to relatives, was not formally condemned by the Church, moreover it seems to have its roots in the Church's hierarchy. Pope Alexander VI (1492–1503) born Rodrigo Borja (Borgia) inherited the position of Archbishop of Valencia after his uncle Alonso de Borja became Pope Callixtus III. He had several mistresses and five legitimate children, perhaps his daughter, Lucrezia Borgia being the most notorious. He appointed his son Cesare, who will serve as a model for Machiavelli's Prince, as cardinal, a position from which he will later resign to follow a military career.

In human history, murder was considered the gravest crime and was always punished with the outmost severity. Christian tradition held that the first crime in history was the murder of Abel by Cain. It is somehow

---

[90] Weber, N., "Simony", The Catholic Encyclopedia. (New York: Robert Appleton Company) Retrieved April 27, 2015 from http://www.newadvent.org/cathen/14001a.htm
[91] Text retrieved from http://www.papalencyclicals.net/Councils/ecum16.htm accessed on 4/27/2015
[92] Jacques Le Goff, *Your money or your life*, tr. Patricia Ranum, (New York: Zone books, 1990)
[93] See www.papalencyclicals.net/Councils/ecum18.htm

surprising to find murder related to the head of the church; popes were either killed or they were directly or indirectly killers themselves. Pope Benedict IX was accused of murder by the Bishop Benno of Piacenza and by Pope Victor III, Gregory V was poisoned, even the death of John Paul I in 1978 spawned a series of conspiracy theories.

One of the greatest achievements of Christianity was that it put an end to the practice of human sacrifices. We are certain that the Gods were not the ones who demanded the sacrifice; the request came from a member of the priesthood class. We also have the certainty that the Gods did not use the priests to communicate their will. But what does this mean? It can only mean that all the human sacrifices in history were done for corrupt purposes, either to obtain the wealth of the victim or to end a line of succession. The sacrifice of wives or slaves of one patron meant fewer mouths to feed for the inheritor of his wealth. The conclusion that the first contract killers were the shamans and priests might be a shocking, but it is, nonetheless, accurate. Ending the human sacrifices is perhaps the greatest contribution of Judaism and Christianity to humanity.

The laws of Noah prohibited adultery, incest and homosexuality. These types of sexual offences had been condemned throughout history and the Christian Church followed the mosaic tradition in condemning this acts as sins. Sexual scandals involving popes are remembered in the history of the church; stories about mistresses, illegitimate offspring, rape and homosexuality are acknowledged even by the official historians of the Catholic Church and they are not just inventions of adversaries. Pope John XII, 955 - 964 was killed by a husband who found him in bed with his wife. Normally such an act is a crime a passion which is not the subject of this thesis. Yet the crime is a consequence of corruption since the Pope as any other cleric had taken an oath of chastity.

Forgery was another crime that was known to the high hierarchy of the church; the most notorious collection of forged documents is the False Decretals or the Pseudo-Isidorean Decretals, from the 9th century.

The most severe sanction under canonical law was excommunication. Today, it is not easy to grasp the consequences of such penalty. For instance, the subjects of an excommunicated king no longer owed him their allegiance.[94] Political and military alliances with other monarchs

---

[94] Luigi Giustiniani, *Papal Rome as it is*, (Baltimore: Publications Rooms 1843), pg. 175

would have been severely affected and any attempt to create new alliances would have been doomed from the start.

The relation between the Church and the State was a complex one. Powerful kings imposed benevolent popes while strengthening the institutions of the State and popes often interfered in laic affairs to secure the stability and influence of the Church. On many occasions the Pope and the King came into conflict, mostly on matters of secular nature and rarely on theological issues.

The human resource for the high hierarchy of the church came from the nobility; since the clerics were not allowed to marry and noble family were the only ones capable to provide an education for their children it is natural that the hierarchy of the church was elected or appointed from nobility. For instance, the Medici family, between 13th and 17th centuries, gave four popes, Leo X, Clement VII, Pius IV and Leo XI. The political position of the bishop or the abbot in the middle ages is again complicated. He is caught between the Pope and the King while struggling to attend to his family interests.

The first major power struggle between the heads of the Church and State occurred in the eleventh century with the investiture controversy between Pope Gregory VII 1072 - 1085 and Henry IV, 1056 - 1106, the Holy Roman Emperor. Carolingian emperors imposed the practice that the emperor (king) had the power to appoint the hierarchy of the Church. These appointments were not cheap and they gave the emperor a power over the nobility since these favors could also be revoked.

The *Dictatus papae,* a document attributed to Pope Gregory VII composed from 27 sentences, asserted in unequivocal terms the powers of the Pope: *"That he alone can depose or reinstate bishops. That it may be permitted to him to depose emperors. That he himself may be judged by no one."*[95]

During this quarrel the Pope excommunicated Emperor Henry thrice, and the emperor appointed his own Pope, the Antipope Clement III. The conflict exceeded the lives of both Pope Gregory and Emperor Henry and ended in a sort of armistice with the Concordat of Worms on September 23, 1122. Henry V and Pope Calixtus II agreed that Emperor will elect the bishops and abbots *"...without simony and without any violence;"*[96]and d the Pope will certify their investiture *"...through ring and staff"*.

---

[95] Henderson, pg. 366
[96] Ibid., pg. 408-409

King Philip IV the Fair reined France from 1285 to 1314. He was a powerful monarch who sought the reformation of the feudal State and the strengthening of the central administration. But King Philip had in Pope Boniface VIII an equal opponent; on 18 November 1302 he issued *Unam Sanctam*, a bull that called for the unity of the Church and stated that the Pope is the absolute head of the Church.

The conflict escalated when he excommunicated Philip; in return the king conveyed an assembly of 29 bishops accusing the Pope of heresy, simony, idolatry and the practice of magic and sent his ministry Guillaume de Nogaret with a small troupe at the pope's residence in Anagni and held the pope hostage for three days. Following the incident, the pope died from a violent fever one month later.

The next Pope, Benedict XI reverted the bull *Unam Sanctam* and annulled Philip's excommunication, but he excommunicated Nogaret for the Anagni incident; he died in 1304 in suspect circumstances. His successor, pope Clement V moved the papal residence from Rome to Avignon under Philip's protection and control.

Philip's reforms as well as his wars with England and Flanders were costly enterprises and, above anything else the king needed money. He had already taxed the Church, expelled the Jews and the Lombards from which he borrowed heavily, debased the French coinage.

The Order of the Knights Templar became renowned for their active role in the Crusades but they also created a financial system with offices all over Europe and the Holy Land. Unable to pay his debts to the Order, on 13 October 1307, in a very well synchronized maneuver, Philip's troops arrested the Grand Master of the Temple, Jacques de Molay and hundreds of Templar knights and, after tortures and trials on charges of heresy, had them burned at the stake, thus dismantling the Order of the Knights Templars.[97]

Another significant event in Church's history happened during the reign of Henry VIII, King of England from 21 April 1509 to 28 January 1547. Unable to have a male heir from his wife Catherine of Aragon, daughter of Queen Isabella I of Castile and King Ferdinand II of Aragon, King Henry sought for a way to divorce, and the only option was to have his marriage annulled by the Pope Clement VII.

Caught in a complicated political equation, Pope Clement refused to invalidate the marriage which determined King Henry to take drastic

---

[97] For a romanced history of the events read Maurice Druon, *The accursed Kings. The iron King.*

measures. A special court headed by Thomas Cranmer, the Archbishop of Canterbury declared that the marriage with Catherine was against the law of God on 23 May 1533. With the Act of Supremacy of 1534, King Henry declared himself the *"the only supreme head on earth of the Church of England"* and asserted the independence of the *Ecclesia Anglicana* from papal authority.

Martin Luther, 10 November 1483 - 18 February 1546 was a Monk of the Order of St. Augustine and Master of Arts and Sacred Theology and lecturer at the Wittenberg University 'Leucorea'. On 31 October 1517 he posted on the door of the Church of All Saints in Wittenberg a document composed of 95 theses (sentences or propositions would be more appropriate) in which he made a vehement critique to the indulgence letters. In a later work The Babylonian Captivity of Church, from 1520 Luther describes indulgences with a single phrase as *"...a knavish trick of the roman sycophants"*.[98]

Luther also mentions the construction of the basilica of St. Peter for which the indulgences sell campaign was gathering funds and ask in thesis 86 *"Why does not the pope, whose wealth is today greater than the wealth of the richest Crassus, build this one basilica of St. Peter with his own money rather than with the money of poor believers?"*

Pope Leo X issued a Bull *Exurge Domine* on June 15, 1520, charging Luther with heresy and threatening him with excommunication in case he doesn't recant his thesis. Luther's reaction was to burn the Papal Bull and several books and, on January 3 1521, he was excommunicated.

In a letter from 6 September, 1520, entitled *"Concerning Christian Liberty Dedicatory Letter Of Martin Luther To Pope Leo X"*, Martin Luther writes *"Your see, however, which is called the Court of Rome, and which neither you nor any man can deny to be more corrupt than any Babylon or Sodom,..."*[99] and *"Is it not true that there is nothing under the vast heavens more corrupt, more pestilential, more hateful than the Court of Rome?"*[100]

In Luther's works we can also find accusations of nepotism, simony, usury, pluralism, beside the sale of indulgences, against the Pope and the high hierarchy of the Church.

---

[98] Martin Luther, *Works Of Martin Luther*, (Albany: Books For The Ages, 1997), vol. 2, pg.121
[99] Ibid., pg. 109
[100] Ibid., pg. 110

The Reformation movement that Luther started expanded in the rest of Europe with the works of Ulrich Zwingli in Switzerland, Jean Chauvin (John Calvin) in France; with the emancipation of the English Church from papal control under Henry VIII and Elisabeth I it created four major branches inside the Christian religion. The answer was a counter reform movement called the Catholic Revival or the Catholic Reformation which led to a series of bloody wars, more or less religious motivated.

From the reformation period onward the power of the Pope gradually diminished despite the success of counter-reformation in France and Spain. The strengthening of the institutions of the State, especially in England, had limited the judicial power of the Church and allowed the development of a secular justice system. In Germany reformation had an entire different effect and that is the merger between the secular and divine law.[101]

The power of excommunication carried less and less weight and the Church no longer had the military power or the political influence to see that other sanctions are imposed. In the 17th and 18th centuries there are no excommunications against a head of State, the last major historical figure that was excommunicated was Napoleon Bonaparte on June 10, 1809 by Pope Pius VII. The bull *Quum Memoranda* had no immediate consequence for Napoleon, but the Pope will spend the next six years in house arrest.

To conclude the story of the Catholic Church in the Middle Ages I shall say that the phenomenon of corruption was present in the high hierarchy of the church just as it was present in the laic State with no significant difference generated by the church's moral and ethical codes.

## 1.6. Rediscovering law in Renaissance

Renaissance is the period between the 14th century and the 17th century; the term is also used to describe a social movement that originated in Italy and spread in the rest of the world. It is the period when humanity changed its view on itself. Everything begins to change, in visual arts the beauty of the human body is rediscovered, architecture becomes

---

[101] Von Bar, *A History of Continental Criminal Law*, pg. 223

grandiose and science begins to substitute superstitions in numerous aspects of daily life.

As the complexity of the legal relations grew, the *Corpus Juris Civils* is gradually reintroduced as it was needed. The law is subsequent to the legal relation which it is called to regulate. The legislators of the Middle Ages had found in the Corpus an excellent resource for all the new legal situations that begun to (re)appear.

Since Justinian already cleared the Roman Law of the pagan aspects, the Church posed no opposition and helped in the recovery of the principles of Roman Law especially those regarding propriety, family, trade, contracts, and, to a certain extent, criminal matters.

In the reign of Charles V, born February 24, 1500, died September 21, 1558, Holy Roman Emperor, the *Constitutio Criminalis Carolina* (based on the *Bambergensis*, a criminal procedure written by Johann of Schwarzenberg in 1507) was enacted by the Reichstag at Regensburg in July, 1532 and was intended unify the criminal law throughout the empire.[102]

According with article 3, the judge is bound to swear that he will not weaver to *"affection, enmity, bribe, gift or anything else."*[103] The CCC went into a great deal of details to define the circumstances when torture is applied; as gruesome as it may seem today, by the time of the enactment these provisions would have serve the propose of eliminating arbitrary acts of torture.

Among the crimes enumerated in CCC we can find treason, murder, poisoning, theft, robbery, arson, forgery, paid and false witnessing, rape, adultery and sorcery. Death penalty involved burning, quartering, drawing to the wheel, drowning and burying alive; corporal punishments meant cutting off tongues, ears, fingers or flogging with rods.

After the reformation, as Von Bar explained compressively, legal science was defending itself from two enemies *"...the bigoted theology and the despotism of the princes....."*.[104] Indeed, between the concept of the crime of lese-majesty and the concept of alliance with the Devil, any action could have been considered criminal and punished accordingly with the outmost severity.

---

[102] Ibid., pg. 215
[103] John H. Langbein *Prosecuting Crime in the Renaissance*: England, Germany, France, pg. 268
[104] Von Bar, pg. 226

Benedict Carpzov the Younger, 1595 - 1666, author of *Practica nova Imperialis Saxonica rerum criminalium,* is one of the founders of the German Criminal Law. As sources of law in regard homicide, Carpzov mentions[105] *jure civili* (*Lex Cornelia*), *jure divino* (Genesis, Leviticus, Exodus) and *caesareo,* which can be translated as the law of the Caesar (*Constitutio Criminalis Carolina*). There are some important distinctions between several forms of homicide committed from resentment, purposeful and deliberate and accidental, depending on intent, and also parricide, infanticide, abortion, depending on the victim.

Questions 44 to 50 concern religious crimes heresy, blasphemy, perjury, sorcery, magic, and making a pact with the devil. Among sex crimes which are answered in questions 51 to 76 we can find adultery, bigamy, incest, seduction, promiscuity, procurement, rape and sodomy. Other crimes mentioned are robbery, arson, forgery of coins, theft, and usury.

Reformation divided the Holy Roman Empire between Catholics, Protestants and Calvinists which caused the Thirty Years' War, between 1618 and 1648; however, these conflicts were not always motivated by religion, in fact, one can say that religion was just a pretext.

Religious superstition and dogmatism led to a series of trials, the witch trials, which lasted between 1580 until 1750. Basically any unfortunate event, war, diseases, famine was considered to be the work of the Devil. Anyone could have been accused of witchcraft, men and women alike, and considered responsible for any undesired event; even suspicion of practice of magic or sorcery would have been enough for conviction.

The book of Heinrich Kramer, *Malleus Maleficarum,* made a career in this period since it provided in its third section a guide on how to conduct a witch trial. The penalty was burning at the stake and sometimes drowning or hanging.

Before the codification process that took place in the time of Napoleon Bonaparte, France was governed by a common law system, similar to the one in England, based on customs and uses. From that period we have a document, a precursor for the codification movement that brings together generals principles of law, criminal, family and feudal law, rules of procedures and sanctions. The document is entitled *The customs*

---

[105] Benedicti Carpzovii, *Practicae Novae Imperialis Saxonicae Rerum Criminalium,* Christiani Kirchneri 1669

of *Bretagne* (*La coutume de Bretagne*)[106] and was drafted in the reign of John III, 1312 - 1341, and was later published in 1480 in Paris.

Several editions were published between 1485 and 1538 in Rennes, Rouen and Nantes. Qualified theft is punishable by death[107] also the theft of horses, cattle and other working animals. Traitors, murderers, assassins, burners and arsonists of houses, rapists must be put to death.[108] Counterfeiters will be boiled and then hanged.[109] All fake sellers, or those who would have sold the same thing to two people, shall be punished as thieves and counterfeiters.[110]

Unlike in Germany or England, the Reformation in France had a different effect and that is a strong alliance between the Catholic Church and the State. The French Protestants or the Huguenots were a religious group influenced by the writings of John Calvin. They had a more violent nature, which led to a civil war with the Catholics.

Most of the Huguenot leaders were assassinated during the St. Bartholomew's Day Massacre of 24 August - 3 October 1572, a severe blow to the movement. During the reign of Henry IV, a former Huguenot himself, they enjoyed a certain freedom under the provisions of the Edict of Nantes. However during the reign of Louis XIII and the regency of Anne of Austria, Cardinals Richelieu and Mazarin, Chief Ministers of France, strengthen the relation between the State and the Catholic Church.

After Mazarin's death in 1661 King Louis XIV assumed the affairs of the State and abolished the position of Chief Ministry. Young and ambitious, the king had found in Jean Baptiste Colbert an excellent collaborator. The King accused his finance minister Nicolas Fouquet of embezzlement and had him imprisoned for life. Colbert embarked in a series of reforms, a truly remarkable enterprise that modernized the French society. Legal reforms came in a series of Ordinances that covered civil law, maritime law, trade and procedural law.

Perhaps the most important document regarding criminal law is the Criminal Ordinance of August 1670.[111] The bulk of the document

---

[106] Marcel Planiol, *La tres Ancienne Coutume de Bretagne*, (J. Plihon et L. Herve, Libraires-Editeurs, Rennes, 1896)
[107] See http://ledroitcriminel.free.fr/la_legislation_criminelle/anciens_textes/coutume_de_bretagne.htm, Article 626
[108] Ibid., Article 632
[109] Ibid., Article 634
[110] Ibid., Article 682
[111] http://ledroitcriminel.free.fr/la_legislation_criminelle/anciens_textes/ordonnance_criminelle_de_

contains rules of criminal procedures but there are few articles worthy to be mentioned here.

Under Title II Article 11 it is forbidden for the constabulary officers to retain some furniture, weapons and horses seized or belonging to the accused under the penalty of losing the office. The entire Title IX is dedicated to the crimes of false and under Title XVII, Article 27 forbids judges, clerks, bailiffs, archers and other officers of the court to take money, furniture, clothes belonging to convicted. Title XIX contains a set of rules on how and when torture should be applied.

A notable event from the time of Louis XIV is the Affair of the Poisons (L'affaire des poisons). It all started with the trial of Marie-Madeleine-Marguerite d'Aubray, Marquise de Brinvilliers who was convicted and executed by beheading for poisoning her father and her two brothers in order to obtain the inheritance.

The next year, in 1677, the fortuneteller Magdelaine de La Grange was charged forgery and murder; she claimed to have knowledge of other crimes which led to a serious investigation among alchemists, fortunetellers and magicians. From 442 suspects, 36 were executed either by beheading, hanging or burning by the stake; several persons were condemned to perpetual imprisonment or exile[112]. Among the clients were dukes and duchesses, counts, marquis, viscounts showing that the practice of magic and sorcery was endemic in the aristocracy.

The next legal reform happened between 1717 and 1750; Chancellor D'Aguesseau[113] attempted to create the first code of laws but he was unable to complete it. Among the laws proposed by D'Aguesseau we shall mention the declaration of 5 February 1731 which limited the rights of Provostships and Presidials due to abuses and the Ordinance of July 1737 on falsification.

The most serious offence in Medieval France is the crime of lèse-majesté,[114] a large concept under which any criminal act may be considered and punished usually by death. Bribery is punished with the loss of office and fine. There are several forms of counterfeiting of money, of royal letters and seals, merchandise. Other crimes are peculation or

1670.htm

[112] Anne Somerset, *The Affair of the Poisons: Murder, Infanticide, and Satanism at the Court of Louis XIV* (St. Martin's Press, 2003)

[113] See Charles Butler, *Memoir of the life of Henry-Francis D'Aguesseau*, (London: John Murray, 1830)

[114] Von Bar, pg. 163

the embezzlement of royal or public moneys, extortion and 'malversation' in office, obstruction of public justice.[115]

Although the term 'renaissance' might be improper to use when we study England, the movement that pulled humanity out of the dark ages was felt under the Tudor dynasty. The legal system is still under the influence of religion despite the clear separation between the spiritual and the temporal.

Sir Edward Coke, 1 February 1552 - 3 September 1634, was one of the most influential English jurists, famous for his Reports and Institutes of the Lawes of England. On his epitaph it is written "*...Most Devoted Investigator of Profound Faithfulness. Integrity Itself, Always the Most Constant Advocate of the Cause of Truth Corrupted Neither by Favor Nor by Gifts.*"[116]

In the period when Sir Edward Coke wrote his Institutes, we can clearly see the advancement made by the criminal law as a science; there are a larger number of crimes compared to those in the time of Glanville and Bracton. There are two types of treason: high treason "*...when a man doth compasse or imagine...*"[117] the death of the King, Queen, Prince, Chancellor, Treasurer, and Justices and petit treason if the act of killing is committed against "*subjects and inferior persons*"[118] Here we can find an interesting concept and that is "*the corruption of the blood*". It was considered that the blood of the traitor is corrupted so the children should not inherit the traitor's propriety.[119]

Killing of humans is classified in murder, which Sir Coke considers to be the most heinous of all felonies especially murder by poisoning "*...the most detestable of all because is the most horrible...*"[120] and homicide or manslaughter. Religious offences are heresy, conjuration, witchcraft, sorcery and inchantment, usury and simony. Among sex crimes, beside rape and carrying away a woman against her will, Sir Coke mentions buggery or sodomy, which includes bestiality, and polygamy.

Bribery is defined by Sir Coke as follows:

---

[115] Ibid., pg. 285
[116] Edward Coke, *The Selected Writings and Speeches of Sir Edward Coke*, ed. Steve Sheppard (Indianapolis: Liberty Fund, 2003), Vol. 3
[117] See Edwardo Coke, *The Third Part of the Institutes of Laws of England*,( London, W. Clarke &Sons, 1817), cap 1
[118] Ibid., pg. 20
[119] Ibid., pg. 210
[120] Ibid., pg. 48

*"... a great misprision (1), when any man in judiciall place (2) takes any fee or pension, robe or livery, gift, reward (3) or brocage (4) of any person, that hath to do before him any way (5), for doing his office, or by color of his office, but of the king only, unlesse it be of meat or drink, and that of small value, upon divers, and grievous punishments."*[121]

Extortion is different from bribery because it may be committed not only by a man in *"judiciall place"* but also by a man in ministerial office[122]. It is *"a great misprision because is accompanied by perjury."*[123] Sir Coke recounts here the case of Sir William Thorpe, chief justice of the King's Bench who, at the assize at Lincoln, stayed the writ of exigent against Richard Saltley and others, for which he was charged with bribery, a crime for which was later pardoned.

Another notable case is the case of Cardinal Thomas Woolsey (1473 – 1530), Lord Chancellor, King's Henry VIII chief adviser for fourteen years. Failing to solve king's divorce, Woolsey failed in disgrace and was removed from office in 1529; in Articles against Cardinal Woolsey,[124] Sir Edward Coke presents a long list of accusations brought against Woolsey in the Court of Chancery, among those, treason, bribery and extortion. On his way to London, Woolsey died at Leicester on 29 November 1530.

The punishments are similar with those in continental Europe; burning, beheading, hanging and drowning for serious offences, imprisonment, pillory or fines, for milder forms of criminality.

## 1.7. The laws of the Revolutions

French Revolution is one of the most remarkable events in human history; a bloodstained, ferocious and gruesome end to an era, but also the genesis of a new social order, intermittently founded on the principles of liberty, equality and fraternity.

French society in the 18th century was divided in three classes, the *Estates-General*; the First Estate represented the clergy, the Second Estate represented the nobility, and the Third Estate was formed by bourgeois and common people. The first two estates enjoyed a series of

---

[121] Ibid., pg. 144
[122] Ibid,. pg. 147
[123] Ibid., pg. 148
[124] See Edwardo Coke, *The Four Part of the Institutes of Laws of England*, (London: W. Clarke &Sons, 1817), pg. 88

privileges, mostly of patrimonial nature but also of legal nature, since the early middle ages.

To explain the animosity felt by the Third Estate, Germaine de Staël wrote: *"Thus the nobility maintained that valor was the exclusive inheritance of their order; and the clergy, that religion could not subsist without the possession of property by the church."*[125] Moreover, *"France has been governed by custom, often by caprice, and never by law"*[126]. Indeed, one of the goals of the revolution was to establish a legal system applicable for all citizens.

In the preamble of The Declaration of the Rights of Man and of the Citizen, August 1789 is stated that *"...ignorance, forgetfulness or disregards for the rights of man are the sole causes of public misfortunes and of the corruption of governments..."*[127]

On August 1789, the National Assembly's decree ended the feudal system of privileges. The tone of the document is quite impressive; the first proposition of the Article 1 states *"The National Assembly destroys the feudal regime completely."*[128] Seigniorial courts are abolished (Article 4), tithes of any nature and taxes are abolished (Article 5), and pecuniary, personal or real privileges are abolished forever (Article 9, 10). In Article 17 the National Assembly proclaims King Louis XVI to be the *"restorer of French liberty"*; at this moment there is no resentment against monarchy, or against the religion.

The French Revolution was not an atheist movement; it was a revolt against the privileges and the wealth accumulated by the clergy or the First Estate. The National Assembly's Decree on the Civil Constitution of the Clergy of 12 July 1790 stated that *"...the only one manner of filling bishoprics and cures will be known, that is through elections"*, an enactment intended to combat nepotism.[129]

Later on, in the second Declaration of the Rights of Man and of the Citizen from the preamble of the Constitution of 24 June 1793 it is stated that the declaration is made in the presence of the Supreme Being. Moreover, in 8 June 1794 Robespierre tried to establish a new State religion in the form of the Cult of the Supreme Being.

---

[125] See Germaine de Staël, *Considerations on the Principal Events of the French Revolution*, ed. trans. Aurelian Craiutu, (Indianapolis: Liberty Fund, 2008), pg.163
[126] Ibid., pg.80
[127] See Philip G. Dwyer and Peter McPhee, *The French Revolution and Napoleon A source book*, (London: Routledge, 2002), pg.24
[128] Ibid., 24
[179] Ibid., 46

Neither atheism nor the new theist movements managed to replace the Catholic faith and, on 15 July 1801, the Concordat of 1801 between Napoleon and Pope Pius VII acknowledged Catholicism as the religion of the great majority of the French people, however, it did not restored the privileges held in the *Ancien Regime.*

One controversial law is the Law Le Chapelier, of 14 June 1791, which banned any form of organization in guilds or corporations. One positive effect of the law was that the prices were now dictated by the market and they were not arbitrarily established by a guild; the negative effects were that the right to strike was also eliminated and that the University and the faculty of medicine were closed, allowing the practice of medicine without medical studies. It was abolished by the Law Ollivier on May 25, 1864, but it shows how confusing things were in that period.

In 1791 Louis-Michel Le Peletier de Saint-Fargeau presented in the National Assembly the draft of new criminal code which was adopted by the Constituent Assembly as the *Code Pénal Du 25 septembre - 6 octobre 1791.* Two innovations deserve a special mention: first, the code was based on the principle stated in Cesare Beccaria's *Dei Delitti e Delle Pene* that the punishment should be proportionate to the crime although disregarded the principle that the State has no right to take life, and second, the religious crimes such as blasphemy, heresy, sacrilege and witchcraft are abolished.

It was followed in 25 October 1795 by the *Code des Délits et des Peines Du 3 brumaire, an 4 Contenant les Lois relatives à l'instruction des affaires criminelles* and by the *Code Pénal De 1810* (published under the name of *Code Des Délits Et Des Peines*) also known as the Napoleon's Penal Code.

The term used by the NCP to describe antisocial behaviors that needed to be sanctioned by the penal law is '*infraction*' which can be, depending on the severity of the punishment '*un crime*' which corresponds to the modern term of a felony, '*un délit*' which is an intermediate category punished, with an afflictive or infamous penalty and '*une contravention*', roughly corresponding to term "misdemeanor" in the modern classification of offences.

Felonies and delicts[130] against the State addressed in Title I of Book III if the Code entitled '*Crimes et Délits contre la Chose Publique*' which

---

[130] Not to be confused with the term delict, a civil wrong used in Scotland, Louisiana or South Africa, the

should[131] be translated as 'Felonies and Delicts against Public Affairs'. The *actus reus* in these offences may be bearing arms against France (art.75), the practicing of machinations or exchanging intelligence with a foreign power or its agents, with the purpose of engaging in hostilities or war (art.76) or betraying to them towns, ports, fortresses etc., acts punished by death.

Corruption is explicitly mentioned in article 82 "*Every other person who, by corruption, fraud, or violence, succeeded to subtract such plans, and shall have communicated them, either to the enemy or to the agent of a foreign power, ...*" referring to the plans of fortifications, arsenals, ports, enumerated in the previous article. For the first time, the legislators unambiguously had incriminated the link between the phenomenon of corruption and an offence against the State, espionage in this case. The author of such crimes may be a public official under art.81, or any person, under article 82. The penalty for espionage is the death penalty by beheading.

Medieval methods of execution were extremely cruel; the wheels, burning at the stake, hanging, beheadings with axes or massive swords were the most used. In 1789, Joseph-Ignace Guillotin, a French physician, proposed in the National Assembly a reform of the capital punishment. A committee was created in 1791 to search for a humane method of execution.

The result was a device designed by Laquiante and Tobias Schmidt, made of a wooden frame and a 45 degree angled blade, inspired by similar devices used in medieval times such as the Halifax Gibbet or the Scottish 'Maiden'. The device nicknamed the Guillotine, after Joseph-Ignace, compared with the previous methods, was indeed 'humane' and remained in use as the official method of execution in France until the abolition of the death penalty in 1981.

Other offence against the safety of the State is plotting or attempting against the life of the emperor, or high treason and is punished as the parricide (right arm cut off before beheading) a penalty which was meant to suggest that the emperor was the father of the people.

---

equivalent of tort, or with the French délit civil, again, a tort. In the following translation from the NCP we shall use the English term delict, to translate the French délit or délit penal which is basically a felony.

[131] The English translation used by several sources is 'crimes against the commonwealth' which I consider to be incorrect.

More interesting for us are the felonies and delicts sanctioned in the Chapter II of the Title I of Book III, Felonies and Delicts against the constitutions of the Empire; a prescription against electoral corruption is stated in article 111 which incriminate the altering of the votes, a delict punishable by pillory (*carcan*) which meant tying the offender to a post with an iron ring around the neck in a public place as subject of humiliation.

The buying and selling of votes was sanctioned under article 113 with the loss of civic rights for 5 to10 years, an article that reminds us of the *de ambitu* laws of the Romans. Arbitrary acts of public officials that create prejudices to the individual liberty or the civic rights are punished with civic degradation (art.114). In Chapter II, Section III, articles 123-126, are incriminated conspiracies by public officers against the rule of law and in Section IV encroachment of administrative and judicial authorities.

Chapter III of the Title I of Book III is dedicated to crimes and delicts against public peace. Section I incriminates forgery and counterfeiting of money, seals, public, private and authentic documents, passports, traveling permits and other certificates.

Section II incriminates Crimes or Delicts committed by Public Officers, in the exercise of their functions, forfeitures, embezzlements, extortions, incompatibilities. Paragraph IV of the Section II is entitled *"About the corruption of the public officials"*; according to article 177 any public official of the administrative or judicial order or any agent or employee of a public administration who shall have accepted any offers or promises, or received any gifts or presents, to do any act of his function or employment is punished by fining and pillory.

A more severe sanction may be applied if the object of corruption is a criminal act sanctioned with a penalty more severe than pillory (art. 178). The corruptor is sanctioned under article 179 with the same penalty as the corrupt official.

The corrupt judge or juror is sanctioned with solitary imprisonment and a fine or, if there was a greater penalty given as a consequence of corruption, that penalty should be inflicted on the corrupt judge or juror (art. 181-182).

The abuses of the public authorities sanctioned in paragraph V are grouped into two classes of delicts, as abuses against natural persons which are sanctioned with fines (ar. 184-187) and abuses against public affairs which are punished with solitary imprisonment, deportation or even more severe sanctions.

The second title of the third Book of the Code is dedicated to crimes and delicts against natural persons (*particuliers*) and is divided in two chapters, the first refers to crimes and delicts against persons and the second is concerned with crimes and delicts against private propriety. Section IV of the first chapter, articles 330 to 340, entitled Attacks upon Morals, incriminates outrageous acts against modesty, rape, debauchery and corruption of youths, prostitution and corruption excited or facilitated by parents and legal guardians and adultery. Section VII, articles 361 to 378, incriminates calumny, slanders, disclosure of secrets by the physicians, surgeons and other officers of health.

Offences against propriety are incriminated in Chapter II of the Title II of Book III. Article 379 of the Section I defines theft very succinctly, "*Whoever has fraudulently abstracted a thing which does not belong to him, is guilty of theft.*", and the punishment was death, if the act was committed in the circumstances described in the article 381.

Various forms of theft are described and incriminated under articles 382 to 401 with less severe sanctions ranging from perpetual hard labor to imprisonment. In Section II, article 402 incriminates fraudulent bankruptcies, Article 405 incriminates the making use of false and article 406 incriminates the abuse of trust. At last, the articles from section III incriminate various forms of arson and destructions.

The extent of the influence that the Napoleonic codes exercised on the other codes of the European continental law is debatable. At its height in 1812, the French Empire and the satellite States covered most of Europe except Great Britain. Napoleon's vision for a unitary law system in his Empire is expressed very clear in a letter to Louis, King of Holland: "*The Romans gave their laws to their allies: why should France not have its laws adopted in Holland?*"[132] The empire lasted until 1814, when Napoleon abdicated at Fontainebleau but undoubtedly his legacy can be seen in the European codes that followed.

In the German States the enlightenment movement was triggered by the French philosophers like Voltaire, Montesquieu and Rousseau and jurists like the Dutch Hugo Grotius and the Italian Cesare Beccaria.

---

[132] See Philip G. Dwyer and Peter McPhee. *The French Revolution and Napoleon A source book* (London: Routledge, 2002), pg. 166

At the end of the Thirty Years War, the tortures and the cruelty of the punishments were challenged in the works of Baron Samuel von Pufendorf, 1632 - 1694, author of *On the Duty of Man and Citizen According to the Natural Law* (1673), Christian Thomasius, 1655 - 1728, author of *Essays on Church, State, and Politics* and Christian Wolff, 1679 - 1754, *The Law of Nations According to the Scientific Method* [133] with little practical success; the theological influence is still omnipresent in their work.

A small advancement is made with the *Codex Juris Bavarici criminalis* of 1751, *Constitutio criminalis Theresiana* of 1769, the Statutes of Frederick II of Prussia, the Prussian Landrecht of 1794 and the Austrian Code of 1803.[134]

The landmark document that changed definitively the German Criminal Law was the Penal Law Code for the Kingdom of Bavaria (1813). Paul Johann Anselm Ritter von Feuerbach (1775 - 1833) was appointed Minister of Justice of Bavaria in 1805 and was commissioned to draft a new code which will be adopted as the Bavarian Criminal Code of May 16, 1813 that used the tripartite classification of crimes similar to the French Code Penal.[135]

Feuerbach's code was followed by similar documents, such as the Oldenburg Criminal Code of September 10, 1814, The Hanoverian Code of August 8, 1840, the Code of the Kingdom of Saxony of March 30, 1838, or the Prussian Criminal Code of April 14, 1851 each one with its own flaws[136] but all sharing the merit of enriching the criminal law as a science.

Following the victory in the battle of Austerlitz (2 December 1805), the Holy Roman Empire was dissolved on 6 August 1806 and reorganized by Napoleon in the Confederation of the Rhine which was followed by the German Confederation after the Congress of Vienna (1815). In 1866, after the Austro-Prussian War the North German Confederation was created and on 10 December 1870 was renamed the German Empire and William I was proclaimed German emperor, thus ending the unification process.

---

[133] Thomas Vormbaum, *A Modern History of German Criminal Law*, Michael Bohlander, ed., Margaret Hiley, tr., (Springer-Verlag Berlin Heidelberg 2014), pg. 20
[134] Von Bar, pg. 250 to 258
[135] Ibid., pg. 330
[136] Ibid., pg.146

Heinrich von Friedberg (1813 -1895), Supreme Counsellor of Justice, wrote the Draft of 1869 of the Criminal Code for North Germany, modeled after the Prussian Criminal Code[137] which, with several changes from the original form will become the Penal Code for the German Reich of May 15, 1871.[138]

A major advancement was the abolition of the death penalty except in cases of high treason and premeditated murder. Perjury is punished under section nine, second part, articles 153-163 and false accusations under section ten. Blasphemy is the only religious offence and is punished with imprisonment up to three years under article 168.

Crimes and offenses against morality are incriminated under section thirteen and include bigamy, adultery, incest, sodomy which include bestiality, indecent assault, pimping. Theft and embezzlement are punished under section nineteen and robbery and extortion under section twenty. Section twenty two concerns fraud and embezzlement, and section twenty third falsification of documents.

Of particular interest for us is section twenty-eighth of the second part, offences and misdemeanors in office. Officials who accept bribes, gifts or other advantages are punished under article 331,332 with imprisonment from five years to six months or fines not exceeding one hundred *thalers*.

A special quality is required under articles 333, 334 for the subject, to be a member of the armed forces or a judge, umpire, juror or lay judge. Article 337 and 338 contain sanctions for priests and minister of religion. Abuses of authorities are punished under articles 339-346. Embezzlement is punished under articles 350, 351.

On July 4, 1776 thirteen British colonies declared their independence from British monarchy and formed a new nation, the United States of America. The Declaration of Independence adopted in Congress, states:

> *"When in the Course of human events, it becomes necessary for one people to dissolve the political bands which have connected them with another, and to assume among the powers of the earth, the separate and equal station to which the Laws of Nature and of Nature's God entitle them, a decent respect to the opinions of mankind requires that they should declare the causes which impel them to the separation. We hold these truths to be self-evident, that all men are created equal,*

---

[137] Ibid., pg. 354
[138] *Strafgesetzbuch für das Deutsche Reich*, ( Nordlingen , Druck und Verlag C. H. der Buchdruckerei, 1871)

*that they are endowed by their Creator with certain unalienable Rights, that among these are Life, Liberty and the pursuit of Happiness...*"[139]

The United States Constitution was drafted on 17 September 1787 and despite criticism expressed in its early days proved to be a success. The Constitution contain one direct reference to the phenomenon of corruption, in Article II Section 4 *"The President, Vice President and all civil Officers of the United States, shall be removed from Office on Impeachment for, and Conviction of, Treason, Bribery, or other high Crimes and Misdemeanors."*[140]

The ultimate legal innovation lay in the fact that the document may be amended; on September 25, 1789 the First Congress of the United States adopted the first 10 amendments, also known as the Bill of Rights, and between 1795 and 1992 sixteen other amendments were added.

The greatest achievements of these documents, is that they focus on human rights as the foundation of the social order. The idea of a codified legal system did not have many supporters in the newly formed United States of America which opted for a common law system based on English common law.

With the victory in the battle of Trafalgar, 21 October 1805, England became the dominant naval power and with the victory in the battle of Waterloo, 18 June 1815, ended Napoleon Bonaparte's political career. The greatest of Napoleon's legacies is the codification process of the laws that he succeeded to export in the rest of the continent.

Perhaps due to the hostility towards Napoleon's person, English jurists and legislators disregarded the benefits of the codification process until the contemporary period.

Sir William Blackstone, 10 July 1723 - 14 February 1780, is the most influential jurist of the common law legal systems. He wrote *Commentaries on the Laws of England*, in four volumes, first volume published in February 1766, followed by volumes two and three on October 1766 and June 1768, and finally ending with the volume four published on 1770 which is dedicated to criminal law.

Sir Blackstone wrote about electoral corruption in Chapter II Of the Parliament, in the form of bribing voters with money, gift, office, employment, or reward. On the note 53 he mentions The Corrupt

[139] See the text on www.archives.gov/exibits/charters/declaration.html
[140] See the text on www.archives.gov/exibits/charters/constitution_transcript.html.

Practices and Prevention Act of 1854 which *"...defines carefully and comprehensively what constitutes Bribery, Treating, and Undue Influence..."*[141]

The issue of electoral corruption will be addressed in later statutes such as the Ballot Act 1872, the Corrupt and Illegal Practices Prevention Act 1883 and the Parliamentary Elections Corrupt Practices Act 1885.

The 'corruption of blood' is another concept that today we can certainly declare to be utterly wrong. Blood is the bodily fluid responsible with the oxygenation and nourishment of the cells and the transportation of the metabolic wastes from the cells; the 'corrupt blood' of a traitor for instance, will not have any effect on his offspring behavior.

The truth behind the doctrine of 'corrupt blood' is that it offered a reason to deny the inheritance rights to the heirs of a person accused and convicted of treason or other crime of lese-majesty. It was just a method used in medieval period to avoid the vengeance of the successors by depriving them of wealth and power.

Sir Blackstone mentions in Chapter XXXIII. Of the rise, progress, and gradual improvements of the Laws of England *"...a hope that corruption of blood may one day be abolished and forgotten"*[142]; the doctrine of corrupt blood was finally abolished by the Corruption of Blood Act in 1814.

Chapter IV of Book IV is dedicated to offences against God and religion. Among those Sir Blackstone mentions apostasy, heresy, the offence of reviling the ordinances of the church, non-conformity to the worship of the church, blasphemy, the offence of profane and common swearing and cursing, witchcraft, conjuration, enchantment, or sorcery, religious imposture, simony, profanation of the Lord's day, lewdness.

In Chapter X we can find several offences against public justice. Embezzling or vacating records, or falsifying certain other proceedings in a court of judicature, obstructing the execution of lawful process, compounding of information upon penal statutes, conspiracy to indict an innocent man, bribery of judges or other persons concerned in the administration of justice, embracery *"...an attempt to influence a jury*

---

[141] William Blackstone, *Commentaries on the Laws of England*, vol.1, (Philadelphia: J.B. Lippincott Company, 1893), pg. 179
[142] Ibid., pg. 440

*corruptly...*", negligence of public officer, the oppression and tyrannical partiality of judges, justices, other magistrates, and extortions.

In Chapter XII Of Offences Against Public Trade we find another offences associated with corruption, smuggling, *"or the offence of importing goods without paying the duties"*, fraudulent bankruptcy, usury, cheating, forestalling the market, regrating, engrossing and monopolies.

And last in Chapter XVII Of Offences Against Private Property, beside larceny or theft, forgery which is defined at common law as *"the fraudulent making or alteration of a writing to the prejudice of another man's right"*[143].

With Sir William Blackstone's Commentaries on the Laws of England we end our journey in the history of laws against the phenomenon of corruption. Much more could have been said about the corrupt deeds of the past and many laws and statutes did not entered in this selection. My purpose was to create a historical perspective on the phenomenon and offer general directions for further explorations on a subject that, as I said in the beginning, may alone fill a library.


## 1.8. Conclusions

The genesis of the phenomenon generally named 'corruption' occurred in the earliest forms of human organization, as the poet said, 'since life begun'; therefore it must be contemporary with the first laws. In order to function, a community must establish, by common agreement or by force, a set of rules, or, in other words, a body of positive laws.

In its entire history the human kind failed to produce a law that will satisfy the needs, the interests and the desires of every single member of the society. When personal desires are contrary to the positive law, an individual will seek ways to break or to elude the law in order to achieve his purpose. Corruption is a natural counteraction to positive law, when the interests and the desires of individuals are in opposition with the law.

Human society, during the ages, was organized in several forms, starting with patriarchy, followed by autocracy, democracy, and oligarchy, depending on the person or the group who held the power to

---

[143] Ibid., pg.246

impose its will to the rest of the members. None of the forms of social organization was immune to corruption; corruption was recorded in the early city-states and kingdoms, in republics and in empires, even religious organizations which are based on strict a moral code, proved to be vulnerable.

Each society felt the ill effects of corruption and took measure against it, but none of these measures proved to be constant successful in the fight against corruption. Sparta's social model of equality is the only social model in history that briefly eliminated corruption, but eventually succumbed to it. There is not a single social model in the recorded history that was able to eradicate it and no form of human organization was immune to it. This leads to the conclusion that it must be a major flaw in the way we design our organizations and until this flaw is properly identified and corrected, we cannot hope for a corruption free society.

Tacitus, in *The Annals of Imperial Rome* observed that *"The more corrupt the State, the more numerous the laws."* Indeed, there seems to be a correlation between the amount of laws and the level of corruption. Even specific anti-corruption laws seem to generate more corruption. And here we can identify the trap in which all the legislators in history unwillingly entered: anti-corruption laws in particular and laws in general address the effects and not the causes. Despite my best efforts, I failed to identify a single law in the entire legal history that tackles the causes of corruption.

In an incipient stage, corruption is not capable to threat the legal order; any justice system, even the oldest ones were capable to address the effects of corruptions, but only *a posteriori*, after the damage has been done. In this stage, cases of corruption are sporadic and they are contained with relative ease.

When corruption exits the embryonic stage, it affects the justice system; without corruption among the magistrates the phenomenon cannot develop. A rapid expansion of the phenomenon occurs when the State or other form of organization acquires an extra wealth suddenly, without a mechanism of control to ensure the equitable management and distribution of that wealth. Paralyzed by corruption, the justice system is incapable to perform its task and corruption begins to spread rapidly on the organizational structure, vertically and horizontally.

In the pre-endemic stage there is a sort of balance, the calm before the storm. The ill effects of corruption are not felt by the society. Corruption seems to be a good business profitable for many. It is the phase when corruption grows unnoticed and unattended.

The collapse of the State occurs when corruption becomes endemic. The instrument of the collapse may be internal, revolution, *coup d'état*, or external, war, followed by the loss of suzerainty in a certain degree. Until a new social order is established, the society is ravaged by anarchy, allowing for the worst atrocities to happen.

The new regime is unable to eradicate corruption but in the immediate period it is able to put it under control. Gradually, the new administration of the State begins to indulge in the same practices as the former regime by neglecting the principles of justice and equality and creating new privileges. In time, corruption regrows and waits for the proper moment to enter in the final stage; it is a never ending cycle.

Sometimes, strong or violent public reaction against corruption are forcing the high hierarchy of the organization to take cleaning measures by expelling the subjects of the revolts; history proved this to be only a temporary measure with limited success. Even radical changes in the hierarchy of the organization never achieved long lasting results. This led us to the conclusion that once the structure of the organization is vulnerable there is no defense against corruption. Each new form of administration inherits the fundaments and a significant part of the human resource from the old administration and by this corruption perpetuates.

From the dawn of civilization actions that bring harm to the social order are punished; today we call those acts crimes or offences. Certain forms of the phenomenon of corruption had been incriminated by the first laws; bribery, embezzlement, forgery were punished in any society.

The severity of the punishment as a deterrent factor doesn't seem to have much effect against corruption. Even the cruelest punishments of the medieval period, usually doubled by the concept of sin for which the penalty was eternal damnation, did not succeeded in eradicating corruption among both clergy and lay men.

The wealth and the power that corruption generates have such an allure that individuals are willing to risk everything, even their lives, to obtain it; we have numerous examples of honest people becoming corrupt, and, unfortunately, only a few cases of corrupt men turning righteous, perhaps Diogenes of Sinope is the best example. Strangely enough, it was not religion that offered comfort for inequality, abuses, injustice and other consequences of corruption, but philosophy, which we shall explore in the next chapter.

*Men are more moral than they think and*
*far more immoral than they can imagine.*

Sigmund Freud

# 2. Ethics and morals - antitheses for corruption

The development of ethical and moral philosophy is a consequence of the phenomenon of corruption. In a society without corruption, ethics and morals would have no subject-matter for study and the society would not have much need of moralists. The purpose of this intrusion in the realm of philosophy is to find the views of the most influential philosophers about corruption and its antithesis, ethics and morals.

Bertrand Russell defined philosophy as *"something intermediate between theology and science"*, placed in *"the No Man's Land between the two"*[1]. Diogenes Laertius wrote that philosophy originated with the barbarians: the Magi, the Chaldaei, the Gymnosophistae and the Druids.[2] The foundations of philosophy as a science were laid by the Greek philosophers, but the principles behind it, the concepts of right or wrong, of justice and injustice, are much older, going back to the beginning of civilization. Indeed, philosophy itself is an evolutionary process.

The term εθικὰ (etika) was introduced by one of Aristotle's most important and influential works, Nicomachean Ethics. The term *moralis* comes from Latin and was used by Cicero to translate the Greek *êthikos*, form *mores* meaning custom, habit.[3]

The term corruption is also considered to be introduced by Cicero; nevertheless it is to be found in The Law of the Twelve Tables, Tabula VIII.27 *"...dum ne quid ex publica lege corrumpant..."*, ca. 451-449 BC, and in *Lex Genucia de Feneratione*, 342 BC, *"...et minus corruptis moribus..."*. Even if these texts come from secondary sources, Gaius and Tacitus, it is safe to assume that the notion of corruption was known to the Romans long before Cicero, in fact the Law of the Twelve Tables contains a very important prescription against corrupt judges.

---

[1] See Bertrand Russell *A History of Western Philosophy, And It's Connection with Political and Social Circumstances from the Earliest Times to the Present Day,* (New York: Simon and Schuster, 1945), pg.1
[2] Diogenes Laertius, The Lives and Opinions of Eminent Philosophers, C.D. Yonge tr., (London: Henry G. Bohn, 1853)
[3] Blackwell, *Dictionary of Western Philosophy*, pg.228

The surplus of resources allowed for trade to develop; the contract of exchange was gradually surpassed by the contract of sale, first inside the community and then between the communities. The early civilizations from the Fertile Crescent begun trading with each other once the resources of a city exceeded the needs of its inhabitants, but the most important commodity that the merchants unknowingly traded was information. The fascinating stories narrated by travelers and foreign traders were passed to the next generation and generations after, and this is why we can see common elements in the mythology of the habitants of the Fertile Crescent.

The Phoenicians and later the Greeks established a chain of colonies around the Mediterranean Sea and the Black Sea and since they benefited from the information gathered from all their trading partners, they became the most advanced civilizations of their time.

It is generally agreed that philosophy begins with Thales. Again, we are in the presence of an evolutionary process; Thales must have been the end product of a school of thought. His mathematical knowledge was acquired in Egypt while his astronomical knowledge came from Babylon through Lydia. This connection is important to remember, because is giving us an understanding about the influence that these centers of civilization, Babylon, Egypt and Greece exercised on each other. The most important contribution of the Milesian School is the fact that philosophy, as an incipient science, began to be separated from religion thru speculation.[4]

There is a succession that must be explained from the beginning. A social organization, in order to function, must enact rules, or positive laws unlike an anarchic society which is ruled by natural law. After the laws are enacted and enforced, particular interests drive individuals to seek ways to break or to elude the laws. And thus corruption is born, as a counter reaction to positive law.

When corruption was no longer a solitary and isolated event, and begun to grow in a form that challenged the rule of law, philosophers sought ways to reestablish the social equilibrium, either in the form of legal philosophy, or in the form of ethical theory and moral philosophy. Corruption causes a positive counter reaction in those individuals

---

[4] Bertrand Russel, *The history of Western Philosophy*, pg.46

affected directly or indirectly by its ill effects, in the form of ethical and moral principles which are developed as antithesis for corruption.

## 2.1. The architects of philosophy

Socrates, 470/469 BC - 399 BC, is considered by many scholars to be the father of Western philosophy. Socrates never wrote anything, so his own work and philosophical ideas are indistinguishable from those of his disciples, Plato and Aristotle, a situation referred to as 'the Socratic problem'. The works of the two, together with the works of Xenophon and the plays of Aristophanes are the main sources on Socrates and his philosophy.

Beside the fact that he was Socrates's student, and is perfectly normal for him to refer to his mentor and to follow in his steps, Plato might have had a more practical reason to use Socrates in his dialogs. Considering that his death sentence for his philosophical ideas might not have raised a public support for philosophy and philosophers in general, it is possible that Plato sought in Socrates an alibi to spread his own theories, which were beyond contemporary reasoning, in order to avoid a similar fate. It is known that Plato left Athens after Socrates death and returned after ten years, so it is common sense to believe that he might have done so out of fear for his own life. An older Plato, recounting his mentor's dialogues, was not much of a threat for the social order.

The Greek term for corruption is διαφθορά[5] (diaftora), meaning destruction, ruin, or when it was used figuratively it describes seduction.

In *Gorgias*, Socrates makes a distinction between three states of corruption; "*...there are three states of corruption, namely poverty, disease, and injustice*"[6] that affects one's finances, body, and soul. Among those, injustice is considered the most shameful because "*...it surpasses the others by some monstrously great harm and astounding badness, since it doesn't surpass them in pain...*"[7] Socrates offers an elegant solution: financial management for poverty, doctors for disease and judges to get rid of injustice and indiscipline[8].

---

[5] Henry George Liddell and Robert Scott, *A Greek English Lexicon*, (Oxford: Claredon Press, 1996), pg. 418
[6] Plato, *Gorgias*, 477c
[7] Ibid 477e
[8] Ibid 478b

In *Protagoras*, Socrates tells us that virtue cannot be taught, providing several examples, the stories of Pericles and Clinias, situations in which the sons of famous individuals failed to follow their fathers model. The sophistic view expressed by Protagoras was that virtue can be taught. However, at the end of the debate, Socrates changes his position, believing that *"...everything is knowledge - justice, temperance, courage - in which case, virtue would appear to be eminently teachable".*[9]

The question: *"Can virtue be taught?"*[10] is raised in another Socratic dialogue, *On Virtue*, considered to be a product of the Athenian Academy, where the author reflects that *"...possession of virtue is very much a divine gift and that men become good just as the divine prophets and oracle-mongers do"*[11] and *"...virtue is neither teachable nor natural, but comes by divine allotment to those who possess it"*[12].

This view, however, is too religious in its nature to be attributed to either Socrates or Plato. Greed is explored by Socrates in *Hipparchus*, another dialogue from an unknown author. *"Profit is good"*, *"everyone always wants good things"*[13], *"all people would be greedy, both the virtuous and the wicked"*[14].

In *Euthyphro*, Socrates is on his way in to answer the charges of 'impiety' brought against him by three younger fellow citizens *"...he says that I am a maker of gods, and on the ground that I create new gods while not believing in the old gods..."*[15] and *"...makes innovations in religious matters..."*[16] Moreover, the accusers claimed that *"...Socrates is a pestilential fellow who corrupts the young"*[17] and *"Socrates is guilty of corrupting the young and of not believing in the gods in whom the city believes, but in other new spiritual things"*[18].

In *Apology*, Socrates defends himself against the accusations of corruption:

> *"If one asks them what he does and what he teaches to corrupt them, they are silent, as they do not know, but, so as not to appear at a loss, they mention those accusations that are available against all philosophers, about "things in the sky*

---

[9] Plato, *Protagoras*, 361b
[10] Plato, *On Virtue*, 376b
[11] Ibid (379c);
[12] Ibid (379d);
[13] Plato, *Hipparchus*, 227c, 227d
[14] Ibid 232c
[15] Plato, *Euthyphro*, 3b
[16] Ibid.
[17] Ibid., 23d
[18] Plato, *Apology*, 24b

and things below the earth," about "not believing in the gods" and "making the worse the stronger argument"; they would not want to tell the truth, I'm sure, that they have been proved to lay claim to knowledge when they know nothing."[19]

Socrates considers this statement to be the only defense he needs, and begins to examine those accusations, point by point. His defense however is ineffective in front of a hostile jury and he is sentenced to death.

In *Crito*, friends of Socrates tried to convince him to escape by bribing the guards. He refuses, perfectly aware of the consequences such an act will bring upon his friends. He chooses to die by poison.

The story of Socrates, as is told by Plato and others, shows as that society in general is reticent to new ideas. Although Socrates doesn't consider himself to be an atheist, he challenges contemporary religious beliefs.

We can say that his trial is a turning point, a moment in human history when philosophy as a science distinguishes itself clearly from religion. Socrates's hypothetic situations that he brings as argument or counter argument shows that in human relations, everything is relative and none of the values that society uphold, good, right, law, justice, are to be exercise in an absolute manner. The position of the observer is what determines what is right, just, moral.

***

Plato, 428/427 or 424/423 - 348/347 BC, Socrates's student, founder the first Academy in Athens, is the most influential philosopher in the Western culture, a position shared with his disciple, Aristotle.

Just as in many of the Dialogues, the *Republic* uses Socrates as the main character; Book I begins with a quest for the definition of justice. The views that justice means to "...*speak truth and pay your debts*"[20] or that "...*justice is nothing other than the advantage of the stronger*"[21] are contradicted by the ideas that "...*justice is soul's virtue and injustice its vice*"[22] and "...*a just person is happy, and an unjust one wretched*"[23] with the conclusion that "...*injustice is never more profitable than justice*".[24]

An interesting parable is used in Book IV to pinpoint the place a philosopher should occupy in society; the philosopher is similar to the pilot of the ship because unlike the captain or the sailors, the pilot is the

---

[19] Ibid., 32d
[20] Plato, *Republic*, 331d
[21] Ibid., 338c
[22] Ibid., 353e
[23] Ibid., 354
[24] Ibid.

66

only one who has the knowledge to steer the ship. Yet we are warned that philosophers and philosophy itself may be corrupted with consequences on the education of the youth.[25]

*Laws* is one of the Plato's later works, a discussion between three elderly men, Clinias a Cretan, Megillus a Lacedaemonian and the Athenian, while they travel on a pilgrimage from Knossos to the cave of Zeus. *Laws* begin with an essential question: the Athenian asks *"Tell me, gentlemen, to whom do you give the credit for establishing your codes of law? Is it a god, or a man?"*[26]

While Clinias claims that Cretan laws were inspired by Zeus and Lacedaemonian laws by Apollo, the Athenian mysteriously remain silent about the Athenian laws. Plato's view is clear, he respects the contemporary opinion and the historic tradition, yet, by remaining silent he places himself in total disagreement.

In Book III Clinias reveals that he is a member of the legal commission entitled to draft the laws for a new colony, Magnesia, and the trio embarks in a quest for the most suitable laws for the perfect colony.    Since the focus of the discussion is a new colony, little mentions to corruption are made. The laws of the new city which the Athenian suggests are in fact Plato's improvements on the existing legislation of Sparta and Athens. He covers several topics, administration of the State, education, and criminal law.

Plato wrote about the education of a child, *"...surrounding him with lots of pleasures..."*[27] is *"...the best way to ruin a child, because the corruption invariably sets in at the very earliest stages of his education."*[28]

Another form of corruption which Plato takes in consideration is sexual corruption; his view is that sex should be performed just for procreation purposes like *"...birds and many other wild animals which are born into large communities and live chaste and unmarried, without intercourse, until the time comes for them to breed."*[29] He acknowledges that such a law will be impossible to obey, so he advocates privacy and decency as the next best thing.[30]

---

[25] Plato., *Republic* 492
[26] Ibid., 609
[27] Plato., *Laws*, 792c
[28] Ibid., 792d
[29] Ibid., 840d
[30] Ibid., 841b

While exploring the laws for commerce Plato wrote: "*...only a small part of mankind - a few highly educated men of rare natural talent - is able to steel itself to moderation when assailed by various needs and desires; given the chance to get a lot of money, it's a rare bird that's sober enough to prefer a modest competence to wealth.*"[31]

Books IX to XII are concerned with criminal matters; offences that are proposed for incrimination are robbery, treason, theft, and murder in various degrees.

***

Aristotle, 384-322 BC, was born in Stagira, Macedonia and joined Plato's Academy in 402 BC; he will become one of the greatest philosophers in history. In his work, Aristotle is using the term corruption both literarily, in *On Generation and Corruption* or in *On the Generation of Animals* meaning alteration, decay, and figuratively, in the sense we use it almost exclusively today.

In *Politics*, Aristotle considers that "*...many are more incorruptible than few*", a principle that is also to be found in the *Athenian Constitution*. Wealth can be acquired in two ways by household management and by trade; usury "*...which makes a gain out of money itself*"[32] is considered the most hated form of making money and the most unnatural mode of acquiring wealth.

In Book II Aristotle searches "*... what form of political community is best of all for those who are most able to realize their ideal of life.*" He criticizes the social model proposed in The Republic and Laws by Plato, sometimes quite ironically: "*Again, if Socrates makes the women common, and retains private property, the men will see to the fields, but who will see to the house?*"[33]

In Book III Aristotle favors large collective bodies over a single ruler because "*... the many are more incorruptible than the few; they are like the greater quantity of water which is less easily corrupted than a little.*"[34]

An interesting concept is presented in Book V: "*....state should be so administered and so regulated by law that its magistrates cannot possibly make money.*"[35] In his view this is the only way to combine aristocracy and democracy. If the office of magistrate offers no benefits

[31] Ibid., 918d
[32] Aristotle, *Politics*, 1258b1
[33] Ibid., 1264b1
[34] Ibid., 1286a25
[35] Ibid., 1308b30

only the notables will be interested to hold it, *"...the poor will keep to their work and grow rich, and the notables will not be governed by the lower class"*[36], *"And honors should be given by law to magistrates who have the reputation of being incorruptible"*.[37]

In Book VI Aristotle argues against numerous assemblies that *"...can hardly be made to assemble unless they are paid ... leading the notables to obtain money ... by a property tax and confiscations and corrupt practices of the courts, things which have before now overthrown many democracies."*[38]

The *Constitution of Athens* is another praised work especially because offers an insight on a dark area, the laws of ancient Greece, which were either unwritten or they were written on perishable mediums, sheep skins or wooden tablets and did not survive.

Aristotle wrote about the phenomenon of corruption among magistrates:

*"The following magistrates also are elected by lot: Five Commissioners of Roads (Hodopoei), who, with an assigned body of public slaves, are required to keep the roads in order: and ten Auditors, with ten assistants, to whom all persons who have held any office must give in their accounts. These are the only officers who audit the accounts of those who are subject to examination, and who bring them up for examination before the law–courts. If they detect any magistrate in embezzlement, the jury condemns him for theft, and he is obliged to repay tenfold the sum he is declared to have misappropriated. If they charge a magistrate with accepting bribes and the jury convict him, they fine him for corruption, and this sum too is repaid tenfold. Or if they convict him of unfair dealing, he is fined on that charge, and the sum assessed is paid without increase, if payment is made before the ninth prytany, but otherwise it is doubled. A tenfold fine is not doubled."* [39]

Aristotle was the author of three treatises on moral philosophy *Nicomachean Ethics*, *Magna Moralia* and *Eudemian Ethics*; their chronology, influence, importance, even their author,[40] were debated ever since antiquity.

*Nicomachean Ethics* is a treatise in ten books, general regarded as the best work from the three mentioned. Of particular interest to us is Book V (which is the same with Book IV of the *Eudemian Ethics*), where

[36] Aristotle, *Politics*, 1309a5
[37] Ibid., 1309a15
[38] Ibid., 1320a209
[39] Aristotle, *Athenian Constitution*, § 54
[40] See Antony Kenny, *A New History of Western Philosophy*, vol. 1, (New York: Oxford University Press, 2006), pg. 80

Aristotle analyzes justice and injustice, especially injustice, a genre in which corruption may be placed.

For Aristotle Justice is *"...that kind of state which makes people disposed to do what is just and makes them act justly and wish for what is just..."* and injustice is *"...that state which makes them act unjustly and wish for what is unjust."*[41] *"Both the lawless man and the grasping and unequal man are thought to be unjust, so that evidently both the law-abiding and the equal man will be just."*[42]

The relativity of good is explored subsequently:

> *"Since the unjust man is grasping, he must be concerned with goods—not all goods, but those with which prosperity and adversity have to do, which taken absolutely are always good, but for a particular person are not always good."*[43]
> *"The unjust man does not always choose the greater, but also the less—in the case of things bad absolutely; but because the lesser evil is itself thought to be in a sense good, and graspingness is directed at the good, therefore he is thought to be grasping. And he is unequal; for this contains and is common to both."*[44]

The law is just and commands us to do just actions; justice is complete excellence, not absolutely, but in relation to others.

Justice is part of virtue, injustice is a part of vice; there is a part of injustice which is contrary to law. If a person acts for a gain he is unjust; Aristotle uses here an interesting example, a person who commits adultery for money compared with the person who commits adultery out of passion which he considers not greedy but intemperate.

There are two types of justice, one that plays a distributive role in the sharing of honors or money, and the other that plays a 'rectificatory' role in transactions. Aristotle considers the 'transactions' to be voluntary (selling, buying, lending at interest, pledging, lending without interest, depositing, and letting) and 'involuntary'( some involving secrecy like theft, adultery, poisoning, procuring, enticing away slaves, treacherous murder and false witness, some involving force like assault, imprisonment, murder, robbery, maiming, slander, and insult).[45]

Justice *"...is found among people who associate in life to achieve self-sufficiency, people who are free and either proportionately or arithmetically equal."*, *"...what is just exists only among people whose relations are governed by law, and law only among those liable to*

---

[41] 1129a9-1129a17
[42] Aristotle, *Nicomachean Ethics*, 1129b1
[43] Ibid., 1129b 5
[44] Ibid., 1129b10
[45] 1130b30-1131a9

*injustice, since legal justice consists in judgement between what is just and what is unjust."*[46]

He wrote:

> *"And between men between whom there is injustice there is also unjust action (though there is not injustice between all between whom there is unjust action), and this is assigning too much to oneself of things good in themselves and too little of things evil in themselves. This is why we do not allow a man to rule, but law, because a man behaves thus in his own interests and becomes a tyrant. The magistrate on the other hand is the guardian of justice, and, if of justice, then of equality also. And since he is assumed to have no more than his share, if he is just (for he does not assign to himself more or what is good in itself, unless such a share is proportional to his merits—so that it is for others that he labours, and it is for this reason that men, as we stated previously, say that justice is another's good), therefore a reward must be given him, and this is honour, and privilege; but those for whom such things are not enough become tyrants."*[47]

Another interesting concept is to be found in chapter seven; there are two parts of political justice, natural justice and legal justice. *"Of things just and lawful each is related as the universal to its particulars; for the things that are done are many, but of them each is one, since it is universal."*[48]

In chapter eight, Aristotle divides human acts, which can be just or unjust, into voluntary acts and involuntary acts: *"...a man acts unjustly or justly whenever he does such acts voluntarily; when involuntarily, he acts neither unjustly nor justly except in an incidental way; for he does things which happen to be just or unjust."*[49].

He considers that there are three kinds of injuries in transactions, mistakes, misadventures and acts of injustice.

> *"When he acts with knowledge but not after deliberation, it is an act of injustice - e.g. the acts due to anger or to other passions necessary or natural to man; for when men do such harmful and mistaken acts they act unjustly, and the acts are acts of injustice, but this does not imply that the doers are unjust or wicked; for the injury is not due to vice. But when a man acts from choice, he is an unjust man and a vicious man."*[50]

In order to determine if a man is unjust or not: *"...if a man harms another by choice, he acts unjustly; and these are the acts of injustice which imply that the doer is an unjust man, provided that the act violates*

---

[46] 1134a24-1134b7
[47] 1134a24-1134b7
[48] 1135a6-1135a7
[49] 1135a16-1135b25
[50] 1135a16-1135b25

*proportion or equality. Similarly, a man is just when he acts justly by choice; but he acts justly if he merely acts voluntarily.*"[51] He considers that some involuntary acts and errors are pardonable and some are not.

In chapter nine, about the 'distributors of justice', Aristotle wrote:

"*...if the distributor gave his judgment in ignorance, he does not act unjustly in respect of legal justice, and his judgment is not unjust in this sense, but in a sense it is unjust (for legal justice and primary justice are different); but if with knowledge he judged unjustly, he is himself aiming at an excessive share either of gratitude or of revenge. As much, then, as if he were to share in the unjust act, the man who has judged unjustly for these reasons has got too much; for, assigning the land on that condition, he received not land but money.*"[52]

In chapter ten Aristotle explores the notion of equity which he considers to be superior to justice because laws cannot prescribe for any particular situation.

He wrote:

"*...the equitable is just, and better than one kind of justice—not better than absolute justice but better than the error that arises from the absoluteness of the statement. And this is the nature of the equitable, a correction of law where it is defective owing to its universality.*"[53]

The equitable person is "*...the man who chooses and does such acts, and is no stickler for justice in a bad sense but tends to take less than his share though he has the law on his side, is equitable, and this state is equity, which is a sort of justice, and not a different state.*"[54]

In his Nicomachean Ethics, Aristotle does not say a single word about corruption, yet there several examples that fit the term very well; the crime of adultery committed for gain, for instance. Here we can conclude that corruption is unjust and unlawful.

Perhaps the greatest philosophical advancement in Greek society, are the separation of science from religion and the separation of law from religion. Greek laws are not inspired by the Gods; the lawgivers of Ancient Greece, Draco, Solon, Lycurgus, are normal humans. They do not possess superpowers, and none of them were raised to the status of Gods or at least demi-gods in their life or after. Unlike their predecessor in Babylon and Egypt, Greek lawmakers did not use Divinity to ensure that their laws are obeyed.

---

[51] 1136a1-1136a4
[52] 1136b33-1137a4
[53] 1137b33-1138a3
[54] 1137b33-1138a3

Religion played an important part in Greek society. They have constructed some of the most impressive temples; the Temple of Artemis at Ephesus was one of the wonders of the Ancient World. The Statue of Zeus at Olympia, another ancient wonder created by Phidias was an object of awe for nearly a millennium.

Religious festivals were held constantly in honor of major deities involving rituals, sacrifices, offerings; the Gods spoke thru the voice of oracles to rulers, citizens, merchants, travelers, and philosophers alike.

The Gods are omnipresent in literature, arts, history and philosophy, yet in the legal domain their presence is quite discrete. An explanation for this situation is that the Greeks used collective bodies in managing the State's affairs. When a decision was made in a trial or about a new law in the presence of hundreds or thousands of people, it was hard to claim any divine inspiration or intrusion in the process. Religious rituals might have preceded or followed the legal process but did not interfere with it.

## 2.2. The philosophers of the Church

Augustine of Hippo, 13 November 354 - 28 August 430, was the most influential Christian theologian and philosopher. He came in contact with Christian believes in his childhood; his mother, Santa Monica was a fervent Christian. In his youth he studied rhetoric to become a lawyer and he admired Cicero. He adhered to the Manichaean sect but he was never an important figure inside the sect; in 386 converted to Christianity, in 391 became a priest and in 395 became Bishop of Hippo.

The *City of God* was written in 410 after Rome was sacked by the Goths, and it is intended to be a reply to the view of the non-Christians that Jupiter no longer protects the city.[55] The Goths, however, were Christians and they spared those who took refuge in churches and, besides Christians, many non-Christians used this escape.

It was such an important event, that from now onwards, people will seek refuge in churches in times of wars.[56] God "...*uses war to correct and chasten the corrupt morals of mankind...*"[57] and "...*a major reason why the good are chastised along with the evil, when God decides to*

---

[55] Bertrand Russel, *A History of Western Philosophy*, pg. 355
[56] Ibid., pg. 356
[57] St Augustine, *City of God*, Henry Bettenson tr., (London: Penguin Classics, 1984) I.1

*punish moral corruption with temporal calamities. Good and bad are chastised together, not because both alike live evil lives, but because both alike, though not in the same degree, love this temporal life.*"[58]

Suicide was common among romans; those defeated in battle or in the political struggle chose to end their own life rather than to suffer the humiliation. For Augustine, such acts are "*...a detestable crime and a damnable sin*"[59] ; his interpretation is that the women who were raped during the war did not lost their chastity and suicide is not the solution to save chastity.[60]

St Augustine thinks that those who oppose the Christian era do not seek peace and general prosperity but "*...an infinite variety of pleasure with a crazy extravagance, and your prosperity produces a moral corruption far worse than all the fury of an enemy.*"[61]

Lust for power and ambition appears in a people "*corrupted by greed and sensuality*".[62] St Augustine praises Nasica[63] for opposing o the construction of a theatre that would have weakened the Roman moral character.

In Book II.16, St Augustine makes very an interesting point: the Romans did not receive moral instructions from their gods, but from the laws of Solon which they improved. He goes even further to blame the gods that they did not protect their worshipers from disasters and points to them as promoters of corruption.

> "*Thus though corrupt thoughts, corrupt lives and corrupt conduct are so dangerous that their most learned men assert that countries come to ruin through them, even when the cities still stand, nevertheless, their gods were not in the least concerned to protect their worshippers from such disasters. In fact, as we have argued, they were most concerned to promote this corruption.*"[64]

More of that can be found in II.22. The Roman Gods were not concerned to prevent the destruction of the commonwealth through moral corruption; "*...they were content that they should live in corruption, provided that they supplied all their wants under the compulsion of fear*"[65].

---

[58] Ibid., I.9
[59] Ibid., I.25
[60] Ibid., I.19
[61] Ibid., I.30
[62] Ibid., I.31
[63] Publius Cornelius Scipio Nasica Corculum (died 141 BC) Pontifex Maximus in 150 BC
[64] St. Augustine, *City of God*, II.22.
[65] Ibid.

Sometimes St. Augustine contradicts himself; on some occasions he does not believe in the Roman and Greek Gods which he sees as fables an tales, while in other occasions he seem to consider them evil, hence they exist.

The criticism towards pagan religion and pagan gods continues throughout the first part; if books I–V concern religion, the criticism in books VI–X is focused on philosophic aspects. The second part of the book is concerned with the City of God and the Earthly City, their genesis, their development and their future.

Corruption resulting from a sin is a punishment;[66] the City of God is free of corruption. As Plato before him, St Augustine uses the term corruption in both senses, figuratively and literally. In the City of God, which is free of corruption, the body of the resurrected becomes eternally incorruptible.

*Confessions* is another work by St Augustine that exerted a significant influence thru the ages. It's an autobiography written around 400 and it is regarded by some scholars as the best writing of Augustine.

In the first books he recounts his childhood, his studies in rhetoric in Cartage and his involvement with the Manicheans. In Book 7 he remembers his struggle to understand God; he wrote:

> *"But since it is of the utmost truth and certainty that the incorruptible is preferable to the corruptible, even as I already preferred it to be, I could now attain in thought to a being better than yourself, my God, if you were not incorruptible.1 Therefore, where I perceived that the incorruptible must be preferred to the corruptible, there ought I to seek you. There, too, ought I to observe where evil itself is, that is, whence comes that corruption, by which your substance can in no way be violated. For absolutely no corruption defiles our God: none from the will, none from necessity, none from any unforeseen chance. He is God, and what he wills for himself is good, and he himself is that same good, whereas to be corrupted is not good."*[67]

In Book 9 he wrote:

> *"Who am I, and what am I? Is there any evil that is not found in my acts, or if not in my acts, in my words, or if not in my words, in my will? But you, O Lord, are good and merciful, and your right hand has had regard for the depth of my death, and from the very bottom of my heart it has emptied out an abyss of corruption"*[68].

---

[66] Ibid., XIV 3
[67] St Augustine, *The Confessions of St Augustine*, John K. Ryan tr., (New York: Image Books, 1960) VII.4.(6)
[68] Ibid., IX.1.(1)

St Augustine's view on creation is that God created the universe out of nothing, unlike his predecessors Plato and Aristotle who saw God as an architect[69] making use of a primitive matter. His understanding of time is astonishing, before creation there was no time.

*On the Free Choice of the Will* is an interesting dialogue between St Augustine and Evodius who ask a very important question: "... *isn't God the cause evil?*"[70] Evodius defines evil as adultery, murder, and sacrilege and "...*others, that time and memory do not permit me to enumerate*".[71] Evodius considers that adultery is not evil because law forbids it, the law forbids it because is evil.[72]

The conclusion that the origin of evil is the free choice of the will is somehow disappointing; St Augustine fail to explain why the criminal chooses the evil action instead of the righteous one and why he chooses lust over virtue.

Towards the end of his career St. Augustine wrote *Reconsiderations On Free Choice of the Will*, where he attempts to bring some clarifications that will distance him from the pelagian heresy. He does so by adding the concept of the "*grace of God*" but his defense seems only to add a new contradiction.

St. Augustine does not have the lucidity of Plato; when Plato uses Socrates in his dialogues, his (or Socrates's) ideas are clear from the beginning and the dialogue is just an excuse for the argument. St. Augustine's entire work is an exploration, he is not certain about his position and first he tries to convince himself about the correctitude of his beliefs.

***

Born at Rocca Secca in the Kingdom of Naples, 1225 or 1227, died at Fossa Nuova, 7 March, 1274, Thomas Aquinas was a Dominican monk, theologian, doctor of the Church (*Angelicus Doctor*), and he is one of the greatest philosophers of the Middle Ages.

If Plato was the dominant influence on St. Augustine's philosophy, Aquinas draws his inspiration from Aristotle and rejects Platonism, despite the fact that he is always mindful to St. Augustine's sayings.

Aquinas was a prolific writer, his entire opera is gigantic. The most important and influential works are *Summa contra Gentiles*, completed

---

[69] Bertrand Russel, *A History of Western Philosophy*, pg. 353
[70] St. Augustine, *On the Free Choice of the Will*, (Indianapolis: Hackett Publishing Co., 1993), I.[1]
[71] Ibid., I.[3]
[72] Ibid.

in 1265 and *Summa Theologiae,* which was never completed because on December 1273, while saying mass, a vision caused him a block and he could no longer write or dictate.[73]

The format of *Summa Theologiae* is unique; the entire work is divided in treatises and each treatise is structured on a number of important topics, called questions. On each topic, the author asks several questions, called articles, for which he provides one or several answers (objections), formed in the opinions of his predecessors or just in general, then presents his opinion on the matter, which in most cases is contrary to the others, and ends by making his argument in replies to the objections. This format was criticized by Russell: *"The finding of arguments for a conclusion given in advance is not philosophy, but special pleading."*[74]

The phenomenon of corruption is present in his entire work; the term corruption is used, as in Aristotle, in two senses, literary, referring to decay, death and figuratively, referring to matters of morals or ethics.

God is incorruptible in the sense that it is simple, perfect, good, and infinite[75] therefor doesn't decay like any other substance and it cannot be corrupted by evil; *"... evil is found in things, as corruption also is found; for corruption is itself an evil."*[76]. Angels are incorruptible[77] unlike man who is corruptible, yet the human soul is incorruptible.[78]

A habit *"either of virtue or of vice, may be corrupted by a judgment of reason, whenever its motion is contrary to such vice or virtue, whether through ignorance, passion or deliberate choice"* and *"a habit of virtue can be corrupted"*[79].

*"The first sin infects nature with a human corruption pertaining to nature; whereas other sins infect it with a corruption pertaining only to the person"* and *"the effect of sin is the corruption of the good of nature"*[80].

For Aquinas *"Law is a rule and measure of acts, whereby man is induced to act or is restrained from acting: for lex (law) is derived from ligare (to bind), because it binds one to act."* and *"...the law belongs to*

---

[73] Antony Kenny, *A New History of Western Philosophy,* vol. 2, pg. 74
[74] Bertrand Russel, *A History of Western Philosophy,* pg. 463
[75] St. Thomas Aquinas, *Summa Theologica,* 2nd edition, tr. Fathers of the English Dominican Province. (London: Burns Oates and Washbourne, 1920) I, Q. 2-10
[76] St. Thomas Aquinas, *Summa Theologica,* I, Q. 48, Art. 2
[77] I, Q. 50, Art. 5
[78] I, Q. 75, Art. 6
[79] I-II, Q. 53, Art. 1
[80] II-I, Q 85

*that which is a principle of human acts, because it is their rule and measure*".[81]

Law can be Devine, Natural or Human. The eternal law "...*is nothing else than the type of Divine Wisdom, as directing all actions and movements.*"[82] Virtue is natural "...*all virtuous acts belong to the natural law.*"[83] Human law "...*is derived from the law of nature*", "... *if in any point it deflects from the law of nature, it is no longer a law but a perversion of law*"[84] and "*human laws do not forbid all vices, from which the virtuous abstain, but only the more grievous vices, from which it is possible for the majority to abstain*"[85].

There are several definitions in Aquinas that interest us in particular. Heresy is defined as "*a species of unbelief, belonging to those who profess the Christian faith, but corrupt its dogmas.*"[86]

Right is the object of justice[87] and justice is "*the perpetual and constant will to render to each one his right*" a definition from Justinian's Digest.[88]

About injustice he wrote:

> "*Injustice is twofold. First there is illegal injustice which is opposed to legal justice: and this is essentially a special vice, in so far as it regards a special object, namely the common good which it contemns; and yet it is a general vice, as regards the intention, since contempt of the common good may lead to all kinds of sin.*" "*Secondly we speak of injustice in reference to an inequality between one person and another, when one man wishes to have more goods, riches for example, or honors, and less evils, such as toil and losses, and thus injustice has a special matter and is a particular vice opposed to particular justice.*"[89]

To the question whether it is lawful to kill a sinner, Aquinas answer is: "*Therefore if a man be dangerous and infectious to the community, on account of some sin, it is praiseworthy and advantageous that he be killed in order to safeguard the common good, since "a little leaven corrupteth the whole lump" (1 Cor. 5:6).*"[90]

Only the authorities may kill an evildoer[91], not even the clerics can do such acts.[92] It was a doctrine that was respected in letter by the clerical

---

[81] I-II, Q. 90, Art. 1, I-II, Q. 90, Art. 2
[82] I-II, Q. 93, Art. 1
[83] I-II, Q. 94, Art. 3
[84] I-II, Q. 95, Art. 2
[85] I-II, Q. 96, Art. 2
[86] II-II, Q. 11, Art. 1
[87] II-II, Q. 57
[88] *Digest.. i, 1; De Just. et Jure 10
[89] St. Thomas Aquinas, *Summa Theologica* II-II, Q. 59.
[90] II-II, Q. 64, Art. 2

authorities in the Middle Ages; the executions of those condemned by the clerical authorities were performed by the secular authorities, sometimes through the institution of the public executioner, sometimes by local authority or even by mobs.

The principle of self-defense is very well expressed: *"...if a man, in self-defense, uses more than necessary violence, it will be unlawful: whereas if he repel force with moderation his defense will be lawful..."*[93]

Theft and Robbery are also considered sins *"I answer that, If anyone consider what is meant by theft, he will find that it is sinful on two counts. First, because of its opposition to justice, which gives to each one what is his, so that for this reason theft is contrary to justice, through being a taking of what belongs to another. Secondly, because of the guile or fraud committed by the thief, by laying hands on another's property secretly and cunningly. Wherefore it is evident that every theft is a sin."*[94]

A man can justly judge one who is not his subject[95], it is unlawful for the judge to deliver judgements contrary to the truth based on evidence[96], and he can sentence only a man that is accused[97].

Usury is considered a sin: *"To take usury for money lent is unjust in itself, because this is to sell what does not exist, and this evidently leads to inequality which is contrary to justice."*[98]

Question 98 is dedicated to perjury: *"Now perjury, of its very nature implies contempt of God, since, as stated above (A. 2), the reason why it is sinful is because it is an act of irreverence towards God. Therefore it is manifest that perjury, of its very nature, is a mortal sin."*[99]

Simony is not clearly defined but the question is *"Whether Simony Is an Intentional Will to Buy or Sell Something Spiritual or Connected with a Spiritual Thing"*. Simony is a heresy *"...by buying or selling a spiritual thing, a man treats God and divine things with irreverence, and consequently commits a sin of irreligion."*[100] It is notable that Aquinas said that even the Pope can be guilty of simony:

---

[91] II-II, Q. 64, Art. 3
[92] II-II, Q. 64, Art. 4
[93] II-II, Q. 64, Art. 7
[94] St. Thomas Aquinas, *Summa Theologica* II-II, Q. 66, Art. 5
[95] II-II, Q. 67, Art. 1
[96] II-II, Q. 67, Art. 2
[97] II-II, Q. 67, Art. 3
[98] II-II, Q. 78, Art. 1
[99] II-II, Q.98.Art. 2
[100] II-II, Q.100.

*"The Pope can be guilty of the vice of simony, like any other man, since the higher a man's position the more grievous is his sin. For although the possessions of the Church belong to him as dispenser in chief, they are not his as master and owner. Therefore, were he to accept money from the income of any church in exchange for a spiritual thing, he would not escape being guilty of the vice of simony. In like manner he might commit simony by accepting from a layman moneys not belonging to the goods of the Church."*[101]

The sign of equivalence between crime and sin is firmly established with Aquinas. From this moment onward, until Cesare Beccaria wrote *On Crimes and Punishments* in 1764, crime will be associated with evil and the criminal with the Devil. The reminiscences of this theory is to be seen even in the modern definition of the crime, an *actus reus*, or a bad, an evil act performed by a person with a *mens rea*, an evil mind.

## 2.3. Philosophers for Revolutions

François-Marie Arouet, 1694 –1778, wrote under the pseudonym Voltaire a gigantic work, however, here we shall limit our analysis only to his *Dictionnaire philosophique*. Voltaire's definitions are not the common doctrine of his time; most of them are in contradiction with the majority of the philosophical concepts drawn from feudalism.

Avarice, is "*...the desire of accumulating, whether in grain, movables, money, or curiosities*"[102] Voltaire argues that an entrepreneur who gathers wealth all his life is not called avaricious, yet a father of a family who saves his money for his children is considered "*avaricious, mean, stingy, a niggard, a miser, a gripfarthing*".[103] The reason for this is that "*men hate the individual whom they call avaricious only because there is nothing to be gained by him*"[104] and admire wealthy individuals, Croesus type characters, because there is something to be gained from them.

Envy is treated quite lightly, as a natural passion, so "*...it is better to excite envy than pity is a good proverb. Let us, then, make men envy us as much as we are able.*"[105]

---

[101] II-II, Q.100 Art.1, Reply Obj. 7
[102] Voltaire, *The Works of Voltaire A Contemporary Version*, tr. William F. Fleming, (New York: E.R.DuMont, 1901), vol. III, pg. 144
[103] Ibid., pg.145
[104] Ibid.
[105] Voltaire, *The Works of Voltaire*, vol. IV, pg. 246

In his definition of Luxury, Voltaire explains the difference between luxury and progress, *"In a country where all the inhabitants went bare-footed, could luxury be imputed to the first man who made a pair of shoes for himself?"* [106] He recounts Cato's advice to the Romans *"Beware of luxury; you have conquered the province of Phasis, but never eat any pheasants. You have subjugated the country in which cotton grows; still however continue to sleep on the bare ground. You have plundered the gold, and silver, and jewels of innumerable nations, but never become such fools as to use them. After taking everything, remain destitute of everything. Highway robbers should be virtuous and free."* and Lucullus reply *"...Wish that Pompey and Cæsar may so far impoverish themselves as not to have money enough to pay the armies."* [107]

Blasphemy was a serious offence in Voltaire times. In his definition, first he criticizes the judicial system *"Punishments are almost always arbitrary, which is a great defect in jurisprudence"* [108], and second, he ridicules diverse Christian denominations that are accusing each other of blasphemy.

Heresy comes from Greek and signifies *"belief, or elected opinion"*. Voltaire wrote: *"It is not greatly to the honor of human reason that men should be hated, persecuted, massacred, or burned at the stake, on account of their chosen opinions..."* [109] He mocks the Latin Church *"...which alone can possess reason, has also possessed the right of reproving all who were of a different opinion from her own."* [110]

He criticizes the penalty for heresy, burning at the stake, with the following argument: if someone if guilty of heresy he will burn in hell for eternity, and burning a heretic in this world is a *"usurpation of the jurisdiction of God"*. Differences of opinions in regard religious matters are natural and the strongest dictates what is orthodox. *"It is a great evil to be a heretic; but is it a great good to maintain orthodoxy by soldiers and executioners?"* [111], asks Voltaire.

In the second section of the definition of heresy, he points out that different denominations or sects, are still Christians and he advocates religious tolerance. *"Bind to the state all the subjects of that state by their*

---

[106] Ibid., vol. VI, pg. 154
[107] Ibid.
[108] Voltaire, *The Works of Voltaire*, vol. III, pg. 256
[109] Ibid., vol. V, pg.36
[110] Ibid., vol. V, pg.37
[111] Ibid., vol. V, pg.42

*interest; let the Quaker and the Turk find their advantage in living under your laws. Religion is between God and man; civil law is between you and your people."*[112]

The definition of Atheism is the longest definition in the dictionary, and is extended with a definition for the Atheist. He begins by setting the distinction between atheism and idolatry. In the second part he presents the arguments of the theists, that the universal order must be the result of forming Intelligence, God the Eternal Geometrician, and the argument of the atheists, that motion alone is responsible for the creation of the universe. Voltaire favors the theist party, though he admits he doesn't know the position of the Eternal Geometrician in the universe.

Last, in section four, the possibility of a society of atheists is put in question, *"In what does the apparent impossibility of a society of atheists consist? In this: It is judged that men without some restraint could not live together; that laws have no power against secret crimes; and that it is necessary to have an avenging God-punishing, in this world or in the next, such as escape human justice."*[113]. Voltaire's opinion is that a society of atheists  will be lacking virtue and it is *"... absolutely necessary for princes and people that the idea of a Supreme Being - creating, governing, rewarding, and punishing - be profoundly engraved on their minds."*[114]

Last, on Crimes or Offences Voltaire criticizes a system where death penalty is imposed for minor, insignificant crimes and the rule that two witnesses are enough to hang a man. The criticism continues in the next definition, the Criminal Prosecution. Beside the witnessing procedure, the Ordinances of Louis XIV, drawn by Colbert, are questioned:

> *"In the first, which refers to civil causes, the judges are forbidden to condemn in any suit, on default, when the demand is not proved; but in the second, which regulates criminal proceedings, it is not laid down that, in the absence of proof, the accused shall be acquitted. Singular circumstance! The law declares that a man proceeded against for a sum of money shall not be condemned, on default, unless the debt be proved; but, in cases affecting life, the profession is divided with respect to condemning a person for contumacy when the crime is not proved; and the law does not solve the difficulty."*

---

[112] Ibid., vol. V, pg.46
[113] Ibid., vol. III, pg.122
[114] Ibid. vol. III, pg.126

Voltaire died on 30 May 1778; he was denied a burial in sacred ground and he was initially buried in Champagne. In 1791 his remains were transferred in the Panthéon.

***

Jean-Jacques Rousseau, 28 June 1712 - 2 July 1778, was a Swiss philosopher, writer, and composer, whose writings will have a significant influence in the French revolution and will shape to a certain extent the socialist and communist doctrines of the 20th century.

Rousseau became famous in 1750, after winning an essay competition at the Académie de Dijon with his *Discourse on the Arts and Sciences*; the task of the competition was to answer the question if *"the revival of the Sciences and Arts contributed to improving morality?"*

The *Discourse on the Arts and Sciences* is hard to defend, if not impossible. Nevertheless, Rousseau's position must be considered from two perspectives; first, his modest condition and troubled personal life and second, his understanding of the words 'science' and 'art' in the historical context.

The argument which Rousseau makes in his two parts discourse is that science and arts are responsible for the decay of morality. In the first part of the discourse, he brings as evidence examples of States that once were successful but later succumbed to corruption.

His view on the events that he recounts is narrow, to say the least. It is hard to blame the fall of the Roman Republic on Ovid; the battle of Actium took place in 31 BC and Octavian became the sole ruler of Rome when Ovid was 12 years old. Martial will be born a century later, and Catullus, the last in *"...that gang of obscene authors, whose names alone make decency blush..."* was not even a minor figure in Rome's politics.

On the same key, Rousseau wrote that Chinese science *"...could not save them from the yoke of the illiterate and brutish Tartar..."*[115] which shows a major confusion between the Tatars and the other nomadic tribes which inhabited the Mongolian plateau. In fact, the military successes of Genghis Khan were founded on the military knowledge he acquired from the Chinese.

His views on sciences are also severely distorted: *"Astronomy was born from superstition; eloquence from ambition, hatred, flattery, and*

---

[115] Rousseau, Jean-Jacques, *The Social Contract and The First and Second Discourses,* Susan Dunn ed., (New Haven: Yale University Press, 2002)

*falsehood; geometry from avarice; physics from vain curiosity; all of them,
even moral philosophy, stem from human pride."*[116]

Perhaps is useless to point that astronomy developed out of the need
to find the best time for seeding, geometry was invented out of the need
to erect durable buildings, eloquence or perhaps the art of rhetoric
emerged in democracy and last, moral philosophy always acted as a
control mechanism against excesses.

Yet, at the end of the discourse is hard to disregard it entirely. The
biggest flaw, the lack of scientific objectivity is perhaps its savior.
Rousseau criticism is not directed against art and science *per se* but
more to the decadence in both. The art in the service of luxury is what is
under criticism here. Scientific progress that doesn't benefit the entire
people but only a few is what Rousseau rejects. From this perspective his
answers, arguments and conclusions are not utterly wrong but pathetic,
a pathetism which draws its substance from the desire to live in a better
world.

Encouraged by his success, Rousseau wrote a second material,
*Discourse on the Origin and the Foundations of Inequality among
Mankind* to answer the question *"What is the origin of inequality among
mankind and does natural law decree inequality?"* He sees two species of
inequalities: physical inequalities dictated by nature and moral or
political inequalities, based *"...on a kind of convention, and is
established, or at least authorized by the common consent of mankind."*[117]

In the first part of the discourse he makes an idyllic portrait of the
savage man in a state of *"primitive innocence"* in opposition to the
portrait of the civilized man and all the predicaments that civilization
brought upon him.

Rousseau thinks that propriety is to blame for inequality; it is a
doctrine that was gladly adopted by totalitarian regimes in a corrupt
form; communist regimes regarded propriety as a threat and tried to
eliminate the private propriety with the well-known disastrous results.

Again, here we shall have to remember the historical context. In the
French society Rousseau had a model of social inequality, with the first
two Estates enjoying numerous privileges. His discourse may be seen as
a plea for the simplicity of life opposed to the quest for luxury.

---

[116] Ibid., pg. 56
[117] Ibid., pg.88

The most important of Rousseau's works is, without a doubt, *Of the Social Contract, Or Principles of Political Right*, which he published in 1762. Explaining his theory in a single phrase, Rousseau defines the social contract as following: "*Each of us puts in common his person and all his power under the supreme direction of the general will; and in return each member becomes an indivisible part of the whole.*"[118]

In his social model propriety is common; the individual has only the right to possess the propriety. It is a doctrine that had an enormous appeal even among fine intellectuals; an absolute equality. In practice however, things were quite different. Communist regimes that implemented this doctrine by force caused the death of millions of people guilty of reluctance to relinquish the patrimony of their families. What Rousseau and a long list of intellectuals after him failed to understand is that absolute equality equals absolute anarchy.

Rousseau honestly believed in 'general will' and considers it to be always right and always tending to the public good. He wrote "*Men always desire their own good, but do not always discern it; the people are never corrupted, though often deceived, and it is only then that they seem to will what is evil.*"[119]

An interesting idea is to be found in Book II, Chapter VI:

"*... if he who rules men ought not to control legislation, he who controls legislation ought not to rule men; otherwise his laws, being ministers of his passions, would often serve only to perpetuate his acts of injustice; he would never be able to prevent private interests from corrupting the sacredness of his work.*"[120]

Another interesting passage from Book III Chapter IV:

"*Nothing is more dangerous than the influence of private interests on public affairs; and the abuse of the laws by the government is a lesser evil than the corruption of the legislator, which is the infallible result of the pursuit of private interests. For when the State is changed in its substance, all reform becomes impossible. A people that would never abuse the government would likewise never abuse its independence; a people that always governed well would not need to be governed.* [121]

Just as many of his predecessors, Rousseau sees in luxury a cause of corruption. Throughout his book he favors the model of a small State, a city State if you like, which he considers to be a better social model than an empire. People may be "*readily assembled*", there will be "*...a great*

---

[118] Ibid., pg.164
[119] Ibid., pg.172
[120] Ibid., pg181
[121] Ibid., pg. 201

*simplicity of customs and morals"*, a *"...considerable equality in class and fortune..."*, and *"...lastly, little or no luxury, for luxury is either the result of wealth or makes it necessary; luxury corrupts simultaneously the rich and the poor, the former by ownership, the latter by coveting; it betrays the country to indolence and vanity; it deprives the State of all its citizens in order to enslave them to one to another, and all to opinion."* [122]

Last, a correct observation is noted in Book IV: *"As the regimen of healthy persons is unfit for the ill, so we should not desire to govern a corrupt people by the laws that suit a good nation. Nothing supports this maxim better than the duration of the republic of Venice, only the shadow of which now exists, solely because its laws are suitable to none but worthless men."* [123]

Indeed, laws are regulating the social relations existing in a certain State and in a certain period in time. States ravaged by endemic corruption will find that, by adopting the legal model of a corruption free State, they will not obtain the desired effects in a short period of time, even more, this import may be counterproductive. Drastic times calls for drastic measures for the society to survive; the only problem here is the establishing of a limit so that personal rights do not get annihilated.

The question to be asked here is that if there is a contract between the State and the individual, the existence of the phenomenon of corruption isn't a failure of the State to perform his obligations? Corruption first suffocates the justice system; a State without corrupt magistrates will have no corruption, any act of corruption would be swiftly settled according to the law in the courts of law.

Subsequently, because of the corruption in the justice system, more corruption is generated. The idea that laws can be broken or eluded without consequences, or with consequences that can be 'dealt' with in a corrupt court of law, will become more and more appealing to a greater number of individuals.

If the State, as an entity, tolerates corruption among its magistrates, doesn't it break the social contract with its citizens? Once the corruption becomes endemic and social order disaggregates, the State enters in a process of reform; yet in the entire human history we are unable to find an example of a State that begun its reformation with the human resource in the justice system. Laws are changed, kings, dictators,

---

[122] Ibid., pg. 201
[123] Ibid., pg. 239-240

presidents, political parties are removed from power, even the justice systems suffers a facelift, yet the core of the magistrates remains in position and the germs of corruption with it.

***

Charles Louis de Secondat, Baron de La Brède et de Montesquieu, 1689 - 1755, was a French lawyer and philosopher who deserve to be placed in a class of his own; it is the reason why I chose to present his works at the end of this subchapter.

No other work, by any other author, better serves our purposes, than Montesquieu's *De l'Esprit des Lois*; nowhere I was able to find a better understanding of the phenomenon of corruption and it's relation with the law and the society.

Laws, considers Montesquieu, are the necessary relations arising from the nature of things; as many of his contemporaries he distinguishes between the Laws of Nature and Positive Laws and three forms of Government: republican, monarchical, and despotic.

Under a democratic republican government, when people "...*are gained by bribery and corruption*"[124], a state of indifference towards the public affairs settle in the public conscience, "...*and avarice becomes the predominant passion.*"[125] Indeed, this effect is observable today in States ravaged by endemic corruption.

It is hard to understand why people continue to support a corrupt leadership. Two of the motives are explained by Montesquieu: in order to ascent to power and to remain there, a corrupt government gain public support by electoral corruption.

Of course that an entire nation cannot be bought, the subjects here are only those who are able to influence the outcome of an electoral process. Since the result of the electoral process is known in advance, the public interest towards elections diminishes and personal survival becomes predominant over the public good.

The term used here, "avarice" seems to be too critical; since the first level of government is corrupt, the second level has little choice but to become corrupt also, spreading the practice downwards in the State's hierarchy. To be corrupt becomes a matter of survival in a corrupt

---

[124] Montesquieu, *The Complete Works of M. de Montesquieu*, (London: T. Evans & W. Davis,1977), Book II, pg. 15
[125] Ibid.

environment, which is by no means an excuse, but it cannot be blame entirely on avarice.

Book VIII is entitled Of the Corruption of the Principles of the Three Governments. Here Montesquieu explains the phenomenon of corruption within the governments, in a manner that cannot be found in any other author. The entire Chapter I of the Book VIII contains a single proposition:

*"THE corruption of each government generally begins with that of the principles."*[126]

In Chapter II he analyzes the corruption of the principles of democracy. He wrote:

*"THE principle of democracy is corrupted, not only when the spirit of equality is extinct, but likewise when they fall into a spirit of extreme equality, and when each citizen would fain be upon a level with those whom he has chosen to command him. Then the people, incapable of bearing the very power they have delegated, want to manage every thing themselves, to debate for the senate, to execute for the magistrate, and to decide for the judges."*[127]

After a brief reference to Xenophon's Banquet, he continues:

*"The people fall into this misfortune when those in whom they confide, desirous of concealing their own corruption, endeavour to corrupt them. To disguise their own ambition, they speak to them only of the grandeur of the state; to conceal their own avarice, they incessantly slatter theirs. The corruption will increase among the corrupters, and likewise among those who are already corrupted. The people will divide the public money among themselves, and, having added the administration of affairs to their indolence, will be for blending their poverty with the amusements of luxury. But, with their indolence and luxury, nothing but the public treasure will be able to satisfy their demands."*[128]

He explains very well extortion, or as we call it today, embezzlement, as the consequence of electoral corruption, or in other words the bribing of voters:

*"We must not be surprised to see their suffrages given for money. It is impossible to make great largesses to the people without great extortion: and, to compass this, the state must be subverted. The greater the advantages they seem to derive from their liberty, the nearer they approach towards the critical moment of losing it. Petty tyrants arise, who have all the vices of a single tyrant. The small remains of liberty soon become insupportable; a single tyrant starts up, and the people are stripped of every thing, even of the profits of their corruption. Democracy hath, therefore, two excesses to avoid; the spirit of inequality, which leads to aristocracy*

---

[126] Ibid., Book VIII, pg.143
[127] Ibid.
[128] Ibid., pg.144

*or monarchy; and the spirit of extreme equality, which leads to despotic power, as the latter is completed by conquest."*[129]

An aristocracy becomes corrupted *"if the power of the nobles becomes arbitrary: when this is the case, there can no longer be any virtue either in the governors or the governed."*[130] He continues:

> *"The extremity of corruption is when the power of the nobles becomes hereditary; for then they can hardly have any moderation. If they are only a few, their power is greater, but their security less; if they are a larger number, their power is less, and their security greater: insomuch, that power goes on increasing, and security diminishing, up to the very despotic prince, who is encircled with excess of power and danger."*[131]

The corruption of principles is to be found also in monarchies:

> *"As democracies are subverted when the people despoil the senate, the magistrates, and judges, of their functions, so monarchies are corrupted when the prince insensibly deprives societies or cities of their privileges. In the former case, the multitude usurps the power, in the latter, it is usurped by a single person."*[132]

Quoting an anonymous Chinese author, Montesquieu identifies the causes of corruption in monarchies:

> *"Monarchy is destroyed, when a prince thinks he shews a greater exertion of power in changing, than in conforming to, the order of things; when he deprives some of his subjects of their hereditary employments to bestow them arbitrarily upon others; and when he is fonder of being guided by fancy than judgement. Again, it is destroyed, when the prince, directing every thing entirely to himself, calls the state to his capital, the capital to his court, and the court to his own person. It is destroyed, in fine, when the prince mistakes his authority, his situation, and the love of his people; and when he is not fully persuaded that a monarch ought to think himself secure, as a despotic prince ought to think himself in danger."*[133]

A despotic government *"...is subject to a continual corruption, because it is, even in its nature, corrupt"* and *"... is ruined by its own intrinsic imperfections, when some accidental causes do not prevent the corrupting of its principles. It maintains itself, therefore, only when circumstances, drawn from the climate, religion, situation, or genius of the people, oblige it to conform to order, and to admit of some rule."*[134]

---

[129] Ibid., pg.144-145
[130] Ibid., pg. 147
[131] Ibid., pg. 147-148
[132] Ibid., pg. 149
[133] Ibid.
[134] Ibid., pg. 152

Last, the effects of corruption in government, as Montesquieu sees them: *"WHEN once the principles of government are corrupted, the very best laws become bad, and turn against the state: but, when the principles are sound, even bad laws have the same effect as good; the force of the principle draws every thing to it."*[135]

*"When once a republic is corrupted, there is no possibility of remedying any of the growing evils, but by removing the corruption and restoring its lost principles: every other correction is either useless or a new evil."*[136]

Montesquieu's explanations' are so clearly stated that they do not need further explanations. The lucidity of his thoughts doubled by an impeccable literary style makes *The Spirit of Laws* one of the best books about laws ever written.

## 2.4. The German idealists

Immanuel Kant, 1724-1804, is the best renowned German philosopher, the founder of a new philosophical current, generally named German Idealism. His most influential works are his *Critics* and the *Metaphysics of Morals.*

Various influences are to be found in Kant's works; the Bible, St Augustine, Aquinas and of course Luther, in theological matters, the stoics in the questions of ethics and morals, Wolff, Leibniz, and later Rousseau and Hume were the contemporary subject of interest.

Kant considered that happiness cannot be the ultimate purpose of morality[137]; his philosophy is based on the doctrine of duty towards God, oneself and others. He defined ethics as *"...the science of actions that are validly imputable before no other forum save the internal one."*[138]

Kant's work is voluminous and difficult to read and understand even for advanced students of philosophy. In this study on the phenomenon of corruption we are trying to make the subject-matter more understandable. For this reason I chose to analyze only one of his later

---

[135] Ibid.
[136] Ibid., pg. 155
[137] See Antony Kenny, *A new history of western philosophy, The rise of modern philosophy*, (New York: Oxford University Press, 2006), vol. 3, pg. 264
[138] Immanuel Kant, *Lecture on Ethics*, ed. Peter Heath, J. B. Schneewind, tr. Peter Heath, (Cambridge: Cambridge University Press, 1997), pg. 8

works, which I considered to serve best our investigation on the phenomenon of corruption.

The story of *Religion within the Bounds of Bare Reason* is quite interesting: after he published the First Piece in Berlinische Monatsschrift, Kant was denied the right to publish the Second Piece by the censure. He managed to publish all four pieces through the University of Jena, but the consequence was a royal order of 1794 from King Friedrich Wilhelm II, banning him to speak or write about religion, which Kant agreed to do *"as long as the King shall live"*.[139]

The First Piece is treating the relation of human nature and evil. *"The human being is (by nature) either morally good or morally evil."*[140] Kant considers this disjunctive proposition to be incorrect and rejects the idea of man in an intermediate position between the two extremes. The human being has a natural predisposition to the good and a natural propensity to evil.[141] He classifies this propensity on three levels, as frailty, impurity and wickedness. He wrote:

> *"Third, the wickedness (vitiositas, pravitas), or, if one prefers, the corruption (corruptio) of the human heart is the propensity of the power of choice to [pursue] maxims whereby one is to put the incentive from the moral law second to other (nonmoral) ones. It can also be named the perversity (perversitas) of the human heart, because it reverses the moral order in regard to the incentives of a free power of choice; and although legally good (lawful) actions can always still consist with this [wickedness], yet the way of thinking is thereby corrupted in its root (as far as the moral attitude is concerned), and the human being is therefore designated as evil."*[142]

On the origin of evil, Kant elaborates on the Christian doctrine of sin; he considers that the moral law as divine law precedes the human being.[143]

In the Second Piece Kant writes about the struggle of the good with the evil principle for dominion over the human being. He considers the development of good insufficient and the location and the combating of evil necessary.[144] It is a universal human duty to elevate itself to an ideal moral perfection inspired by God.[145] The old religion  which made

---

[139] Immanuel Kant, *Religion within the Bounds of Bare Reason* , Werner S. Pluhar tr., introduction by Stephen Palmquist, ( Indianapolis/Cambridge: Hackett Publishing Company, 2009)
[140] Ibid., pg. 22
[141] Ibid.,  pg. 31
[142] Ibid., pg. 33
[143] Ibid., pg. 46
[144] Ibid., pg. 62
[145] Immanuel Kant, *Religion within the Bounds of Bare Reason*, pg. 67

use of miracles to gain authority[146] is to be replaced by a moral religion, one that does not need miracles.

The Third Piece describes the society in which the good overcomes the evil. The coercive element in the law is no longer necessary, each person legislate himself, judge himself and there is no need for a public authority.[147] The man lives the ethical state of nature and becomes a member of an ethical community.[148]

The Forth Piece is dedicated to the service and pseudoservice under the dominion of the good principle. The ethical community is united by a special kind of duty, a sum of each member's individual duties without a special agreement among them. The community united under the moral law must be strong to resist *"...the challenges of the evil principle (which human beings are otherwise tempted, even by one another, to serve as instruments)."* The *"...kingdom of God, can be undertaken by human beings only through religion..."*[149]; God is *"...the originator of the constitution, but human beings as members and free citizens of this kingdom are yet in all cases the originators of the organization..."*[150]

Kant was a profoundly religious man; he grew up in a Pietist family and was educated Collegium Fridericianum by Pietist teachers. Strict education, later troubles with the censorship of ecclesiastical authorities did not strayed him from his belief in God. The entire theory of morality that Kant developed is based on the idea that God exists. Although he is critical sometimes towards the Church, his criticism does not come from a mild form of agnosticism but from the desire for a perfect church.

One of the problems with Kant's theory of morality is the fact that the belief in God is just a belief, and it is not shared by all humans. Therefore, faith becomes a condition placed at the foundation of the Kantian morality.

For the atheist, the agnostic or even for the theist from a different religion, the perfect model is quite irrelevant. But that doesn't mean an agnostic or an atheist is immoral or that he cannot perform his duty in society.

Moreover, the dynamic of human beliefs caused by personal experiences may cause a person to 'migrate' from theism to atheism and

---

[146] Ibid., pg. 95
[147] Ibid., pg. 104
[148] Ibid., pg. 106
[149] Ibid., pg. 166
[150] Ibid.

back without any consequence on his ethics. Kant seems to persist in the medieval mentality that a man can be either sinful or righteous.

Kant did not have a passion for travelling; he spent his entire life in and around Konigsberg.[151] His interactions with other cultures, religions, ideas, peoples came from literature, and no matter how much one reads there is no substitute for personal experiences. What seems to be lacking in Kant's moral philosophy, is life itself; perhaps this is what is making Kant so abstract, so dogmatic.

***

Georg Wilhelm Friedrich Hegel, 1770 –1831, was the German philosopher who had the most influence in legal sciences; Hegel's Philosophy of Right[152]was published in 1821. Unlike his predecessors, Hegel was in a privileged position. The Napoleonic Codes, either by acceptance or rejection, had already became known all over Europe, setting a definitive course for Continental Law. Although Hegel is credited for introducing the term *volksgeist*, and supports German legal tradition, he is certainly in favor of codification. In the Third Part - Ethics, he wrote:

> *"No greater insult could be offered to a civilized people or to its lawyers than to deny them ability to codify their law; for such ability cannot be that of constructing a legal system with a novel content, but only that of apprehending, i.e. grasping in thought, the content of existing laws in its determinate universality and then applying them to particular cases."* [153]

Hegel is one of the critics of the Anglo-Saxon legal system. One particular point is the role of the judge as a legislator. He wrote:

> *"The authority of precedent is binding on them, since their predecessors have done nothing but give expression to the unwritten law; and yet they are just as much exempt from its authority, because they are themselves repositories of the unwritten law and so have the right to criticize previous judgments and pronounce whether they accorded with the unwritten law or not."*[154]

A discussion was initiated among legal scholars about which system is superior; Hegel provided here a solid argument in favor of codification. When we consider the phenomenon of corruption among judges, what is clear is that neither system is perfect.

---

[151] Bertrand Russell, pg. 704
[152] The original title is *Naturrecht und Staatswissenschaft im Grundrisse and Grundlinien der Philosophie des Rechts*
[153] Georg Hegel, *Philosophy of Right*, T.M. Knox tr., (Oxford : Oxford University Press, 1978), pg. 136
[154] Ibid., pg. 135

One of the most important concepts that are to be found in Hegel is the election of the magistrates. The procedure to become a judge is different from country to country and usually involves some extra knowledge beyond the law school, either in the form of an extensive practice as counselor, or by special magistracies schools or some mixed form.

I've pointed out that corruption first infects the justice system; it's a condition that allows corruption to enter in the development stage.

The formula by which one becomes a judge thru bureaucratic procedures is the most susceptible to corruption. Once one becomes judge thru corrupt means he will have favors to return or money to recover and certainly profits to make.

Hegel's idea of direct election by the public of the magistrates, or at least the heads of the core is something worth considering as a method to combat corruption. An electoral process held only among the magistrates core may also be counterproductive, remembering Aristotle, smaller bodies are more susceptible to corruption than larger bodies.

Hegel's *Philosophy of Right* is structured in three parts: the first is dedicated to abstract right, the second to morality and the third to ethical life. Contractual relationship is *"...the mediation of the will to give up a property, a single property, and the will to take up another, i.e. another belonging to someone else; and this mediation takes place when the two wills are associated in an identity in the sense that one of them comes to its decision only in the presence of the other."*[155]

Wrong, referring to contracts, is considered by Hegel to be of three kinds: non-malicious wrong, fraudulent and coercive or criminal. Hegel defines fraud as follows *"...we have fraud when the universal is set aside by the particular will and reduced to something only showing in the situation, primarily in contract, when the universal will is reduced to a will which is common only from the outsider's point of view."* He considered that man cannot be coerced, *"Only the will which allows itself to be coerced can in any way be coerced."*[156]

About crime he writes:

*"...it makes a difference to the objective aspect of crime whether the will so objectified and its specific quality is injured throughout its entire extent, and so in the infinity which is equivalent to its concept (as in murder, slavery, enforced*

---

[155] Ibid., pg. 58
[156] Ibid. pg. 66

*religious observance, &c.), or whether it is injured only in a single part or in one of its qualitative characteristics, and if so, in which of these."*[157]

He continues on the subject *"The subjective, moral, quality of crime rests on the higher distinction implied in the question of how far an event or fact pure and simple is an action, and concerns the subjective character of the action itself..."*[158] *"...If crime and its annulment (which later will acquire the specific character of punishment) are treated as if they were unqualified ends, it must, of course, seem quite unreasonable to will an evil merely because 'another evil is there already'...The annulling of crime in this sphere where right is immediate is principally revenge, which is just in its content in so far as it is retributive."*[159]

In other words, Hegel sees punishment as a retribution for the crime and not as a vengeance, with the justification in the will of the criminal himself going against the general will; it is the end of the right of vengeance coming from the ancient Greeks thru the middle age knight.

The Second Part is dedicated to morality and the focus is placed on purpose intention and good. He considers that *"The externalization of the subjective or moral will is action."* [160] and *"The right of the moral will involves three aspects: Purpose, Intention and Good."*[161] Here we can find the principle of personal responsibility: *"The deed can be imputed to me only if my will is responsible for it."*[162] There is an interesting observation regarding Good:

*"In this Idea, welfare has no independent validity as the embodiment of a single particular will but only as universal welfare and essentially as universal in principle, i.e. as according with freedom. Welfare without right is not a good. Similarly, right without welfare is not the good; fiat justitia should not be followed by pereat mundus. Consequently, since the good must of necessity be actualized through the particular will and is at the same time its substance, it has absolute right in contrast with the abstract right of property and the particular aims of welfare. If either of these moments becomes distinguished from the good, it has validity only in so far as it accords with the good and is subordinated to it."*[163]

The Third Part is concerned with Ethical Life, which *"...is the concept of freedom developed into the existing world and the nature of self-consciousness."*[164]

---

[157] Ibid., pg. 68
[158] Ibid.
[159] Ibid.
[160] Hegel, *Philosophy of Right*, pg. 78
[161] Ibid., pg. 79
[162] Ibid., pg. 80
[163] Ibid., pg. 87

For Hegel, ethical life concerns family, civil society and the State. Family means marriage, a common patrimony and the education of children. Hegel finds divorce ethically acceptable if it is pronounced by an authority, secular or clerical.

Civil society contains three moments, a system of needs, the exercise of justice and the police and corporation. Hegel's view on the role of the police and the corporation to protect particular interests is indeed idealistic.

The State is governed by the constitution or the constitutional law in internal matters and by international law in relation with other States.

Perhaps the greatest innovation in Hegel's philosophy is the fact that he established a dialectically dynamic model[165]: thesis (Aristotle - happiness) → antithesis (Kant - duty) → synthesis (Hegel - right). Just as Kant, Hegel is also a deeply religious man, placing religion in the center of his moral and ethical system; his *Phenomenology of Spirit* is his best known work. He is critical towards the Catholic Church but not in anything regarding faith.

Hegel is hard to understand by the common law lawyer and maybe it will be useful to explain why. The *Philosophy of Right* uses two languages: the normal language, the one that is to be found in any book and the legal language, which is contained in the legal codes, statutes and legal doctrine. Some of the words have different meanings or are used in a slightly different manner in the two languages. In translation, most of the subtleties are lost, and Hegel becomes hard to follow in English.

***

Friedrich Nietzsche, 1844 - 1900, was a German philosopher, philologist, poet, cultural critic and composer; he is perhaps the most controversial philosopher in history. He has been associated with national-socialism, communism, anarchism despite the fact he is equally critical towards any doctrine.

The phenomenology of corruption covers, in Nietzsche's work, three main areas: corruption in the Christian Church and in the State, the corruption of morals and cultural corruption.

*Human, All Too Human: A Book for Free Spirits* was first published 1878; it was completed with a second part *Assorted Opinions and*

---

[164] Ibid., pg. 106
[165] Ibid. pg. 267

*Maxims* in 1879 and a third part, *The Wanderer and his Shadow*, in 1880. In chapter two, On the History of the Moral Sensations he opposes the idea that man is fundamentally evil and corrupt or the opposite, that he is fundamentally good, implying that these ideas are induced for profit.[166]

In chapter 8, A Glance at the State, he wrote:

> *"When abuses (for example defects in an administration, corruption and arbitrary favouritism in political or learned bodies) are painted in greatly exaggerated colours, the representation may fail in its effect among the knowledgeable but will produce all the stronger an effect upon the unknowledgeable (who would have remained indifferent to a cautious, sober representation). Since these are markedly in the majority, however, and harbour within them stronger willpower and a more impetuous desire for action, that exaggeration will lead to investigations, punishments, undertakings, reorganizations. - To this extent it is useful to paint abuses in exaggerated colours."*[167]

Another interesting idea is to be found in this chapter: "*Innocent corruption. - In all institutions that are not open to the biting air of public criticism an innocent corruption flourishes like a fungus (as, for example, in learned bodies and senates)*".[168] It is true that transparency is corruption worst enemy.

The concept of decadence and its definition is quite interesting. *"Waste, decay, elimination need not be condemned: they are necessary consequences of life, of the growth of life. The phenomenon of decadence is as necessary as any increase and advance of life: one is in no position to abolish it."*[169]

Nietzsche believes that no one can or should abolish decadence; he sees society as a body that after birth experiences natural aging, disease, vice in an natural process that cannot be interfered by a social construction *"in which vice, disease, prostitution, distress would no longer grow.- But that means condemning life"*.[170]

He highlights a confusion regarding the nature of decadence: *"its supposed causes are its consequences."*[171] *"The whole moral struggle against vice, luxury, crime, even disease, appears a naivete and superfluous...."*.[172] He thinks the fight against decadence should focus on

---

[166] Friedrich Nietzsche, *Human, All Too Human*, R. J. Hollingdale tr., (Cambridge: Cambridge University Press, 1996), pg. 41
[167] Ibid., pg.164
[168] Ibid. pg.170
[169] Ibid., pg. 25
[170] Ibid.
[171] Ibid.

protecting the healthy parts of the organism. The consequences of decadence are skepticism, the corruption of morals, and curing is impossible; *"...the "cured" are merely one type of the degenerates."*[173]

Nietzsche is committing an error when he compares the human society with the human body; they share similar characteristics, a parallelism may be drawn for effect, parts of the human body may be used as a metaphor, the head of the State for instance, yet the human body and the human society are fundamentally different things.

The eradication of vice, decadence, corruption, all terms are synonyms here, is achievable and it should be desired. I don't see that as a weakening of human race, but, on the contrary, an affirmation of its power; eradicating corruption should be seen as a new beginning for humanity.

Nietzsche is one of the most famous critics of religion; his criticism is not only towards the catholic Church as in the works of Luther or Calvin, but also towards God and the Christian fate, especially Christian morality. Is hard to say if Nietzsche was an atheist, he seems to believe in soul, spirit.

In *The Gay Science* he wrote: *"At the time of the great corruption of the Church, the Church in Germany was the least corrupt; that is why the Reformation occurred here, as a sign that even the beginnings of corruption were felt to be intolerable."*[174]

It is impossible to know if the German Church was less corrupt in the time of Luther than the French Church for instance, from what we learned about corruption so far, I tend to disagree. Corruption was not the only motive behind the Reformation, any type of reform or revolution cannot be attributed to a single cause, there is always a complex of factors.

The Catholic Church, *"the last Roman construction"*[175] as Nietzsche himself labels it, had passed thru the Dark Ages and Renascence, virtually unchanged. If we apply Nietzsche's theory here, the reformation of the Church was an unavoidable event that had to have a place of beginning.

In the *Ecce Homo* he writes:

---

[172] Ibid.
[173] Friedrich Nietzsche, *Human, All Too Human*, pg. 26
[174] Friedrich Nietzsche, *The Gay Science*, Bernard Williams, ed., Josefine Nauckhoff, tr.( Cambridge: Cambridge University Press, 2001), pg. 130
[175] Ibid., pg. 221

> *"Christian morality the most malignant form of the will to He, the real Circe of humanity - that which corrupted humanity. It is not error as error that horrifies me at this sight - not the lack, for thousands of years, of "good will," discipline, decency, courage; in matters of the spirit, revealed by its victory: it is the' lack of nature, it is the utterly gruesome fact that antinature itself received the highest honors as morality and was fixed over humanity as law and categorical imperative.*
>
> *To blunder to such an extent, not as individuals, not as a people, but as humanity."*[176]

He considers that humanity itself is not decadent and it does not degenerate, but the degeneration comes from *"that parasitical type of man - that of the priest"* who uses Christian morality to come to power. His definition of morality: *"Definition of morality: Morality-the idiosyncrasy of decadents, with the ulterior motive of revenging oneself against life-successfully."*[177]

In *Will to Power* he wrote *"it is an error to consider "social distress" or "physiological degeneration" or, worse, corruption, as the cause of nihilism"*, *"it is in one particular interpretation, the Christian-moral one, that nihilism is rooted"*. Ignorance and not vice corrupts the race and *"Virtue is our greatest misunderstanding."*[178]

Russell saw in Nietzsche's ethics similitudes with the ethic of Machiavelli's Prince;[179] perhaps the two belong to the same gender but they are certainly not of the same specie.

## 2.5. The British enlighteners

David Hume, 1711-1776, historian, economist and philosopher, was the most illustrious exponent of Scottish Enlightenment. He wrote *A Treatise of Human Nature* in 1739, a book considered by many authors as one of the most important books in Western philosophy.

His second major work is *The History of England* started in 1745 and completed in 1762 can also be a source interesting for our research.

His last works *An Enquiry Concerning Human Understanding* (1749), *An Enquiry Concerning the Principles of Morals* (1751) and *Dialogs*

---

[176] Friedrich Nietzsche, *On the Genealogy of Morals Ecce Homo*, tr. Walter Kaufmann and R. J. Hollingdale (New York: Random House, 1967), pg. 322
[177] Ibid., pg. 333
[178] pg. 34
[179] Bertrand Russel, *A history of western philosophy*, pg. 762

*concerning Natural Religion* (1779) published posthumously are also interesting for our subject-matter.

*A Treatise of Human Nature* is divided in three books, Of Understanding, Of Passions, and Of Morals. In the third book, he wrote:

> "...*nothing is ever present to the mind but its perceptions; and that all the actions of seeing, hearing, judging, loving, hating, and thinking, fall under this denomination. The mind can never exert itself in any action which we may not comprehend under the term of perception; and consequently that term is no less applicable to those judgments by which we distinguish moral good and evil, than to every other operation of the mind. To approve of one character, to condemn another, are only so many different perceptions.*"[180]

He considers that our perceptions are divided into impressions and passions. He asks:

> "... *whether 'tis by means of our ideas or impressions we distinguish betwixt vice and virtue, and pronounce an action blameable or praiseworthy?*"[181]

> "*Since morals, therefore, have an influence on the actions and affections, it follows, that they cannot be derived from reason; and that because reason alone, as we have already proved, can never have any such influence. Morals excite passions, and produce or prevent actions. Reason of itself is utterly impotent in this particular. The rules of morality, therefore, are not conclusions of our reason.*"[182]

Moreover, he writes "*Moral distinctions, therefore, are not the offspring of reason.*"[183] The main idea here is that morality is not entirely rational but also emotional, and that moral approval is an emotional response. Hume's theory has been revisited by scholars in recent years, and we can foresee a revival of some authors that for whatever reason had been forgotten in modern times.

In *Enquiries Concerning Human Understanding* he wrote:

> "*Luxury, or a refinement on the pleasures and conveniencies of life, had not long been supposed the source of every corruption in government, and the immediate cause of faction, sedition, civil wars, and the total loss of liberty. It was, therefore, universally regarded as a vice, and was an object of declamation to all satirists, and severe moralists.*" [184]

David Hume also wrote several essays in a collection first published as *Essays Moral and Political* (1974) and later as *Essays Moral, Political and Literary* in 1958. Essay II is entitled *Of the Liberty of the Press.*

---

[180] David Hume, *The Philosophical Works of David Hume*, (Edinburgh: Printed For Adam Black And William Tait And Charles Tait), vol.2, pg. 220
[181] Ibid.
[182] Ibid., pg. 221
[183] Ibid., pg. 223
[184] David Hume, *The Philosophical Works of David Hume*, vol. 4, pg. 251

After comparing the liberty of the press in Great Britain with France, an absolutist monarchy and Holland, a republic, he wrote:

> "*Thus it seems evident, that the two extremes of absolute monarchy and of a republic, approach near to each other in some material circumstances, In the first, the magistrate has no jealousy of the people; in the second, the people have none of the magistrate: Which want of jealousy begets a mutual confidence and trust in both cases, and produces a species of liberty in monarchies, and of arbitrary power in republics.*[185]

> *It is apprehended that arbitrary power would steal in upon us, were we not careful to prevent its progress, and were there not an easy method of conveying the alarm from one end of the kingdom to the other. The spirit of the people must frequently be roused, in order to curb the ambition of the court; and the dread of rousing this spirit must be employed to prevent that ambition.*"[186]

A free press is indeed the worst enemy for corrupt politicians and magistrates. It is almost natural for an absolutist form of government to restrict the freedom of the press. It is important to highlight that the free press may be silenced in two ways: either by violence, meaning intimidation, arrest, deportation, murder, either by corruption. Sometimes is far more rewarding to buy a journalist than to kill him.

Hume also wrote an interesting essay entitled *On Avarice*: "*Accordingly, we find no vice so irreclaimable as avarice; and though there scarcely has been a moralist or philosopher, from the beginning of the world to this day, who has not levelled a stroke at it, we hardly find a single instance of any person's being cured of it.*"[187] Hume's observation is correct; is hard to find a relevant example of a person turning from avarice to generosity or from corruption to honesty.

The essay ends with a wonderful fable:

> "*Our old mother Earth once lodged an indictment against Avarice before the courts of heaven, for her wicked and malicious counsel and advice in tempting, inducing, persuading, and traitorously seducing the children of the plaintiff to commit the detestable crime of parricide upon her, and, mangling the body, ransack her very bowels for hidden treasure. ... Avarice, being called before Jupiter to answer to this charge, had not much to say in her own defence. The injury was clearly proved upon her. The fact, indeed was notorious, and the injury had been frequently repeated, When, therefore, the plaintiff demanded justice, Jupiter very readily gave sentence in her favour; and his decree was to this purpose-That, since dame Avarice, the defendant, had thus grievously injured dame Earth, the plaintiff, she was hereby ordered to take that treasure, of which she had feloniously robbed the said plaintiff*

---

[185] David Hume, *The Philosophical Works of David Hume*, vol.3, pg.9
[186] Ibid., pg. 11
[187] David Hume, *The Philosophical Works of David Hume*, vol. 4 pg. 534

*by ransacking her bosom, and restore it back to her without diminution or retention. From this sentence it will follow, says Jupiter to the by-standers, that in all future ages, the retainers of Avarice shall bury-and conceal their riches, and thereby restore to the earth what they take from her."*[188]

Hume was considered an atheist by his contemporaries; he was almost charged with heresy and he was denied nomination as professor of philosophy at Glasgow University for his religious views.

***

Jeremy Bentham (1748 - 1832) was a British philosopher and jurist, is considered the head of Philosophical Radicals, and one of the founders of modern utilitarianism. His work was influenced by Helvetius and Beccaria and it was based on two principles, the principle of association and the principle of greatest happiness.

In *Principles of Judicial Procedure*, Chapter XXIII Jury-Trial, Bentham brings a very important clarification:

*"The act by which temptation of this nature is applied, and applied with success, is, if it be in a pecuniary and tangible shape, termed bribery; or if in a less tangible shape, corruption; though even in any case in which the word bribery is employed with propriety, so may the word corruption: corruption being the genus, bribery one species of it."*[189]

Today, almost everyone is using the two terms bribery and corruption as synonyms which is a gross mistake. Indeed, bribery is just a form that corruption embodies and is a part of corruption regarded as an antisocial phenomenon.

Chapter X of Bentham's *Constitutional Code* is dedicated to corruption. In the beginning, He explains that the term corruption, is used in two senses one in a physical sense *"the breaking up the texture of a mass of animal or vegetable matter"*[190] and the other in a moral sense meaning *"...the breaking up for the worse, the texture of the mental frame"*.[191]

Corruption is:

*"... an operation in which two persons are concerned: one the agent in the operation, corrupting the other, and thereby rendering himself a corruptor: the other, the patient in the operation, being corrupted by the former, and by the having been so corrupted becoming and continuing corrupt."*[192]

---

[188] Ibid., pg. 538
[189] Jeremy Bentham, *The Works of Jeremy Bentham*, 11 vol., ed. John Bowring, (Edinburgh: William Tait, 1838-1843), vol. 2, pg. 127.
[190] Jeremy Bentham, *The Works of Jeremy Bentham*, vol. 9, pg. 64.
[191] Ibid.

This is perhaps one of the best definitions of corruption ever written, yet it is still incomplete. In Bentham's view, there are two parties, a corruptor and a corruptee. His definition does not include those situations where there is only one corrupt perpetrator. In cases of embezzlement for instance, or in cases of abuse of power, there is only one party that acts in a corrupt way.

Bentham considers that the corruptor exercises a corruptive inducement, which is an inducement of intimidative kind, over the corruptee. He wrote *"Say, for example, the fear of death: intimation being given, that if the party meant to be corrupted will not do the sinister service desired at his hands, he shall be put to death,—in the opposite case, not."*[193]

It is true that specific forms of corruption may imply the use of threats, thus inducing a state of fear in the corruptee, but here the party which is threatened is not part of the operation of corruption, is the victim of it.

The principle of separation of powers is a key element of a democratic system; Bentham points that *"A system of government in which an irremoveable functionary possesses an indispensable share in the supreme legislative power, and at the same time the whole or the greatest part of that branch of the supreme executive power... is a system in which corruption is systematically seated."*[194]

Bentham wrote *"In itself corruption is no evil, for neither is the receipt, nor the conferring of a benefit, in any shape an evil; in so far as it is an evil, corruption is so, only in respect of the evil effects produced by it: abstraction made of these effects, it is even a good."*[195]

I consider this assertion to be utterly wrong, corruption being the 'ultimate evil' not only in its effects but in all its aspects. We cannot consider corruption to be 'a good' under any circumstances. Even in the absence of an 'evil' effect, since corruption is an act or acts against the law, the rule of law itself is the victim. The primordial purpose of corruption is to break or to elude the law.in order to procure a benefit. However, Bentham's position is understandable when he explains corruption as a choice between a lesser good and a greater good or a greater evil in preference to the less.

---

[192] Ibid.
[193] Ibid., pg65
[194] Ibid.
[195] Ibid., pg. 66

The question that must be asked when we are considering corruption from a utilitarian perspective is if corruption causes pleasure for the corrupted. And I'm not talking about the fruits of corruption, the luxury, the money, the power, but corruption itself. I think that it is of outmost importance to determine if corruption in itself is a source of pleasure.

I believe that there are two circumstances. First, a person becomes corrupt if the system is corrupt. The other broken wheels of the system eventually break the good wheel. In those circumstances, fear is the key factor; the person that becomes corrupt against his will or with his free will somehow diminished, is incapable of feelings of pleasure.

An honest individual who is forced to accept or to give a bribe for instance, or who becomes part in traffic of influence, will be consumed by the fear of the consequences of his acts and by the internal conflict between his acts and his moral sense. It is evident that in these circumstances the feeling of pleasure is out of the question.

The second circumstance is when an individual draw pleasure from his corrupt acts. In these cases corruption becomes a source of pleasure in itself. Fear of being caught becomes another source of pleasure, similar to the fear we feel in a roller coaster, skydiving or bungee jumping.

Fear of being caught sometimes disappear entirely, no wonder individuals arrested for corruption sometimes show surprise, stupefaction, they cannot process what happened. Nevertheless, in these cases the moral barrier is absent.

Corruption becomes the sole source of pleasure, the material object money, luxury items, becomes secondary, and this is why we see individuals degrading themselves to petty bribes. It is not the amount of the bribe that counts but the trill, the adrenaline rush of taking a bribe.

\*\*\*

Bertrand Russell 1872-1970, was a British philosopher, historian and political activist. He belongs to modern philosophy considering his work and the timeframe; however, by placing him in a chapter dedicated to enlightenment, subsequent to Hume and Bentham, I don't think I am committing an unpardonable error.

In 1932 Russell published a remarkable book entitled *Education and the Social Order*. From what we learned so far about the phenomenon of corruption, I cannot see a more effective weapon against it other than education; this is the reason why we shall include it in our analysis.

In the first chapter Russell ask the following question: should the education system train good individuals or good citizens? The individual should mirror the world: *"...knowledge and comprehensiveness appear to me glorious attributes, in virtue of which I prefer Newton to an oyster"*[196].

He wrote:

> *"The issue between citizenship and individuality is important in education, in politics, in ethics, and in metaphysics....The education of the young of a whole community is an expensive business, which, in the main, is bound to fall to the lot of the State. The only other organization sufficiently interested in forming the minds of the young to have any really important share in education is the Church."*[197]

In the next chapters Russell explores other interesting issues, such as the negative theory of education, emotion and discipline and home education versus school education.

In chapter eight, Russell writes about the role of religion in education. He defines religion as *"...a complex phenomenon, having both an individual and a social aspect."*[198] Here, rather contradictory for a philosopher like Russell, he admits the myth that religion was the generator of the moral code *"Nevertheless, although the moral codes resulting from religion have been curious, it must be admitted that it is religion that has given rise to them. If any morality is better than none, then religion has been a force for good."*[199]

Religious based ethics can be harmful by discouraging intelligent children, limiting the teaching profession and limiting science itself. *"For such reasons as we have been considering, any creed, no matter what, is likely to be harmful in education when it is regarded as exempt from the intellectual scrutiny to which our more scientific beliefs are subjected."*[200]

Other objection that Russell states: religion is conservative thus conserving errors thru generations, once faith is lost there is no comfort, if taken seriously it leads to the neglect of this life in favor for the next, and last it can lead to the denial of any form of moral together with religious moral.[201] He later wrote:

> *"The fundamental defect of Christian ethics consists in the fact that it labels certain classes of acts 'sins' and others 'virtues' on grounds that have nothing to do with their social consequences. An ethic not derived from superstition must decide first*

---

[196] Bertrand Russell, *Education and the Social Order*, (London: Routledge, 2010) pg.2
[197] Ibid., pg. 7
[198] Ibid. pg. 69
[199] Ibid., pg. 70
[200] Ibid., pg76
[201] Ibid., pg. 78

*upon the kind of social effects which it desires to achieve and the kind which it desires to avoid. It must then decide, as far as our knowledge permits, what acts will promote the desired consequences; these acts it will praise, while those having a contrary tendency it will condemn."*[202]

It seems that Russell had already set the premises for the much sought science of moral and ethics independent from religion.

History showed us that there are three possible scenarios about the relationship between religion and education.

In the first scenario, religion is denied to play any role in school. The State assumes the role of the educator and religion becomes a taboo subject. Here we can find an interesting effect; since religious education is denied by the State, people become interested in the subject from an early age and actually become more religious. The lack of formal religious education forms a sort of personal religion, often distorted, perverted and mingled with superstitions, *"the natural ally of injustice"*.[203] This scenario was displayed in absolutist regimes where the governing class wants to hold all the power; the communist regimes are the best examples.

The second scenario, the most common around the world, is the one where the Religion as an institution and the State share the role of an educator. The problem in this system is the unresolved conflict between religious teachings about the origins of the universe and the origins of man or natural phenomena, and science. Since Religion is unwilling admit any error in its teachings and Science offers more and more verifiable answers, the conflict will eventually become unresolvable.

In the third scenario, Religion holds all the power and education is entirely religious, with disastrous effect for Science and the rejection of anything that is not contained in a religious text.

By no means, the study of Religion should be denied to anyone, and by no means should antiquated doctrines prevail over the scientific truth. The ultimate goal of Education should be to create Moral individuals and Ethical citizens.

In the following chapters Russell presents other issues that need to be addressed in education, sex, patriotism, class-feeling, competition or propaganda.

---

[202] Bertrand Russell, *Education and the Social Order*, pg. 79
[203] Ibid., pg169

We shall also note the chapter on the education in communism. Despite the fact that communist regimes are on the verge of extinction, communist like systems are beginning to reemerge in several forms of oligarchies, masked under an appearance of democracy and capitalism; what is certain is that this Hydra has not lost all heads.

Last chapter is dedicated to the reconciliation between individuality and citizenship. Russell is so modern that we can easily forget that the year is nineteen thirty. Here is an example:

> *"When the authorities also are stupid (which may occur), they will tend to side with the stupid children, and acquiesce, at least tacitly, in rough treatment for those who show intelligence. In that case, a society will be produced in which all the important positions will be won by those whose stupidity enables them to please the herd. Such a society will have corrupt politicians, ignorant schoolmasters, policemen who cannot catch criminals, and judges who condemn innocent men. Such a society, even if it inhabits a country full of natural wealth, will in the end grow poor from inability to choose able men for important posts. Such a society, though it may prate of Liberty and even erect statues in her honour, will be a persecuting society, which will punish the very men whose ideas might save it from disaster. All this will spring from the too intense pressure of the herd, first at school and then in the world at large."*[204]

However, something extraordinary happened since Russell's time and that is the internet revolution. Today Google University rules the educational system. In terms of accessibility and quantity, information can be transmitted today almost without restriction. But there is also a great danger, in terms of control and censorship; with the entire world online, an Orwellian social model at a global scale can be functional in less than a decade, a total victory for the absolute corruption.

## 2.6. Currents of thought in modern philosophy

My purpose from the beginning was to make the phenomenon of corruption more understandable; entering in the domain of analytical philosophy to explain the phenomenon of corruption is a path on which I do not dare to venture at this point and we will save that journey for some other time. I do not wish to complicate an overly complicated matter with a sterile analysis.

---

[204] Ibid., pg.171

Much has been written in recent years about morals and ethics but little had been said about corruption. I was unable to identify a single major modern philosopher that treated the phenomenon of corruption exhaustively.

Since the beginning of history, human society was organized by the State (call it kingdom, empire, republic), responsible for law and order, and by the Church (again, use the appropriate name for each religion), responsible for morals and ethics.

The role of religion as an educator for moral and ethical living came under dispute in recent years, but this time the challenge did not come from the State as it was the case in totalitarian regimes, it came from Science which contradicted the basic religious beliefs such as the creation of man or the universe.

The atheist movement is now focused on a quest for a science of morals and ethics, a quest which I see to be incomplete without addressing two other aspects beside religion, namely the law and the phenomenon of corruption.

Science does not provide all the answers at once because we cannot ask all the right questions at once. And science is cruel; it provides the answers that are true, not the answers we want to be true.

There is a major problem with all immaterial beings, call them souls, sprits, angels, gods. In order to move a single atom you need mass; immaterial beings have zero mass by definition, that's why they are called immaterial. All the immaterial beings in the universe united will weigh zero mass. Therefor all the immaterial beings in the universe are incapable of moving one single atom on a distance of one single micron.

Sir Isaac Newton, 1642 - 1727, wrote in *Philosophiæ Naturalis Principia Mathematica* in 1687, the laws of motion; these three laws or axioms, the law of inertia, the law of acceleration and the law of reciprocal actions should have ended any discussion about any form of immaterial beings. Then how can we still believe that something immaterial can have any influence on our morals and ethics, or, if we look at the opposing party, on our vices and corruption?

If the role of religion is put into question, maybe it will also be a good time to question the role of the State. Democracy is a system in which the laws of the country are enacted by those mandated by the people thru the electoral process. But once a majority is formed in the Parliament, democracy ceases to exist; I do not know of a single example from history when a majority decided, against its interests, in favor of a minority.

If the modern man does not need a priest to tell him what is right or what is wrong, maybe he does not need a politician to write a law that determines what is right and what is wrong.

In law, hypocrisy is supreme. While documents like the Universal Declaration of Human Rights or the Constitution (choose any that you like) proclaims the principle of equality before the law, there is a multitude of laws, in any legal systems, that institute exceptions and privileges. The concept of exception shows either a corrupt system or a poorly written law, in either case, a deficiency in the legal system.

At the end of the 19th century, the German physicist Wilhelm Conrad Röntgen discovered the X-rays and made the first radiography, an image of his wife Anna's hand. It was one of the greatest inventions in history; from now on, doctors were able to see inside the human body without a dissecting it first.

Half a century later, Sir Godfrey Newbold Hounsfield, a British engineer had the brilliant idea to unite a computer with X-rays, thus inventing the first CT scanner. The impact of tomography was enormous; doctors are able to construct a 3-D model of a living human body.

Understanding the human brain is the new challenge not only for medicine but also for philosophy. A new discipline, Neuroethics, devised in Ethics of Neuroscience and Neuroscience of Ethics[205] will offer definitive answers in areas that were explored only by philosophy. Notions like good or happiness will be explained by the levels of dopamine or serotonin discharged in the brain. With the help of CT and MRI scanners we are now able to record how the process of thinking takes place.

Philippa Foot, 1920 - 2010, was a British professor of philosophy with a special interest in ethics and morals, and she was influenced in her work by Aristotle. She wrote almost nothing about corruption, the term is mentioned only once in *Virtues and Vices and Other Essays in Moral Philosophy*. However, she raised an interesting ethical dilemma known as the tram problem. First, she imagined a situation for a magistrate:

---

[205] Neil Levy, *Neuroethics Challenges for the 21st Century*, (Cambridge: Cambridge University Press, 2007)

*"Suppose that a judge or magistrate is faced with rioters demanding that a culprit be found for a certain crime and threatening otherwise to take their own bloody revenge on a particular section of the community. The real culprit being unknown, the judge sees himself as able to prevent the bloodshed only by framing some innocent person and having him executed."*[206]

In this case there is a special quality requirement from the active subject involved, the quality of a judge; asking a person without knowledge of the law is useless because it gives false results.

The ethical course of action for the judge is to resign and not to give any judgement, because he is in impossibility to perform his duty as a judge freely; I consider that any judge will point to this answer. If he cannot resign and he is forced to make a judgement, then his decision has no relevance because is obtained by force, it is no longer his.

The main ethical problem raised by Foot is the tram (trolley, train) problem, which caused quite a stir in the academia:

*"...the driver of a runaway tram which he can only steer from one narrow track on to another; five men are working on one track and one man on the other; anyone on the track he enters is bound to be killed."*[207]

Here Foot assumes that anyone will choose to save the five men, and the question is *"...why we should say, without hesitation, that the driver should steer for the less occupied track, while most of us would be appalled at the idea that the innocent man could be framed."*

Again, in the second scenario, the answer is crystal clear for the lawyer. The ethical course of action is not to act, because killing is illegal, the only difference is that there will be a greater sanction for multiple deaths.

If forced to act, we cannot speak about the free will of the active subject, he will not suffer any legal consequences for his acts and his 'choice' will have no relevance because it is not a choice. If the driver of the train is not forced in any way but he has a choice between track A, thus killing one and track B, thus killing five, he must choose the track designated to him in his travel plan, in other words he must perform his duty.

Law, at a certain moment in time is the expression of the preceding moral and ethical principles. A moral dilemma cannot be solved making abstraction of the law. The answer is complicated for the philosopher, for

---

[206] Philippa Foot, *Virtues and Vices and Other Essays in Moral, Philosophy*, (Oxford: Oxford University Press), pg. 23
[207] Ibid.

the medic or for the engineer yet it so clear for the lawyer. One has to choose to kill in order to save other lives. No matter his choice, killing is illegal. If he kills one to save five he will answer for one crime. If he kills five to save one he will answer for five crimes.

People cannot answer this type of questions by ignoring the sanction completely. The choice of saving five may be based on the fear of sanction and not on utility. The moral and ethical choice here is not to intervene. Thus, the active subject will be spared of any sanction, no judge in his right mind can condemn a person for walking away from a situation like this, he will avoid any subsequent moral conflict and ethically he is immaculate. The principles of legal responsibility are the key to these riddles.

One can imagine even better scenarios, for instance a fireman walks into a building on fire and finds an old woman and a pretty young girl; which one shall he choose, supposing he only has the time and the physical capability to save only one. This problem is harder to solve because for the fireman, inaction is not a choice, he has the duty to save lives.

The trolley problem got a new dimension in Greene's *Moral Tribes*[208], even got a new name 'trolleyology'. Green summarizes the problem in a *"Kant versus Mill"* dilemma; he engaged in a serious study of the brain activity during the solving of two variations of the Foot's tram problem called the 'switch' and the 'footbridge'.[209]

The study made use of functional magnetic resonance imaging (fMRI) to measure the activity in the brain while the subjects were trying to solve the above mentioned problems. The conclusion was:

> *"We see evidence for dual-process moral psychology in the lab and in the field, in healthy people and in people with severe emotional deficits, in studies using simple questionnaires and in studies using brain imaging, psychophysiology, and psychoactive drugs. It's now clear that we have dual-process moral brains."*... *"In an ideal world, moral intuition is all you need, but in the real world, there are benefits to having a dual-process brain."*[210]

The trolley problem is not related with the phenomenon of corruption studied in this book but was included to point out a direction where further studies can bring a new light.

[208] Joshua D. Greene, *Moral Tribes, Emotion, Reason, and the Gap between Us and Them* (New York: The Penguin Press, 2013), pg. 113
[209] Ibid., pg. 119
[210] Ibid., pg. 131

Any new studies on the phenomenon of corruption must avoid the following trap: the subjects of the studies similar with that of Green's must be corrupt individuals, persons that actually had the experience of taking a bribe, for instance.

Asking the subjects from the general public will produce false results. In my opinion it will be important to definitively determine if corruption brings happiness for the corrupt and if and to what extent fear plays a role here.

Our understanding of the brain will cause a new set of problems in the near future. Computer controlled brain implants are no longer science fiction, they are about to become science fact. Beside morality, will we be able to have another controller, an artificial one, for our actions and reactions? And is that artificial controller, which I foresee to become technically possible, desirable?

Imagine a device inserted in a child's brain after birth; it will insure that his growing process will be flawless, it will cure any disease it will feed his brain with any information he desires and prolong his life for millennia. If one thinks such a device is a fiction, there is enough space in the cranial cavity to accommodate a processor, all is needed is a direct interface between the brain and the processor.

Will the child of tomorrow be human? Is technology capable of offering humans a perpetual state of happiness? Is technology able to eliminate crime, including here corruption? Will it be ethical to fit a criminal with an artificial controller? These are questions for the new discipline, ethics of neuroscience to answer.

Biology is another area where we should expect further developments in the near future. The Human Genome Project was successful in mapping all the genes of human beings.[211] The study of genes raised a new class of ethical dilemmas, which we shall not explore in depth here.

The main fear is that the manipulation of the human genes will create non-human creatures, superhuman, monsters and so on. A series of laws were quickly passed around the world, either banning experiments or severely restricting them.

The advancement in biology, genetics in particular, will sooner or later be beneficial for medical sciences, in a new generation of drugs, vaccines, treatments for vary diseases. Corruption has often been seen as a disease, one that can be eradicated. I do not consider this view to be

---

[211] www.genome.gov/12011238

accurate, even in cases when the term is used as a metaphor. Corruption is not a disease.

The recent scientific advancement in the field of biology will provide, no doubt, a better understanding of the chemical processes in our bodies. If the desire to accumulate money and power is generated by fear and insecurity, then perhaps it will be useful to search for a 'cure'. Since I am not a biologist I do not know if corruption may be 'cured' with a pill or a vaccine in the near future.

All this information given in this chapter, which is not even the size of a snowflake on the tip of the proverbial iceberg, compared with what it was written about morality and ethical living in recent years might be confusing for the reader.

I think the modern man has a more accurate understanding of the world than Plato did. One should try to study and to express the world as it is reflected to him; we cannot keep searching for definitions and quotes in ancients or utilitarians or idealists every time we encounter a philosophical problem.

## 2.7. Conclusions

The phenomenon of corruption was an object of study for all philosophers. Despite my best efforts I was unable to find a clear and complete definition. Because the term corruption was used in two senses, the first literally meaning destruction, decay, ruin, deterioration in reference to a substance and figuratively with the same meaning but in relation to something immaterial such as soul, morals, spirit, the term is easy to understand, yet the phenomenon is hard to define.

Corruption is subsequent to law and precedes ethics and morals. This simple fact explains why corruption endures in society. When a law is enacted and put into force, it regulates those aspects that are present in that society, at that particular moment in time; legislators cannot foresee the future.

Corruption consists in actions that are directed against a legal order. When corruption exceeds a certain level, philosophers conceive moral principles and ethical norms in order to correct the ill effects of corruption. Legal philosophy provides new principles for new laws, which are enacted by legislators.

Here we have the following succession, placed in never-ending cycle:

→ LAW → CORRUPTION → MORALS & ETHICS → NEW LAW →

Morality, ethics and law are subject to evolutionary processes that are exercising an influence on each other. The question if morality influences law or if law determines morality is just as silly as the question which came first the egg or the hen. At a particular moment in time and space (it doesn't matter the historical period or the geographic location) people organize themselves in a particular manner or form, by establishing rules of behavior or, in other words, by enacting laws.

Corruption, as a counteraction to positive law leads to the development of ethical and moral principles in order to preserve the common good. In a sense, moral and ethics are a counteraction to the natural law because they call on humans to restrain natural impulses, and act in conflict with their immediate interest.

The common good is more rewarding for the individual on the long term than the immediate personal good that corruption provides. It all comes down to choice between moral and ethical way of living and the corrupt way of living. The main problem in the choice is that often people fail to see the long term benefits and are blinded in their choice by the instant reward and therefore they chose corruption.

Luxury was blamed by several authors as the main cause of corruption. Luxury, and by this we mean all the forms of wealth that grossly exceed one's needs is not a cause for corruption but the object of men's desires. The profits, the gain, obtained thru corrupt actions are, in most cases, exchanged for luxury items.

Luxury items, in general, are also works of art involving fine craftsmanship, rare materials and many hours of highly specialized labor. Therefor luxury is not something 'bad' or 'evil', quite the contrary; it helped the technological advancement of our society. The acquisition of luxury thru corrupt means is indeed condemnable.

The most important question to be asked is why men become corrupt. Perhaps the best answer was given by Epicurus: "*Some men want fame and status, thinking that they would thus make themselves secure against other men.*"[212] Could it be true that the corrupt do not seek money, luxury and power, but security? Shall we see a corrupt individual as a person worthy of pity and not envy? It is a very interesting idea,

---

[212] See Epicurus, *Principal Doctrines*, on http://www.epicurus.net/en/principal.html

that will not only explain the motives behind corruption, but it will explain the repetitive behavior of the corrupt.

Another question is if corruption provides happiness for the corrupt. The obvious answer is yes, but things are not that simple. In the beginning the corrupt will enjoy his new acquired wealth, or he will find delight in using his power, but this is only a temporary gratification.

Soon, he will begin to experience the fear of losing his money, privileges, power and he will become more rapacious. His sense of security is frail because it is a false security that money and power brings; he will always seek ways to strengthen his position, to acquire more wealth.

During the entire history, corrupt men were also great builders of temples, pyramids, cathedrals, castles, fortresses; the construction of some of the greatest edifices in human history is linked with stories of corruption. If Epicurus is right, all these constructions served but one purpose, to hide and to protect a scared corrupt man.

The contemporary corrupt man is also hiding, inside exclusivists clubs, behind the walls of mansions and villas, on yachts or up in the air, in private jets or helicopters. Unknowingly, he places himself in a prison, a luxurious prison indeed, but still, just a prison. He interacts with society only thru the members of his staff, thus depriving himself of normal human interactions.

In my opinion, imprisonment is not a sufficient penalty for corruption. Once inside the real prison, the corrupt will use the remaining wealth, or just a promise, to obtain privileges by corrupting the personnel or other inmates. The real punishment is the complete loss of any privileges and social status, especially inside the penitentiary. The process of reeducation should focus on teaching the corrupt that he does not need wealth to feel secure and happy.

In the end, because it is a natural phenomenon, the fate of corruption is hard to predict. At the present moment in the development of human society, corruption is very hard to control and eradication is, for now, a utopic objective.

Nevertheless, we should not abandon the fight against corruption; on the contrary we shall acknowledge the fact that current efforts are insufficient even for containing the phenomenon and increase our efforts. An optimistic view is that eventually we will be able to eradicate corruption. The pessimistic alternative is that corruption will be the final doom of the human race.

A key element in the fight against corruption is a clear definition that will help in making the phenomenon understandable. In the next chapter we shall explore the definitions in use and examine a new definition, followed by an analysis of the phenomenon from a legal perspective.

*Each problem that I solved became a rule,*
*which served afterwards to solve other problems.*

Rene Descartes

# 3. Defining corruption

One may ask why defining and redefining corruption is of any importance; the definitions in use seem to cover almost every aspect or form of the phenomenon, why should we declare ourselves dissatisfied.

The problem with contemporary definitions is that they define corruption in general terms or from a sociological perspective. What seems to be lacking is a definition from a legal point of view, one that will define corruption as a legal phenomenon, a definition based on the philosophy of law.

A clear definition is necessary in the study of any phenomenon because it allows for a thorough analysis, which in the end gives a better understanding of the phenomenon in question.

New definitions are usually born in the academic environment and subsequently they find their place in the legal system and in the daily practice of the law. The absence of a proper legal definition is a source of confusion and divergent interpretations and a cause of disharmony in the legal environment.

For a prosecutor or a judge, a good definition is a useful tool; the phenomenon of corruption is characterized by an elusive side, a hidden dimension that one can easily identify intuitively, yet is hard to prove in a court of law.

For the legislator, clear definitions are necessary to enact laws that are easy to understand, applied and obeyed. The lack of a proper definition is reflected in poorly written laws and a deficient law can cause more problems than its absence.

The term corruption is wildly used in media, in most cases in a proper manner. In the modern period the role of the press as a guardian of democracy was proven in countless occasions. For the journalist is difficult to expose corruption unless he has the certainty that the story he recounts is an act of corruption. A clear definition will be helpful in revealing the elusive side of the phenomenon.

Most of our knowledge on the phenomenon of corruption comes from sociological studies. Again, the lack of a comprehensive definition left out the hidden part of the phenomenon in question, a part that cannot be quantified by the classical sociological methods.

The students from a large variety of disciplines will benefit from a definition of corruption, since the phenomenon is present in all aspects of life and affects any organization.

Finally, I do not see how the fight against corruption can be effective if we do not know what we are fighting. In order to be successful, any fight needs a strategy and without a strategy any government will find that the efforts against corruption are spent in vain.

In this chapter we shall explore the definitions in use, we shall identify their deficiencies and we shall suggest and examine a new definition. The second part of this chapter is dedicated to a legal analysis of the phenomenon, based on the proposed definition.

## 3.1. Definitions in use

In theory, defining corruption should be a facile exercise, yet it seems that no definition is suitable enough to comprehensively capture such a multifaceted phenomenon. But before we begin we must note that "*No jurist has yet achieved a definition of law that does not require the use of the idea of law, either implied or expressed, as a part of the definition.*"[1]

In its essence, corruption is a breach of laws, and, probably, because is so hard to define a law, its breach might be even harder to define. Nevertheless, I shall give an account on the definitions in use, not to exacerbate the confusion, but to create a wider view.

The search for the term corruption in Oxford's Law Dictionary shows: "corruption n. See BRIBERY AND CORRUPTION" and if we continue the search we can find a rather complicated definition:

> "*bribery and corruption Offences relating to the improper influencing of people in certain positions of trust. The offences commonly grouped under this expression are now statutory. Under the Public Bodies Corrupt Practices Act 1889 (amended by the Prevention of Corruption Act 1916) it is an offence, if done corruptly (i.e. deliberately and with an improper motive), to give or offer to a member, officer, or servant of a public body any reward or advantage to do anything in relation to any matter with which that body is concerned; it is also an offence for a public servant or officer to corruptly receive or solicit such a reward. The Prevention of Corruption Act 1906 (amended by the 1916Act) is wider in scope. It relates to agents, which include not only those involved in the business of agency but also all employees, including anyone serving under the Crown or any public body. Under this Act it is an offence to corruptly give or offer any valuable consideration to an agent to do any act or show any favour in relation to his principal's affairs; like the 1889Act, it also creates a converse offence of receiving or soliciting by agents.*"[2]

---

[1] John Maxcy Zane, *The Story of the Law*, (Indianapolis: Liberty Fund, 1998)
[2] Elisabeth A. Martin, A Dictionary of Law, 5th ed., (Oxford: Oxford University Press, 2003)

In Black's Law Dictionary corruption is defined as follows:

> "*1. Depravity, perversion, or taint; an impairment of integrity, virtue, or moral principle; esp., the impairment of a public official's duties by bribery. [Cases: Officers and Public Employees 121.C.J.S. Officers and Public Employees §§ 329–334.]*
>
> "*The word 'corruption' indicates impurity or debasement and when found in the criminal law it means depravity or gross impropriety.*" *Rollin M. Perkins & Ronald N. Boyce, Criminal Law 855 (3d ed. 1982).*
>
> *2. The act of doing something with an intent to give some advantage inconsistent with official duty and the rights of others; a fiduciary's or official's use of a station or office to procure some benefit either personally or for someone else, contrary to the rights of others.*"[3]

A more succinct definition is to be found in Collin's Dictionary of Law:

> "*corruption n. dishonest behaviour such as paying or accepting money or giving a favour to make sure that something is done.*"[4]

Maybe it would be wise not to limit our search for a definition for corruption to law dictionaries and to widen our search area to the more generalist dictionaries and encyclopedias.

Encyclopaedia Britannica defines corruption as:

> "*Improper and usually unlawful conduct intended to secure a benefit for oneself or another. Its forms include bribery, extortion, and the misuse of inside information. It exists where there is community indifference or a lack of enforcement policies. In societies with a culture of ritualized gift giving, the line between acceptable and unacceptable gifts is often hard to draw.*"[5]

while Wikipedia defines it as:

> "*There is no globally accepted definition of corruption. In philosophical, theological, or moral discussions, corruption is the abuse of bestowed power or position to acquire a personal benefit. Corruption may include many activities including bribery and embezzlement. Government, or 'political', corruption occurs when an office-holder or other governmental employee acts in an official capacity for personal gain.*"[6]

In Merriam Webster's on-line edition corruption is:

> "*...dishonest or illegal behavior especially by powerful people (such as government officials or police officers)*"[7]

---

[3] Black's Law Dictionary 8th ed. 2004 pg. , 1047
[4] P.H. Collin, Dictionary of Law, 4th edition, (London: Bloomsbury Publishing), pg.75
[5] "corruption." Encyclopædia Britannica Ultimate Reference Suite. (Chicago: Encyclopædia Britannica, 2011)
[6] https://en.wikipedia.org/wiki/Corruption
[7] http://www.merriam-webster.com/dictionary/corruption

Attempts to properly define corruption were made by International Organizations, thus, World Bank defines corruption as:

> "...*the abuse of public office for private gain.*"[8]

while Transparency International defines it:

> "*Generally speaking as "the abuse of entrusted power for private gain". Corruption can be classified as grand, petty and political, depending on the amounts of money lost and the sector where it occurs.*
>
> *Grand corruption consists of acts committed at a high level of government that distort policies or the central functioning of the state, enabling leaders to benefit at the expense of the public good. Petty corruption refers to everyday abuse of entrusted power by low- and mid-level public officials in their interactions with ordinary citizens, who often are trying to access basic goods or services in places like hospitals, schools, police departments and other agencies.*
>
> *Political corruption is a manipulation of policies, institutions and rules of procedure in the allocation of resources and financing by political decision makers, who abuse their position to sustain their power, status and wealth.*" [9]

Perhaps it would be useful to extend our search for a definition in laws and international conventions.

In the forward of the United Nations Convention against Transnational Organized Crime is stated:

> "*If the enemies of progress and human rights seek to exploit the openness and opportunities of globalization for their purposes, then we must exploit those very same factors to defend human rights and defeat the forces of crime, corruption and trafficking in human beings.*"[10]

and that the Convention

> "*... will constitute an effective tool and the necessary legal framework for international cooperation in combating, inter alia, such criminal activities as money-laundering, corruption, illicit trafficking in endangered species of wild flora and fauna...*"[11]

Article 8 of the Convention contains provisions regarding the criminalization of corruption, considering to be a criminal offence the promise, offering or giving or the solicitation by a public official of an undue advantage in order to act or to refrain in the exercise of his official duties. Although the Convention can be considered a milestone in the fight against transnational and organized crime, corruption is defined in general terms.

---

[8] http://www1.worldbank.org/publicsector/anticorrupt/corruptn/cor02.htm
[9] http://www.transparency.org/what-is-corruption/#define
[10] http://www.unodc.org/documents/treaties/UNTOC/Publications/TOC%20Convention/TOCebook-e.pdf
[11] Ibid.

The Convention against Transnational Organized Crime was followed by a specific document that addresses corruption, the United Nations Convention against Corruption, adopted by the United Nations General Assembly on 31 October 2003 by Resolution 58/4, but even this document doesn't offer us a proper definition. From the preamble we learn that corruption is a serious problem and poses a threat...

> "...*to the stability and security of societies undermining the institutions and values of democracy, ethical values and justice and jeopardizing sustainable development and the rule of law.*"[12]

Moreover, the Convention acknowledges the fact that there is a link between corruption and organized crime, that corrupt activities involve vast quantity of assets and is no longer an isolated matter but a transnational phenomenon.

European Union Law is a hybrid between international law and national law, which has produced a series of documents in regard corruption and specific mechanisms, policies and institutions necessary to combat the phenomenon. Despite the appetence of the European legislators for producing regulations and directives, we are unable to find a proper definition, thus the Civil Law Convention on Corruption Strasbourg, from 9/4/1999, in Article 2, defines corruption as:

> "... *requesting, offering, giving or accepting, directly or indirectly, a bribe or any other undue advantage or prospect thereof, which distorts the proper performance of any duty or behaviour required of the recipient of the bribe, the undue advantage or the prospect thereof.*"[13]

As a last resort, we shall try to find a definition for corruption in academic books. There are several books regarding the white collar criminality, however, despite my best efforts, in none of them I was able to find a definition for corruption. The manuals treating criminal law are equally silent on the subject, probably because corruption is not incriminated *per se*.

The best definition to be found in academic books is the one proposed by Ian Senior in *Corruption - the World's Big C*:

> "...*Corruption occurs when a corruptor (1) covertly gives (2) a favour to a corruptee or to a nominee to influence (3) action(s) that (4) benefit the corruptor or a nominee, and for which the corruptee has (5) authority.*"[14]

---

[12] https://www.unodc.org/documents/treaties/UNCAC/Publications/Convention/08-50026_E.pdf
[13] http://conventions.coe.int/Treaty/en/Treaties/Html/174.htm
[14] Ian Senior, *Corruption – the World's Big C. Cases, Causes, Consequences, Cures* (London: The Institute of Economic Affairs, 2006)

Again we must admit that the question 'what is corruption?' remains unanswered.

## 3.2. Criticism of the definitions in use

After this long exposé on the definitions used today, perhaps it will be useful to highlight the key points where these definitions fail to fulfil their purpose.

The definition in Oxford's Dictionary of Law is the most confusing because it associates bribery, an offence, with corruption, a phenomenon. The result is a group of statutory offences that is defined by this expression. Beside bribery, it is an offence to give, receive or solicit a reward, advantage or favor by a member, officer, or servant of a public body or by an agent or employee. The definition covers bribery and trafficking in influence but we shall see that corruption is much more than that. The definition is incomplete because it does not include unilateral corrupt acts such as embezzlement for instance.

Black's Law Dictionary is equally confusing. It adds a moral dimension to the phenomenon, depravity, perversion, taint, impairment of integrity, virtue, or moral principle but it describes only the receiving of an undue advantage. It is also incomplete because it refers only to an official.

The Collin's Law Dictionary definition is short and to the point, if we were searching for a definition for bribery and undue advantages. Beside clarity, I do not see any other merits for this one.

In Encyclopaedia Britannica is one of the best definitions I was able to find. First, corruption is an 'improper and usually unlawful conduct'. The observation is correct because not always what is improper is also unlawful. The second part of the phrase 'intended to secure a benefit for oneself or another' should have been left out; the corrupt always intents to obtain a benefit for himself even if it is by obtaining a benefit for other first.

Another good point here is it that it presents bribery, extortion and the misuse of inside information as forms of corruption, implying that these are not the only ones. The fact that corruption exists 'where there is community indifference or a lack of enforcement policies' does not explain why corruption exists in developed societies. The reference to 'societies with a culture of ritualized gift giving' is not quite true; here we can find some of the harshest penalties for corruption.

Wikipedia is not always a reliable source of information, but then again, because it is free, it has become in recent years one of the most searched encyclopedias. Its popularity is the reason for which it was included here. Corruption is defined as 'the abuse of bestowed power or position to acquire a personal benefit', thus limiting the definition to a person in power. A good point is that beside bribery, it includes embezzlement among its forms.

The UNTOC places corruption on the same level with crime and trafficking in human beings and later places corruption among other criminal activities such as money-laundering, illicit trafficking in endangered species of wild flora and fauna.

The UNCAC was intended to be the main weapon against corruption, so is hard to understand why such an important issue, the definition of corruption remained unresolved.

The definitions written in academic books about corruption or the white collar criminality make use of the contemporary definitions, sometimes with minor modifications, or they simply ignore the problem. Professor Senior developed a theory, a model based on the five conditions expressed in his definition of corruption, which might be considered useful in the attempt to classify a certain action as corruption, his definition comes short on the key point of any definition...what is it?

I wonder if any of the modern authors had the curiosity to read Bentham; in the previous chapter we have seen a clear definition and also an important explanation regarding the position of corruption in relation with the criminal phenomenon, which we will explore in detail in the next chapter.

One common mistake is to associate corruption with bribery; it is true that the most common form of corruption is bribery, but by placing the sign of equivalent between the two, the result will be an incomplete definition. As we shall see later on, corruption comes in a variety of shapes or forms; some of them are not even incriminated by the Penal Law or are masked under a legal or legitimate appearance.

This type of association is dangerous because it is severely limited; trafficking of influence, fraud, embezzlement, other forms of corruption are not covered by this definitions. It also gives the wrong impression that corruption is always performed by two parties, while in fact we can find numerous corrupt acts that are performed by individuals for their own interests.

Another common mistake is to limit the definition to a person in power, such as a public official, a policeman, a judge. In fact, any person may be part in an affair of corruption. An official position is not a *sine qua non* condition for corruption to exist.

These definitions overlook a major part of the corrupt affairs, those that take place in the private sector. In theory, corruption generates more corruption and one of the generators of corruption in the public sector is, obviously, the corruption in the private sector.

Corruption in the private sector cannot exist without the corruption in the public sector; in a utopic system with zero corruption among policemen, judges and other public officials, corruption in the private sector will be swiftly eradicated.

Even this distinction between public and private corruption is utterly wrong. In fact, a cause-effect relation between the two is impossible to establish because they are different forms of the same phenomenon. So, from a philosophical standpoint it is impossible to tell which one generates the other or which one came first; they are the same thing.

The difference rest in the quality of the persons involved who, in some cases, may hold a public position. A private person may corrupt a public official in order to satisfy his interests, on the other hand we also have situations when public officials seek undue advantages, thus corrupting private individuals.

If we acknowledge the fact that corruption can affect any individual, a general definition for corruption should focus on the phenomenon itself and not on a special quality of its subjects.

Both the UNTOC and UNCAC share a common fallacy; they fail to offer a definition for corruption. In both documents corruption is defined indirectly and only in general terms.

This situation creates a significant problem, because it leaves to the signatory States the task to define corruption, thus allowing for different interpretations and divided views.

It is hard to understand why the legislators left this important issue unresolved. The quest for uniform laws finds itself in front of another obstacle, raised by the same documents that were supposed to bring uniformity. Furthermore, these documents laid the foundation for the construction of specialized institutions to combat corruption, for conceiving and implementing of anti-corruption policies that are supposed to bring corruption under control. How can these policies and institutions be effective against an unknown and undefined enemy?

Another aspect deserves a critical exploration. Sometimes, in legal texts, corruption is mentioned beside bribery, trafficking of endangered species, drugs and human beings, fraud, as a category on its own.

Nothing can be further from the truth; corruption is a phenomenon that incorporates the above mentioned criminal activities. Any form of bribery, no matter the specific circumstances, is part of the phenomenon of corruption. The same thing can be said about any form of trafficking regardless their objects, being them influence, humans, animals or radioactive materials; they are still a form of corruption.

This shows clearly the level of misunderstanding; on one hand we use corruption as a synonym for bribery, on the other we consider corruption an independent category. When these types of wrong placements are found in academic books or dictionaries the situation can be easily corrected in the next edition, but when these mistakes find their way in international conventions, it's a real tragedy. The procedures to correct fallacies in any legal documents in any country are extremely complicated and consume financial resources on a long period of time. When these fallacies are to be found at a philosophic level in international conventions, the adjective catastrophe comes to mind.

The term 'complex phenomenon' it's also used to describe corruption. It is true that there are many aspects that a proper definition must cover which made the challenge to define corruption an interesting one. Finding a definition was the easiest part of this work; the real difficulty is to explain corruption in all its forms.

## 3.3. Definition

Corruption is an antisocial phenomenon which manifests itself in the form of an illegal or immoral unilateral act or as an agreement between two parties, aiming to break or to elude a law or a social norm, for a personal gain.

## 3.4. Characteristics

At present, legal systems around the globe can be classified as belonging either to the civil law family or to the common law family of legal systems. The two families share a common ancestor, the Roman Law, but they have evolved differently.

Even in systems from the same family we can find differences, which were caused by socio-political factors and not by the legal science. In order to make a legal analysis of the phenomenon of corruption we must resort to the legal theory regarding legal acts and legal contracts.

In countries belonging to the Continental Law such as France and Germany, the legal theory was constructed on the foundations of the definitions existing in the civil codes, respectively the *Code Civil des Français* and the *Bürgerlichen Gesetzbuches*. Each country belonging to the so called 'civil law family' adopted a civil code that was influenced either by the CCF or by the BGB.

When it comes to the legal analysis in countries with legal systems based on the common law, such as Great Britain or the United States of America, the absence of legal definitions of some of the key institutions of law employed here makes the analysis a bit more difficult.

Nevertheless, our primary purpose is to make the phenomenon of corruption more understandable, and this is why, by comparison, we will use the legal theory and the laws or statutes of the above mentioned countries. With just a handful of exceptions, our legal analysis of the phenomenon of corruption should be intelligible worldwide, no matter the specific legal system.

The definition I suggested here provides the general characteristics of corruption. First, corruption is an antisocial phenomenon. Second, it is illegal or immoral. Third, it can be an act or an agreement between two or more parties. Forth, it has as scope the breaking or the evading the law in order to obtain a personal gain.

There are only two conditions for an act or an agreement to be defined as corruption. First, it must be illegal or immoral. Second, the act or the agreement must aim to break or to elude a law or a social norm. In the absence of these conditions, no act or agreement can be considered corruption.

### 3.4.1. Antisocial phenomenon

Corruption is considered by many authors, especially by those with a sociologic background, a social phenomenon. Car racing is also a social phenomenon. Formula One or World Touring Car Championship are social events, performed on specialized circuits, by professionals, under strict regulations and with respect for the safety of people involved. Because of their popularity it is safe to call them a 'social phenomenon'.

In recent years though, a new form of the phenomenon of car racing emerged in our society, the illegal car races, performed on streets by amateurs, putting not only their lives in danger, but also the lives of innocent bystanders. To describe in two words these illegal events, nothing is better than the term 'antisocial phenomenon'.

Drawing a parallelism from the example above, we can say that corruption is an antisocial phenomenon as opposed to the obeying the laws, which is a social phenomenon.

In its essence, corruption, in most cases, is just a contract, an illegal contract indeed but still a contract. Therefore, if we are to consider lobby as a social phenomenon, because it is a regulated form of contract, trafficking of influence should be considered an antisocial phenomenon. The similarities between the two contracts are evident, yet one is legal and the other not. The illegal character it's what gives corruption in general its antisocial character.

Moreover, selling coke (a soft drink), is legal, but selling coke (slang term for cocaine), is obviously illegal. The contracts here are absolutely identical; yet, the object of the sale is what makes the former illegal.

Drug trafficking, another form of corruption, therefor, cannot be referred to as a social phenomenon. It is obvious that these forms of corruption, such as drug trafficking or trafficking of illegal substances are antisocial phenomena because they are directed against values of the society.

An antisocial phenomenon is a negative phenomenon that occurs in human society and puts the members of the society in a grave danger. War for instance is another antisocial phenomenon that causes great losses of human life and material resources. There is an intricate relation between corruption and war. In times of war corruption flourishes; on the other hand we can say that the generator of war is corruption itself.

Corruption is an antisocial phenomenon that generates other antisocial phenomena from the most dangerous ones such as war, terrorism, human trafficking and slavery down to milder forms of antisocial behavior such as illegal car racing.

Corruption is just beginning to be perceived as something so dangerous that it puts the entire humanity at risk. Not so long ago corruption was considered 'good for business' because it eased the bureaucratic burden, it 'greased the wheels' was a widely used expression.

In fact corruption is bad business. An entrepreneur might be tempted to think that is profitable to pay a bribe to start a business. What he doesn't realize is that by paying the first bribe, he has opened the Pandora's Box. If he pays a bribe for a license, he will soon be paying a bribe for a construction permit; once his business is functional he will have to pay other bribes to keep it running. In order to raise the money for all these bribes he will cheat his customers or he will commit tax evasion. It is a vicious circle from which it is very hard to break free. The short terms benefits will be annulled by the medium and long term losses and thus corruption is bad business.

Moreover, as an antisocial phenomenon, corruption acts against the economic principles on which a State's economy is founded. A free market, fair competition, property rights, all the fundaments that make a State's economy sound and prosperous are affected by corruption and the entire economic environment suffers.

The consequences of corruption can be seen in famine, epidemics, savage exploitation of natural resources; in a global society all this consequences add up and their impact is no longer a regional matter, but a global one.

Famine for instance cannot be blame solely on weather or poor agricultural management but also on the deficient distribution of the existing food reserves, and here corruption is to blame.

The situation is similar in cases of epidemics; outbreaks of diseases for which the medical science can provide prevention and treatment are still common and the only explanation why vaccines do not reach every person on the planet is again corruption.

When resources of a region are over exploited, the bulk of the profits do not feed the poor, they satisfy the greed of the few, a situation that cannot be named otherwise than corruption.

128

The question 'How much corruption costs?' has been asked before and several studies conducted by international organizations such as World Bank, International Monetary Fund etc., came up with different figures. The truth is that we don't know how much corruption costs.

The estimation depends on how many factors we put in the equation, and no study or estimation so far, was able to integrate all the factors. An accurate estimation on the costs of corruption will have to integrate the costs of other antisocial phenomena generated by corruption; it will have to add the costs necessary to keep the social order functional and most important it will have to take in to account its effects.

Bribery was estimated by the World Bank at 1.3 trillion U.S. dollars per year[15]. If we accept this estimation as accurate, although we have no scientific reason to do so, and we add the cost of all the other offences related to corruption, plus the costs of all the other antisocial phenomena generated by corruption, plus the costs of the effects ... the figure will be simply terrifying.

## 3.4.2. The illegal and the immoral character

In order to produce a legal or juridical effect, a human action must have legal relevance. When a man stares at the stars thru a binocular, his action does not have any legal relevance. If he points the binocular towards his neighbor house, his action has legal relevance because it interferes with his neighbor's right for privacy. The actions are identical but one is legal because there is no law against watching the stars, the second is illegal because the law protects the right for privacy even if it does not define each and every illegal action specifically: 'it is forbidden to watch your neighbor thru a binocular'.

In the previous chapter we have seen how new laws come into being in the sequence Law→ Corruption→ Morals and Ethics → New Law. The main problem here is that the legislators did not discover a modality to legislate for the future. Laws are regulating only those aspects that are present in the society at the moment they are enacted. There could not have been laws regulating the use of binoculars before the invention of the binocular.

---

[15]http://web.worldbank.org/WBSITE/EXTERNAL/NEWS/0,,contentMDK:20190187~menuPK:34457~p agePK:64003015~piPK:64003012~theSitePK:4607,00.html

Here morality plays a key role. In the absence of a law that specifically forbid an action or grants a certain right, it is our moral common sense that determines if the action is acceptable or not in our society. Once a common view is formed, that an action is unacceptable, it takes materiality in the form of a law that can forbid the unacceptable action.

Corruption is subsequent to law. This is why some actions are morally wrong, yet legal. A good example here would be the issue of computer piracy. After the invention of the internet, laws were enacted to regulate this activity. File sharing could not have been made illegal at the moment when the first generations of computer laws were enacted. Gradually, people begun to share movies, music, books, thus avoiding paying royalties for those entitled. Only when the phenomenon reached a certain critical mass, the legislators began a process to regulate this part of the activity that is interfering with the intellectual propriety rights of the authors. Which raised another set of ethical dilemmas: 'Is the buyer of a book allowed to lend the book to a friend?' or 'By buying the book, the buyer has the right of disposition over the book?', and so on.

The definition of corruption presented above covers these aspects with two terms 'immoral' and 'social norm'. Even if an action is not forbidden by law it is not necessarily moral or ethical and if that is the case, the action breaks a social norm. By the term 'social norm' here I mean those norms or rules that exist in our society but they are not contained by the legal form. For instance compassion is not mandatory by law yet is morally correct. Adultery was once strictly incriminated, now is no longer considered an offence. Lying is considered an offence if it is an act against the duty to tell the truth in a court of justice for instance; on other circumstances lying is not a crime. From our moral tradition we define lying as something immoral and it is a social norm that binds us to tell the truth in any situation, not the positive law.

Human actions are illegal if there is a law that forbids them. Since laws are classified in different disciplines, the illegal character may be determined by a criminal law, a civil law or even laws from others disciplines such as administrative law or trade and commerce law.

Another very important source of law that determines the illegal character of a certain human action is the international law. For instance the main document against corruption, the UNCAC in article 15 Bribery of national public officials, states:

*"Each State Party shall adopt such legislative and other measures as may be necessary to establish as criminal offences, when committed intentionally:*

*(a) The promise, offering or giving, to a public official, directly or indirectly, of an undue advantage, for the official himself or herself or another person or entity, in order that the official act or refrain from acting in the exercise of his or her official duties;*

*(b) The solicitation or acceptance by a public official, directly or indirectly, of an undue advantage, for the official himself or herself or another person or entity, in order that the official act or refrain from acting in the exercise of his or her official duties."*

After the adoption of an international convention, it takes a period of several years until the prescriptions are implemented in the internal law of the signatory States. For this reason any legal system is subject to changes. The text presented above can be found now in the FCP or the StGB[16]. International Conventions also bring a legal uniformity for the signatory States; once a convention is adopted the internal laws of the states will be similar.

But there is also the problem of harmonizing the internal legislation of the State with the international law. In order to facilitate the transition, international conventions use general terms and general principles that may be integrated in any legal system.

This set of issues, meaning the internal legislation and the international legislation, the quest for harmonization and uniformity, the differences in the legal doctrine and jurisprudence, sometimes makes the identification of the illegal character of a certain act or contract, a difficult process.

There is another aspect worth considering. It is the problem with masked corruption. The term 'masked' used here aims to nominate those acts and contracts that are legal yet underneath them a corrupt intent is hidden. In areas like lobbying or consultancy, bribery can be very easily disguised in a form of a legit contract, for which even taxes are paid.

It is very important to note that by paying taxes, illegal contracts do not become legal. The tax system is not a stamp of approval for corrupt activities. In determining the illegality of a contract, one must also consider the morality of the contract.

---

[16] See next chapter.

The issue of immorality was addressed in the German Civil Code, the BGB. Thus, Section 138 Legal transaction contrary to public policy; usury, states:

*"(1) A legal transaction which is contrary to public policy is void.*

*(2) In particular, a legal transaction is void by which a person, by exploiting the predicament, inexperience, lack of sound judgement or considerable weakness of will of another, causes himself or a third party, in exchange for an act of performance, to be promised or granted pecuniary advantages which are clearly disproportionate to the performance."*

The CC, in Article 1131 and Article 1133 states:

*"An obligation without cause or with a false cause, or with an unlawful cause, may not have any effect."*

*"A cause is unlawful where it is prohibited by legislation, where it is contrary to public morals or to public policy."*

By declaring any legal transaction contrary to public policy void, the German law covers virtually any aspect of immorality that may be present in a contract. By declaring the obligation with a false or unlawful cause ineffective and cause unlawful if it is prohibited by law or contrary to public morals and public policy, the French law covers the same area.

In common law systems the term 'immorality' is used in a slightly different manner and it usually refers to sexual offences. In UK the Sexual Offences Act 2003, Section 57-59 incriminates trafficking for sexual exploitation, undoubtedly a form of corruption. It is important to notice that the terms 'morality' and 'public policy' in continental law covers a wider area than their common law counterparts.

## 3.4.3. Corrupt acts and corrupt contracts

From the poposed definition we can notice that corruption comes in two forms, the form of a unilateral illegal or immoral act that aims to procure a benefit for the perpetrator or in the form of an illegal or immoral agreement between two parties, each seeking a benefit.

In other words corruption may be an act or an agreement that is either illegal or immoral; as a literary convention we shall call those corrupt acts and corrupt contracts. By the term 'act' here we shall consider any form of exterior manifestation of the human will, not just a legal document.

For obvious reasons, law treatises and books are focused on analyzing the legal characteristic of an act or a contract. Definitions, classifications, validity conditions, all of them were written to explain what is legal. When an act or contract is illegal they are brought before a court of law, where their crooked effects are corrected or annulled. Therefor there was no reason for legal scholars to develop a theory for illegality.

One of the most important principles of law is the principle of contractual freedom because it allows the creation of a *lex partes*. It was subject of critique[17] in common law doctrine; in fact the object of criticism is not the principle of the contractual freedom but the abuse of freedom to contract, especially in labor law.

The general idea here is that humans enter in legal relations with good, honest intentions in mind, in the large majority of cases. Law provides prescriptions for those situations when individuals are driven by dishonesty but it does not recognize the illegal act or the illegal contract as an institution. From a legal point of view, the contracts to kill or the contracts to sell drugs are not contracts and they are not enforceable in a court of law. Yet contract killing and drug trafficking are undeniably realities of life. Thus, I believe that these types of illegal human relations may be called illegal acts and illegal contracts.

Illegal agreements were classified into *"those which are contrary to positive law, those which are contrary to morality, and those which are contrary to public policy"*[18]; this classification was considered of little importance, an assertion that cannot be further from the truth.

Another aspect resulting from the definition is that of immorality. The concept of illegal is contained in the concept of immoral. Acts or contracts may be legal but immoral; it's a situation that occurs when a new type of legal relation emerges in society there are no laws to regulate such relation, or when the authors of the act or the parties in the contract are concealing their corrupt intentions under a legal document.

---

[17] Roscoe Pound, Liberty of Contract, Yale Law Journal, Volume 18, pg. 454 on
https://archive.org/stream/ jstor-785551/785551#page/n1/mode/2up
[18] Samuel Williston, The law of contracts, vol. 3(New York: Baker, Voorhi s& Co., 1920), §1628

### 3.4.3.1. Corrupt acts

The juridical act is a notion well known in continental law, yet the majority of the Civil Codes, modeled after the French Civil Code, do not define the juridical act. The term 'act' is used in continental law in two senses, as a juridical operation (*negotium*) or in the sense of a written legal document (*instrumentum*).[19] The third sense used in practice is that of an action, a manifestation of the human will.

The French doctrine developed a solid theory on the validity condition of the juridical acts, based on the general theory of obligations interpolated with the relevant notions from the CC. Thus, the validity conditions for the juridical act are similar to the validity conditions for contracts; an act is considered illegal when it fails to comply with the general validity conditions: legal capacity, consent, object and scope.

In the new definition it is stated that corruption may come in the form of an illegal or immoral act that is made with the purpose to break or to elude a law or a social norm in order to obtain a personal gain. The definition covers all three senses in which the term act may be used. An illegal act might be an illegal juridical operation, an illegal document or an illegal action. The key element is the existence of a law that forbids a behavior. In the absence of a law that institutes a restriction, general or specific, any act is legal.

For a person to commit an act of corruption the legal capacity is not necessary; a 15 years old, Jonathan Lebed[20], was the youngest person charged with stock market fraud. Between August 23, 1999 and February 4, 2000 he traded stocks on the internet and obtained a profit of $272,826. Stock marked fraud is a form of corruption; from the perpetrator of a corrupt act, only the mental and physical capacity to conceive and to perform the act is required.

The second validity condition for acts is consent. In the absence of consent or if the consent is vitiated, the act is illegal, *"l'acte existe en fait, mais non en droit."*[21] It is somehow counterintuitive, but the rules regarding consent apply to corrupt acts as well. In order for a person to perform an act of corruption, his consent must be valid. Corrupt acts are always intentional, so the perpetrator must act from his own free will; if

---

[19] Marcel Planiol, *Traité Elémentaire de Droit Civil*, vol.1, (Paris: Librairie Cotillon, 1904), pg. 103
[20] See www.sec.gov/litigation/admin/33-7891.htm
[21] Planiol, *Traité Elémentaire de Droit Civil,*vol.1, pg.105

his free will is vitiated by violence, for instance, he cannot be held accountable for the corrupt act.

The third validity condition for acts regards the object; the object must exist, must be determinate or determinable, it must be possible, and it must be licit and moral. With the exception of the last condition, corrupt acts are illegal and immoral by definition, the rest of the rules regarding the object of the act applies for corrupt acts as well.

The forth validity condition for an act to be legal is a lawful scope. Law prohibits acts that have an illegal or immoral scope; by definition, the scope of a corrupt act is either illegal or immoral.

For certain acts (in the sense of *instrumentum*), law requires a written form. A corrupt act does not necessarily require a form, but it might involve altering the required legal form of a document, in order to give an appearance of legality, for example in cases of forgery.

Corrupt acts might not be illegal but they certainly are immoral; what is illegal is also immoral but what is immoral it is not necessarily illegal.

Determining the immoral character of an act is not always easy. Simulation is a juridical institution well known in continental law. Even though it is more related to contracts, simulated unilateral acts are a reality. These are those acts that hide the true intention of their author under a legal public document.

From a legal point of view, those types of acts may be perfectly legit, but from a moral point of view they are acts made with a different intention than the one stated by the act. For instance, we have the simulated donations, when the donor's real intention is to hide certain valuable, which otherwise might be subject to let's say confiscation, by donating them to a third party. The immoral character of such act is obvious yet the act is legal.

When the courts are evaluating simulation, the judges are considering the public act void, and are concerned with the hidden act, the one that expresses the true will of the author.

A corrupt act is an act that intentionally breaks or eludes a law or a social norm in order to obtain a gain. The key element is intention. There is a variety of reasons for which a juridical act may be illegal or immoral, mistake of fact, mistake of law, material error. The author of a corrupt act is aware that there is a law or a social norm that forbids the act yet he acts against it in order to procure for himself a gain.

### 3.4.3.2. Corrupt contracts

Pothier defined a contract as *"...a kind of agreement"* and an agreement or a pact is *"... the assent of two or more persons, to form an engagement between them, or to dissolve or modify one already formed."* [22]

This definition precedes *Le Code civil des Français* of 21 March 1804, the Napoleon's Civil Code. Article 1101 states: *"The contract is a convention by which one or more persons oblige themselves towards one or more other persons to give, to do or not to do something."*

In common law systems the doctrine of the contract law has constantly evolved, the latest definition of a contract was presented in US Restatement of the Law of Contracts *"a contract is a promise or a set of promises for the breach of which the law gives a remedy, or the performance of which the law in some way recognizes as a duty."*[23]

Both doctrines have developed a set of essential conditions for a contract to be considered valid or legal and therefor enforceable in courts. For a contract to be valid in continental law it must meet, simultaneous, four condition, legal capacities for the contracting parties, a non-vitiated will, a licit or legal object or cause[24]. In common law systems, for a contract to be binding, three requirements must be fulfilled, and those are offer and acceptance, consideration and an intention to create legal relations.[25]

In the matter of illegal contracts, in common law legal systems there is a distinction between contracts that are illegal by statute and contracts that are illegal at common law. The contracts illegal by statute are considered valid contracts, yet, because they are made void by a statute, they will not be enforced by a court of law. Contracts that are illegal at common law, e.g. a contract to commit a fraud, are void because they are contrary to the public good. Contracts of corruption, therefor, from an Anglo-Saxon perspective, are illegal either by statute, or by common law, specific circumstances of each case determining in which category they belong.

---

[22] Pothier, *Obligations considered in a Moral and Legal View*,1st vol., ( Newbern: Martin & Ogden, 1802)

[23] http://www.lexinter.net/LOTWVers4/definition_of_contract.htm

[24] Planiol, *Traité Elémentaire de Droit Civil*,vol.2, *Les contrats*, pg.315

[25] Geoffrey Samuel, *Law of Obligations and Legal Remedies*, 2nd ed., (London: Cavendish Publishing, 2001) pg. 299

In continental law the existence of a special category, that of illegal contracts, is debatable. If an agreement doesn't comply with the general validity conditions is void by law, therefor it is not a contract. Paulus set the rule *"We can enter into agreements with reference to matters which are lawful, and from them alone the obligation of a contract arises"*. Moreover, *"We cannot make a contract which is contrary to the laws or to good morals."*[26] These opinions have influenced the juridical thinking in the last two millenniums, yet it seems that the later had a bigger influence in continental law, while the former was favored by the common law.

Since the times of the Roman Jurists, scholar's focus was placed on defining legal contracts and developing a contract law theory for them. A little attention was paid to illegal contracts, but that doesn't mean that they don't exist. People enter in illegal contracts all the time, courts all over the world are kept busy annulling contracts for failing to comply with the general validity conditions set by the contract law; this reality is undisputable.

There is however a thin line of separation between illegal contracts in general and corrupt contracts. Some contracts are illegal because they are objectively affected by a vice, contracting parties being unaware about the situation when they form the contract; even if it's illegal, the parties have no evil intentions. In corrupt contracts, at least one of the parties involved has an intention to break or to elude a law or a social norm. In cases where the intentional element is missing, we cannot speak of corruption.

In a corrupt contract one party, the corruptor, gives or promises to give, a gain to its counterpart. The gain may be of a patrimonial nature such as money or goods, or a non-patrimonial nature such as a favor or the performance of a service. In return for this gain, the corruptor expects a performance from the corruptee, which is an action that breaks or eludes a norm or a law, and by doing so he procures a benefit for the corruptor.

In other words, a corrupt contract is a contract by which the corruptor gives or promises to give, to do or not to do something in the benefit of the corruptee, for which the corruptee gives, does or doesn't do something, by breaking a law or a social norm, for the benefit of the corruptor.

---

[26] Julius Paulus, *The Opinions of Paulus*, Book I, 1,4

The corruptor's action of 'to give' is the most common form of corruption and it usually comes in a form of a sum of money. It also may be materialized as other goods, such as cars, jewelry, virtually anything that holds a patrimonial value. In Criminal Law this contract is defined as bribery.

Nevertheless, the corruptor's performance in the agreement may come in a non-patrimonial form, such as an action that will bring a benefit for the corruptee. In an even more complicated form, the corruptor's performance may come as a lack of action, which is in his power and, if acting, it will cause a loss to the corruptee.

In order to obtain a gain, either patrimonial or non-patrimonial, the corruptee must perform an action in the benefit of the corruptor. The essence of a corrupt contract is the fact that the actions are illegal or they are directed against a value of the society. In the absence of the illegal characteristic, bribery for instance is just another contract.

The fact that a certain contract might not be incriminated in a specific manner by the Criminal Law raises difficulties in distinguishing a corrupt contract from a legitimate contract. The ultimate test is the fact that the corruptee's action comes against a social value.

The corruptee's performance may come as a non-action, e.g. the intentional failure to perform his duty. In this situation the corruptee is bind by his role in society to carry out a certain task. In exchange for a personal benefit, he intentionally fails to perform, or performs inappropriately, a task, with the consequence of procuring a benefit for the corruptor.

The corruptee's performance may also be an act of giving a patrimonial gain to the corruptor, or even to a third party indicated by the former. To exemplify such situation, let us consider the case when an official acquire goods for his organization, for a price above the market price, upon receiving a bribe.

From a moral standpoint, due to the complexity of human relations, sometimes is difficult to properly identify who is the corruptor and who is the corruptee. In complex situations, the bilateral character of the agreement may lead to confusions on who is who, even more, their position may be interchangeable, but in those situations we are in the presence of multiple agreements.

As a rule of thumb, we shall consider as the corruptee, the person whose performance comes against a social value, protected by a law, a moral tradition, a custom and so on. Thus, the corruptor is the person who, in order to obtain a personal benefit, needs that a rule, a law or a social norm is broken or circumvented.

Continental Law distinguishes between civil contracts and commercial contracts. The civil contracts are regulated by the civil codes while the commercial contracts are defined in commercial codes or in special laws. The theory presented here covers any type of contract, civil or commercial.

The CC, in Article 1108 states the validity conditions for a contract and those are: the consent of the party who binds himself, capacity to contract, a definite object which forms the subject-matter of the undertaking and a lawful cause in the obligation.

Here we are concerned with only the last two conditions, object and cause. For a contract to exist *"Only things which may be the subject matter of legal transactions between private individuals may be the object of agreements."*[27] The legal character of the cause is regulated by the art. 1131 and 1133 *"An obligation without cause or with a false cause, or with an unlawful cause, may not have any effect.", "Cause is unlawful where it is prohibited by legislation, where it is contrary to public morals or to public policy."*

It is important to notice that the validity conditions of a contract are necessary only on those situations when a contract is to be enforced by the power of the law. If two parties form an agreement and the agreement is carried out, each party fulfilling his obligation, the contract is completed.

A contract with an illegal object or an unlawful or unmoral cause is still a contract nevertheless. The power of the law cannot be called upon to enforce such contracts, because, in the eye of the law, those contracts are void due to failure to comply with general validity conditions.

It is the law that determines which objects, things, are legal and which are not. Also the law determines which causes are legal and moral. In the absence of such laws, all the objects and causes are legit.

A drug deal is still a buy-sell contract no matter how we look at it, but in cases when one party fail to fulfill his obligation, such a contract cannot be brought to court because it's illegitimate object and cause. Therefor a drug deal must be classified in a special category that of

---

[27] French Code Civil, Art. 1128

illegal contracts, which are contracts in every sense but they are illegal because a specific law declares their object or cause or both, illegal.

In continental contract law theory, simulation is also a juridical operation composed by two contracts, a hidden, undisclosed, unpublicized contract which contains the true will of the parties, and a public contract that creates an appearance of legality. The secret contract stipulates that the public contract doesn't produce any effects and that the true will of the parties is contained in the hidden contract. A court will enforce the hidden contract only if the contract is legal.

I have said earlier that a corrupt contract is a contract by which the corruptor gives or promises to give, to do or not to do something in the benefit of the corruptee, for which the corruptee gives, does or doesn't do something, by breaking a law or a social norm, for the benefit of the corruptor. All corrupt contracts are illegal but not all illegal contracts are corrupt contracts. Therefor corrupt contracts are contained in the larger category, that of illegal contracts.


### 3.4.3. The purpose of corruption

The general opinion is that corruption's purpose is to procure an undue benefit, money, luxury items or other things of a patrimonial value such as cars, or real estates. From the definition suggested above we can see that corruption is an illegal or immoral unilateral act or agreement, aiming to break or to elude a law or a social norm, for a personal gain. Therefor, corruption has two purposes: an initial one and a subsequent one. The initial or the immediate purpose of corruption, manifested either as a corrupt act or a corrupt contract, is to break or elude a law or social norm, while the subsequent purpose is to procure a benefit.

Primary, corruption is directed against a rule, which must be made ineffective before the perpetrator can achieve his goal. Between the desires or interests of individuals and their materialization there is a law or a social norm that raises an impediment. A law determines what kind of human behaviors are permitted or forbidden in society.

Some of these laws are taught to us in our infancy; a child in his cradle has the natural tendency to grab anything he can reach. From parents we learn that we cannot have anything with a phrase that I think it was said by every parent in human history 'You can't have that'.

We also acquire our sense of propriety in childhood, and we often assert our right with the phrase 'It's mine!'

The notion of theft is also taught to us from childhood; children often take possession of things, and this time some sort of sanction is applied. After the first sanction we learn that is better to hide our misbehaving from parents and tutors and we learn to lie to protect ourselves from sanctions. So we learn how to effectively break and elude rules in our childhood. All these interactions are part of every child's upbringing in any culture.

Our desire and fascination for things does not end when we reach adulthood. Then again, as adults, we also have a better understanding of the law, of what it is legal and illegal, even if we do not know the specific text that forbids a certain action.

The perpetrator of a corrupt act is always aware that there is a law that forbids his act, even if he has no specific knowledge of the law.

Corruption is always committed with direct intent, so the perpetrator knows that in order to obtain the object of his desires, he must break some sort of law. If he has a specific knowledge of the law he will be seeking ways to elude the law or to find ways to make the law inapplicable to him.

Corruption may manifest itself not only against a law or statute or other type of legal document, but also against a social value that is expressed through a social norm.

Beside laws, human behavior is controlled by other social norms, such as customs, habitudes, religious rules, ethical and moral principles, that are not laws in the proper sense, yet they are respected by the members of society without the existence of an explicit legal sanction.

Breaking a social norm may not bring any sanction in the form of imprisonment or a fine, but it is still an antisocial behavior because it goes against a social value. The term social norm, in lack of a better one, it is used here to describe any type of regulated human behavior that is not prescribed by a law, but it is considered mandatory by the general public.

There is a conditional relation between the immediate purpose and the subsequent one; the achievement of the subsequent purpose of corruption is conditioned by the accomplishment of the initial purpose, the breaking or the eluding of a law or a social norm.

The subsequent purpose is to obtain an undue advantage, the term preferred by the authors of UNCAC. In my definition I've used the term 'personal gain'; the perpetrator of corrupt acts is aiming to obtain something, to gain something. I believe that the term 'gain', is better suited to describe the subsequent purpose of corruption because the perpetrator knows what he desires. The term undue advantage might leave the impression that the object of desire is unknown, which obviously it is not the case.

Last, in UNCAC Article 15 - Bribery of national public officials, the object of bribery is defined with the phrase "*an undue advantage, for the official himself or herself or another person or entity.*" I believe that the extension to "*other person or entity*" is misused here.

No one accepts a bribe but for himself. If he or she pays a part or the entire bribe to a third party we are in the presence of another corrupt act or corrupt contract. If he or she accepts the bribe on behalf of a third party, than the act of acceptance is complicity to bribery and not bribery.

Therefore, I believe that the term 'personal gain' is accurate in describing the subsequent purpose of corruption, and that corruption itself, in any form may come, is a personal action in personal interest. The idea of corruption in the interest of other seems unrealistic.

## 3.4.4. The material object of corruption

The material object of corruption is the object that the perpetrator seeks to obtain by breaking or eluding a law or a social norm. It may be the sum of money in a case of embezzlement. Bribery can have as material object money, but also luxury items such as jewelries, expensive watches, cars, and so on. In the majority of the cases that we define as corruption, the material object is something that holds a patrimonial value.

Criminal law uses the term 'proceed of the crime' to describe the money given as bribery, for instance. In Article 3 of the UNCAC, the scope of application of the convention is "*...the prevention, investigation and prosecution of corruption*" and "*...the freezing, seizure, confiscation* *and return of the proceeds of offences established in accordance with this Convention."*

This term, in my opinion, may be used only after a criminal trial has been concluded with a final verdict and not before. In order to define a sum of money as the product of a criminal activity one must establish first that a criminal activity had happened.

Another term used to describe the material object of corruption is the term *"undue advantage"*; Article 15(a) of UNCAC uses the term when it defines bribery *"The promise, offering or giving, to a public official, directly or indirectly, of an undue advantage, for the official himself or herself or another person or entity..."* The term *"undue advantage"* covers a large area, virtual anything can be called an undue advantage.

Several articles in UNCAC contain important provisions regarding the material object of corruption such as Article 23 Laundering of proceeds of crime, Article 31 Freezing, seizure and confiscation and Article 35 Compensation for damage. In Chapter V, Article 51 states that asset recovery is one of the fundamental principles of UNCAC.

Indeed, one of the fundamental principles of the fight against corruption is the recovery of assets obtained thru corrupt means. Corruption may offer large financial rewards, sometimes exceeding what the individual is capable to earn in several lifetimes. It is natural for individuals to consider the benefits against the losses; few years in prison against several millions might seem like a good deal for many. The fact that asset recovery is the rule, and in any circumstances, the products of corruption will be recovered, may be a powerful deterrent.

In the definition of corruption proposed here, I have used the term *"personal gain"* to describe the object that the perpetrator of corrupt acts or corrupt contracts seeks to obtain. I believe that the term *"personal gain"* is better suited to describe the object of corrupt desires.

Because the majority of definitions and laws placed the sign of equivalence between corruption and bribery, a large part of the phenomenon of corruption was neglected. This deficiency was corrected in recent legal instruments such as UNCAC up to a point. The general view now is that corruption is aimed to procure something of patrimonial value.

We shall consider also if the object of corruption may be immaterial. For instance, in cases of nepotism, if one uses his power or influence in order to obtain a favor for a protégée. Here, there are no objects of patrimonial value that exchanges hands. Thus, we might be tempted to believe that there is no material object. It is not the case.

In cases of nepotism or other forms of trafficking of influence, there is also a material object. The material object in this case is the payments the protégée receives as long he holds that position. These payments would have been inaccessible for him otherwise.

The protégée is also in a special relation with the person in power by which, he will provide some forms of gratitude, either material or in form of favors. In any case, sooner or later, the person in power will receive some sort of benefits; he will gain something out of his relation with his protégée.

## 3.5. Active Subjects and Passive Subjects

General legal theory usually classifies the subjects of legal relations in active subjects and passive subjects. The active subjects are legal or natural persons that act in a legal relation. In other words the positive action or inaction of a legal or natural person gives birth, modifies or extinguishes a legal relation. The passive subject is a legal, a natural or a community of persons that are not involved in a legal relation but their rights or duties are somehow affected by a legal relation.

In order to perform a corrupt act or a corrupt contract the active subject does not need any legal capacity. All is needed is the intellectual and physical ability to perform such acts. It is hard to imagine a 4 year old bribing his kindergarten teacher, nevertheless, in theory, such corrupt contract is perfectly possible.

In all jurisdictions insanity makes an act or a contract null or void by law. But this does not prevent a person with a mental illness to draw documents or to enter in contracts, situation in which such acts and contracts are annullable. The general rule is that in order to have legal effects, mental illness must be acknowledged by the court, following a psychiatric evaluation.

The rules regarding legal capacity may play here another role. Legal acts or contracts performed by persons without legal capacity are usually void or voidable. Every illegal act or illegal contract is also void if a person lacks legal capacity. The lack of legal capacity or a diminished legal capacity may also interfere with the responsibility of the active subject.

The rules regarding capacity are also important in the relation between the active subject and the passive subject. There are situations in contracts where only one party is driven by a corrupt intent. The passive subject might be under the impression that he is entering in a legal transaction; in these cases the good faith of the passive subject is the key element that determines the consequences of the corrupt contract.

The current view is that a corrupt person is also a person in power, a public official, or someone entrusted with a certain activity. In trafficking of influence for instance, the offence is not possible if the author doesn't have a power of influence.

But there are situations when a person only claims to have an influence, or in more simple terms, he lies about his powers, social position, official quality, and so on.

Both parties in a corrupt contract of trafficking in influence are active subjects; one is 'selling' influence and one is 'buying'. But since it is a corrupt contract, the 'seller' may be also dishonest; in fact here we may have two offences on the part of the 'seller'.

The UNCAC in article 2 offers the definitions for 'public official', 'foreign public official' and 'official of a public international organization' and focuses on the incrimination of bribery (art.15, 16), embezzlement (art. 17) trading in influence (art. 18) illicit enrichment (art.22) as offences if committed by one of the qualified active subjects enumerated above.

Even more, in Article 21 Bribery in the private sector, the active subject is "*...any person who directs or works, in any capacity, for a private sector entity...*" I believe this to be a major deficiency of the UNCAC and the national legislators should correct it if possible by extending the quality of active subject in cases of corruption to any person.

The passive subject is a legal, a natural or a community of persons whose rights are affected by a corrupt act or a corrupt contract. For instance when one embezzles money from the company for which he works, the passive subject is the company itself as a legal person. In cases of bribery the passive subject is the community; in cases of counterfeiting, the buyer of fake merchandise is the passive subject only if he has bought the goods in good faith.

From the point of view of the criminal science or of the criminal law, the passive subject is called the victim. Usually, the passive subject may be any person; in the definition of the certain crimes, the law may require a certain quality for the victim.

The law offers protection for any person; the rights of the passive subject or of the victim of a corrupt act or a corrupt contract are protected regardless of his legal capacity. A lack of or a diminished capacity in part of the passive subject might be an aggravating circumstance for the active subject in criminal cases.

The passive subject has at his disposal two types of legal actions. First, there is a criminal action if the corrupt act or the corrupt contract is an offence. The passive subject can make the legal action himself in the form of a criminal complaint or he can intervene in a trial if the complaint was made by someone else. The other persons may be the prosecutor, another injured party, or any legal or a natural person who is suing for himself.

The second type of legal action is a non-criminal action and it can be founded on civil, commercial, administrative, financial laws. The competent court and the law applicable depend on the circumstances of each case.

The most important thing to remember here is that the subject in cases of corruption may be any person or even a group of persons that either benefit from corruption as the active subjects or suffer loses as the passive subjects.

## 3.6. Effects

The most important effect of a corrupt act or a corrupt contract is the fact that it will make the active subject criminally responsible. But this will happen only if the corrupt act or corrupt contract is defined as a crime, offence or misdemeanor, by the criminal law.

There is a window of opportunity here for corruption to develop; immoral or unjust human relations are born before the criminal law will define such relations as crimes. Today, criminal law covers the vast majority of human behaviors that are considered inacceptable in society.

The advancement of the human society however, gives birth to new relations, that may be regarded as immoral and some of those will be incriminated under criminal law.

Humans are held responsible by the law for their actions and any type of human action may bring a form of legal responsibility; corrupt acts and corrupt contracts may bring a criminal responsibility for the active subject when the action is considered to be a crime by the criminal law or a non-criminal liability when the actions are either not regulated by the law or they are regulated by laws from other domains such as civil, administrative, commercial laws.

## 3.7. Criminal liability

One of the consequences of a corrupt act or contract is that it may bring a criminal liability for the perpetrators.

The first condition for the active subject in a corrupt act or a corrupt contract to be held criminally responsible is that the corrupt act or the corrupt contract is defined as a crime (offence) by the criminal law. The second condition comes from the rules of legal capacity, in other words he must have the capacity to be judged in a criminal trial and, the third condition, is that the active subject must not be in a situation when criminal liability does not apply.

In order to explain criminal liability we shall take bribery as an example, mentioning that this line of reasoning may be applicable to other forms of corrupt contracts.

In a corrupt contract both parties may be held criminally liable; in an illegal contract such as bribery, the payer of the bribe seeks to obtain something from a public official. They form an illegal contract by which one pays a sum of money and the other performs an act, e.g. issues a license or a permit. In this situation they are both guilty of an offence, they are both active subjects in a crime.

There are also situations when a party enters in a corrupt contract in good faith. Even if he seek to obtain a profit, a gain, after all this is the reason why onerous contracts are formed, he may be acting believing he is a part in a legitimate, a legal contract. The key element here is good faith.

The quality of active subject in a corrupt contract may be changed by good faith in that of a passive subject, a victim. In a case of 'bribery' for instance, if the official demands a 'tax' and the other party genuinely believes that there is a legal tax that he must pay, he cannot be held accountable for bribery.

The lack of knowledge of the law is not accepted as a defense in any legal system, but in this case he has no reason to believe or to suspect that the public official's request is illegitimate. In fact here we are in the presence of another crime, extortion.

The prosecutor must establish if the public official deceived the other party to pay. On the other hand, if the payer has knowledge that there is no such tax, or if he understands that the public official is requesting a bribe and he makes the payment, he is guilty of bribery. The only thing that would differentiate bribery form extortion in a case like this is the payer's good faith.

The UNCAC in Article 15 Bribery of national public officials states:

> *"Each State Party shall adopt such legislative and other measures as may be necessary to establish as criminal offences, when committed intentionally:*
> *(a) The promise, offering or giving, to a public official, directly or indirectly, of an undue advantage, for the official himself or herself or another person or entity, in order that the official act or refrain from acting in the exercise of his or her official duties;*
> *(b) The solicitation or acceptance by a public official, directly or indirectly, of an undue advantage, for the official himself or herself or another person or entity, in order that the official act or refrain from acting in the exercise of his or her official duties."*

This model of incrimination was implemented with slight modifications in the German Strafgesetzbuch and the French Code Pénal and also in the rest of the European continent. There are two forms of incrimination here, the giving of bribes and the solicitation of bribes.

Where continental criminal law seems to be deficient is the situation when a person is forced or coerced or manipulated to pay a bribe. In practice, no public official in his right mind will openly 'solicit' a bribe. The solicitation is almost never explicit; there are always some forms of innuendos or allusions, which are hard to prove in court.

Moreover, even the act of giving a bribe may not be always voluntarily. A person might become aware, from interacting with people who went to similar experiences, that in order to obtain a certain document from a certain public official, a bribe is required.

So the subject is faced with a dilemma, either to pay the bribe and have the situation resolved, either abandon the project. There is, of course, a third choice, too often neglected, and that is to report the situation to the competent authorities. But this course of action will lead to a testimony in a long criminal trial and, in many cases, to the sufferance of repercussions, a situation no one desires.

In realistic terms, the individual considers only the first and the second choices presented above. I believe that in these circumstances the free will of the individual is diminished. So, to conclude, the act of giving a bribe must be voluntarily in order to be considered an offence.

## 3.8. Non-criminal Liability

In general, criminal liability is the principal form of liability for corrupt acts or corrupt contracts. However, there are also other forms of liability regulated by the norms of the civil law, administrative law, commercial law, etc. There are several possible situations that deserve an analysis.

In the first scenario, the offence exists, but the author cannot be held accountable because he is not criminally responsible or he has a valid defense. Sometimes criminal organizations use persons that are not criminal responsible in their activities; children are used in carrying or selling of drugs or individuals with intellectual disabilities are used in economic crimes, for instance. Here we can find situations in which there is a valid defense and the author will not suffer any criminal sanction.

In the second scenario, the act or the contract is not defined as a crime by the criminal law, yet is illegal or immoral. In continental law, the criminal or the penal code is not the only source of criminal law. International law, European Union Law, and virtually any other branch of law such as Administrative Law, Business Law, Environmental Law, and so on, are also sources of criminal law. Definitions of certain actions as criminal are to be found in any branch of law, in laws or in other codes. However, there may be occasions where a human action is not defined as a crime, neither by the criminal codes, nor by other special laws, yet they are, by common sense, illegal or immoral.

In a third scenario the perpetrator of a crime may benefit from a mistrial or from a technicality or from a flaw in the law. There are various reasons for which a mistrial may occur, a mistake or an error on the part of prosecution, a hang jury or the death of juror. The annulment of a criminal decision in a superior court based on a procedural error or situations where the law is unclear or contradictory can also end a trial without a criminal sanction.

The general rule, in all legal systems, is that the injured party has at his disposal a civil action by which he can address the effects of a corrupt act or a corrupt contract.

The Article 35 - Compensation for damage of the UNCAC states:

> *"Each State Party shall take such measures as may be necessary, in accordance with principles of its domestic law, to ensure that entities or persons who have suffered damage as a result of an act of corruption have the right to initiate legal proceedings against those responsible for that damage in order to obtain compensation."*

There is another important article in UNCAC, Article 26 - Liability of legal persons which states:

> *"1. Each State Party shall adopt such measures as may be necessary, consistent with its legal principles, to establish the liability of legal persons for participation in the offences established in accordance with this Convention.*
>
> *2. Subject to the legal principles of the State Party, the liability of legal persons may be criminal, civil or administrative.*
>
> *3. Such liability shall be without prejudice to the criminal liability of the natural persons who have committed the offences.*
>
> *4. Each State Party shall, in particular, ensure that legal persons held liable in accordance with this article are subject to effective, proportionate and dissuasive criminal or non-criminal sanctions, including monetary sanctions."*

In article 2 of the French Code de Procédure Pénale is stated: *"The civil action in reparation of the damages suffered because of a felony, a misdemeanor or a petty offence is open to all those who have personally suffered damage directly caused by the offence."* Under the French law, the criminal courts may acknowledge the existence of an offence, yet for other reason may acquit the offender.

In this situation article 2 CPP offers the possibility for an action in the civil courts; the text was limitative in the sense that the existence of an offence is necessary. It was extended by the prescriptions of article 4-1:

> *"The absence of a non-intentional criminal liability within the meaning of Article 121-3 of the Criminal Code does not bar the exercise of an action before the civil courts with a view to obtaining compensation for damage pursuant to article 1382 of the Civil Code where the existence of civil liability under that article is established, or under that of article L.452-1 of the Code of Social Security where the existence of a strict liability under this article is established."*

Article 3 CPP states *"The civil action may be exercised at the same time as the public prosecution and before the same court. It is admissible for any cause of damage, whether material, bodily or moral, which ensue from the actions prosecuted."*

In the CCF, Article 1371defines quasi-contracts as *"...purely voluntary acts of man, from which there results some undertaking towards a third party, and sometimes a reciprocal undertaking of both parties."* and article 1382 defines the civil wrongs as *"Any act whatever of man, which causes damage to another, obliges the one by whose fault it occurred, to compensate it."*

The rules regarding civil wrongs are slightly different in Germany than their French counterparts; the bulk of the rules regarding civil wrongs are contained in the civil code, the BGB, under section Title 27 Torts, sections 823 to 853.[28]

In the German Code of Criminal Procedure, the Strafprozeßordnung, under Section 262 - Preliminary Civil Law Questions, it is stated:

*"(1) If the criminal liability for an act depends on the evaluation of a legal relationship under civil law, the criminal court shall also decide thereon according to the provisions applicable to procedure and evidence in criminal cases.*

*(2) The court, however, shall be entitled to suspend the investigation and to set a time limit within which one of the participants is to bring a civil action, or to await the judgment of the civil court."*

The main difference is that in German law, the civil action can suspend the course of a criminal trial. Chapter III of the StPO contains the rules applicable to the wounded persons; thus, under Section 403 Conditions it is stated:

*"The aggrieved person or his heir may, in criminal proceedings, bring a property claim against the accused arising out of the criminal offence if the claim falls under the jurisdiction of the ordinary courts and is not yet pending before another court, in proceedings before the Local Court irrespective of the value of the matter in dispute."*

The rules from civil procedure are applicable *mutatis mutandis* in criminal cases; it's a rule included in several sections such as Section 37 or Section 111c, g, h, o.

In the common law systems, the civil liability is based on common law or on statutory law. If a corrupt act or contract is defined as an offence by the criminal law, the situation is simple enough, and it will follow the

---

[28]Sir Basil Markesinis, and Hannes Unberath, *The German Law of Torts A Comparative Treatise,* 4th ed., (Oxford: Hart Publishing, 2002), pg.14

rules of criminal law and criminal procedure. If we are in one of the scenarios presented above, and the injured party is seeking reparation for the damage suffered from corruption in a non-criminal court, in common law systems the situation is more complicated than in the continental counterpart.

English doctrine distinguishes between two types of wrongs: *"Wrongs are divisible into two sorts or species: private wrongs and public wrongs."*[29] From medieval times onwards, the English courts developed the law and established precedents that were used in similar cases; in the matter of civil liability, the institution of precedent plays a key role in common law systems.

Depending on the specifics of the case, the claim may be based on contract law or on tort law; sometimes these two branches of law overlap or are in conflict with each other.

In this chapter we defined corruption as a corrupt act (action) or a corrupt agreement. We must remember that corruption is always intentional; therefor, an action based on negligence should be inadmissible. Intentional and strict liability torts are the only categories of torts where corruption may be included.

This area of law is under reform in common law systems; in cases of corruption, when we are dealing with an uncertain situation, we can make use of the norms of international law, norms that are found in conventions such as UNCAC, the Rome Convention[30], the UNCTOC and other similar instruments.

## 3.9. Unjust and illicit enrichment

The concept of unjust enrichment draws its roots from Roman law; Ulpian wrote: *"The Governor of a province must suppress illegal exactions, including such as are committed with violence, as well as sales and obligations extorted by fear, and those where the money is not paid down. He must also provide against anyone unjustly obtaining profit, or suffering loss."*[31]

---

[29] William Blackstone, *Commentaries on the Laws of England*, (Philadelphia: J.B. Lippincott Company, 1893), vol. 2, pg. 1
[30] For more on the subject see J. G. Collier, *Conflict of laws*, (Cambridge: Cambridge University Press, 2001), pg. 189
[31] Digest I.XVIII.6

In continental law the concept is very well known, the civil law doctrine uses the term 'unjust enrichment' to describe in general any increase in one's patrimony without a right or without a just cause.

In the French Civil Code, unjust enrichment or 'enriching without a cause' is a quasi-contract. The norms regulating quasi-contracts are contained in Articles 1371 to 1381. The prescriptions of the code were found insufficient and jurisprudence developed the theory for unjust enrichment. In the decision in Julien Patureau contre Boudier, 15 June 1892, the Court of Cassation stated *"...driving from the principles of equity which prohibits enrichment at other's expense..."* and it was established as a general principle of law by the Council of State in 1961 and therefore it became applicable to public law as well, in criminal matters for instance.

In the German BGB, title 26 is dedicated to the unjust enrichment which is defined in section 812 Claim for restitution, as follows:

*"(1) A person who obtains something as a result of the performance of another person or otherwise at his expense without legal grounds for doing so is under a duty to make restitution to him. This duty also exists if the legal grounds later lapse or if the result intended to be achieved by those efforts in accordance with the contents of the legal transaction does not occur.*

*(2) Performance also includes the acknowledgement of the existence or non-existence of an obligation."*

The institution of unjust enrichment was formally acknowledged by the House of Lords in a landmark case, Lipkin Gorman v Karpnale Ltd.[32] There are four conditions for a claim in unjust enrichment which were set in another case, Banque Financière de la Cité v Parc (Battersea) Ltd[33]: the defendant was enriched, the enrichment was at the claimant's expense, the enrichment was unjust and if there aren't any defenses. Under the term unjust, the English law includes the vitiating factors for contracts such as mistake, duress, failure of consideration, illegality, lack of capacity and so on.

In U.S. following the decision of the New York Court of Appeal in Georgia Malone & Co. v. Rieder in 2012,[34] a claimant must prove a direct relation with the defendant, that the enrichment was at plaintiff's expense and *"...that is against equity and good conscience to permit the other party to retain what is sought to be recovered"*.

---

[32] See www.bailii.org/uk/cases/UKHL/1988/12.html

[33] See www.bailii.org/uk/cases/UKHL/1998/7.html

[34] http://www.courts.state.ny.us/Reporter/3dseries/2012/2012_05200.htm

Article 20 of UNCAC recommends for signatory states to adopt the necessary measures establish illicit enrichment as a criminal offence. The problem here is the definition of illicit enrichment *"... a significant increase in the assets of a public official that he or she cannot reasonably explain in relation to his or her lawful income"*.

Corruption may increase the assets, or a better word, the patrimony, of a public official but also the patrimony of a person who is not a public official. The quality of public official should be irrelevant here; the concept of incrimination of illicit enrichment should be covering any person.

But there is a bigger problem with the term illicit enrichment used by UNCAC. The meaning of the term unjust is different from the term illicit; they should not be used as synonyms. Unjust means the absence of a right while illicit means contrary to a positive law.

The concept of unjust contains the concept of illicit; one's patrimony may be increased unjustly yet licit, legally, without breaking any positive law. Therefor the term illicit enrichment used by UNCAC only comes to complicate a matter that should have been really simple.

I believe that the authors of the convention meant *"the incrimination of the unjust enrichment"*; it is an assumption based on Article 34 of UNCAC entitled Consequences of acts of corruption states *"...States Parties may consider corruption a relevant factor in legal proceedings to annul or rescind a contract, withdraw a concession or other similar instrument or take any other remedial action."*

The subject of unjust enrichment is too vast to explain in depth here and this is not our purpose. However, it is very important to highlight the relation between corruption and unjust enrichment. Once the material object of a corrupt act or a corrupt contract is obtained, it will increase the patrimony of the author of the act or of the parties in the contract with its value. I consider that an action based on the principle of unjust enrichment is available in any case of corruption.

## 3.10. Nullity

In many cases, to achieve his corrupt purpose, the perpetrator makes use of documents, such as written unilateral acts and written contracts. The legislators prescribed general validity conditions for unilateral acts and contracts which make the act or contract void or null by law, if those conditions are not met.

The nullity of the act or contract may be invoked by an injured party or by prosecution. In other cases, the corrupt act or contract may produce its effects until it is declared as void in a court of law.

The matter of nullity was addressed in Article 34 Consequences of acts of corruption of UNCAC which states:

> *"With due regard to the rights of third parties acquired in good faith, each State Party shall take measures, in accordance with the fundamental principles of its domestic law, to address consequences of corruption. In this context, States Parties may consider corruption a relevant factor in legal proceedings to annul or rescind a contract, withdraw a concession or other similar instrument or take any other remedial action."*

It is a very important article because it allows for the national legislators and judges to annul any corrupt act or any corrupt contract.

In French civil law the institution of nullity[35] is to be found in several places in the civil code, for instance, agreements regarding the human body are null by law (art. 16-5, 16-7 CC). The rules regarding nullity are concerning inheritance, divorce, donations, contracts, sales and so on.

Article 1108 of the CC states:

> *"Four requisites are essential for the validity of an agreement: The consent of the party who binds himself; His capacity to contract; A definite object which forms the subject-matter of the undertaking; A lawful cause in the obligation."*

These are the general validity conditions for any bilateral contract and for any act or unilateral contract in general. The person must consent to act/contract, must have legal capacity, the object must be definite and the cause lawful.

Corruption is a phenomenon that has many forms therefore it can affect not only the fourth validity condition, a lawful cause, but also the previous three. For instance obtaining the consent by error, duress or deception[36], using a person without capacity for corrupt purposes[37] or trading illegal objects[38] are also manifestations of the phenomenon of corruption.

---

[35] In English translations of the French Civil Code we find the term 'void' used to translate the French '*nulle*'. This will later lead to the terms 'avoid, avoidance' used to describe an action to cancel an act. 'Avoid' is also used in the sense of eluding or circumventing something. For this reason I find the terms null, nullity, to annul, better suited and less confusing.

[36] Article 1109 CCF

[37] Article 1124 CCF

[38] Article 1128CCF

There are also several prescriptions that may make an act/contract null or annullable in a court of law regarding the mandatory form for certain documents, clauses, or obligations assumed. If there is no special provision, the right for an action in annulment or rescission of an agreement is lost after five years.[39]

The German civil law is similar with the French civil law only in some aspects. The German legislators regarded contracts as void if inconsistent with the rules regarding capacity, illegality, and public policy and voidable if they violate rules of consumer protection, mistake, the removal or disappearance of the foundation of the transaction, fraud, and duress.[40]

The German law also acknowledges the institution of illegal contracts, or contracts contrary to public policy, which are void *ab initio*[41] and are governed by the rules regarding unjust enrichment. The most relevant rules for our subject matter are to be found in Division 3 Legal transactions of the BGB.

Thus, under Section 105 (1) *"The declaration of intent of a person incapable of contracting is void"*[42]. Section 123 provides the rules for annulment on the grounds of deceit or duress while Section 125 regulates the annulment resulting from a defect of form. Under Section 134, *"A legal transaction that violates a statutory prohibition is void, unless the statute leads to a different conclusion"*.

Under Section 138 (1) *"A legal transaction which is contrary to public policy is void."* and *"(2) In particular, a legal transaction is void by which a person, by exploiting the predicament, inexperience, lack of sound judgement or considerable weakness of will of another, causes himself or a third party, in exchange for an act of performance, to be promised or granted pecuniary advantages which are clearly disproportionate to the performance."*

If the matter of nullity is complicated in codified legal systems, in common law systems it may seem to be even more complicated. The historic development of two systems of courts of law and of equity, terms like illegal, void and null used interchangeably in statutes, doctrine and daily practice, the mixture of commercial law and civil law in contracts

---

[39] Article 1304CCF
[40] See Sir Basil Markesinis and Hannes Unberath, *German Law of Contract*, pg. 228
[41] Ibid., pg. 228
[42] English translations of the BGB also uses the terms void, voidable, to avoid; I still believe that terms such null, annullable or to annul are better

are enough reasons to make the subject hard to understand. Our purpose is to make the phenomenon of corruption understandable so I will attempt to keep the explanation as simple as possible.

In common law systems a contract may be void, voidable or unenforceable.[43] In all three hypothesis corruption may play its role in making a contract either void or null by the effect of the law, voidable or annullable in a court, or, last, unenforceable in a court of law. The common law doctrine places the focus on offer and acceptance, consideration, and an intention to create legal relations for a contract to be considered valid.[44]

However, a contract may be affected by five vitiating factors which are misrepresentation, mistake, duress, undue influence and illegality. Depending on the circumstances of a certain case of corruption, either the rules regarding the validity of the contract or the vitiating factors may interfere with the outcome of the case.

From the aspects presented above we can see that the rules regulating null or void acts or contracts are present in all legal systems. It is important to remember that corrupt acts or corrupt contracts will almost certainly violate one of the general rules regarding the conditions of validity of acts and contracts, but it is not a *sine qua non* condition for corruption to exist. Corruption may be hidden under acts or contracts that are legit in form or in respect the general validity condition, a situation in which they are very hard to detect, to prosecute and to annul.

## 3.11. Prescription and limitation

Prescription and limitation may be very well called the 'saviors' of corruption. In both continental law and in common law systems, prescription may be acquisitive, when a right is obtained by its effects or extinctive, when a right is lost by the effects of prescription. In U.S. the term adverse possession is also used for acquisitive prescription.

The concept of prescription comes from Roman Law: *usucapio* was one of the modalities to acquire propriety recognized by the *jus civile*.[45] The

---

[43] Geoffrey Samuel, *Law of Obligations and Legal Remedies*, 2nd ed.( London: Cavendish Publishing, 2001), pg. 318
[44] Ibid., pg. 297,298
[45] Stephenson, *A History of Roman Law*,(Boston: Little, Brown and Co., 1912), pg. 390

concept migrated from civil law to criminal law that instituted extinctive terms for the prosecution of certain crimes.

In the next chapter we shall see how virtually any crime, from treason to trespassing, may be linked to corruption or in other words may be a crime of corruption. The terms for prescription and limitation are very important for the investigative bodies and prosecutors but also for the injured parties that may have at their disposal a civil action. Corruption also may benefit from the rules regarding the limitation on certain crimes and from the rules regarding the acquisitive prescription.

In Germany the limitation period is set in Section 78 of the StGB. The maximum period is 30 years for offences punishable by imprisonment for life. Depending on the severity of the sanction, the other terms may be twenty years, ten years, five years and last three years. In civil law under Section 937(1) of the BGB:

> *"A person who has a movable thing in his proprietary possession for ten years acquires the ownership (acquisition by prescription). (2) Acquisition by prescription is excluded if the acquirer on acquiring the proprietary possession is not in good faith or if he later discovers that he is not entitled to the ownership."*

In CP limitation is regulated under articles 133-2 to 133-6 and 213-5; the terms are twenty years for felonies, five years for misdemeanors and three years for petty offences.

Article 213-5 makes crimes against persons imprescriptible: *"Criminal liability for the felonies set out under the present title is imprescriptible, as are the sentences imposed."* Article 133-6 states:" *Civil obligations resulting from a final criminal decision are barred by limitation according to the rules set out in the Civil Code."*

Article 712 CC states:

> *"Ownership is also acquired by accession or incorporation, and by prescription."* and Article 2262 states *"All claims, in rem as well as in personam, are prescribed by thirty years, without the person who alleges that prescription being obliged to adduce a title, or a plea resulting from bad faith being allowed to be set up against him."*. Article 2233 prescribes that *"Acts of duress may not give rise to a possession capable of bringing about prescription either. Possession begins to produce effects only from the time the duress has ceased."*

In UK the matter of limitations is governed by the Limitation Act 1980; the time limit for actions founded on tort is six years (I.2.) except theft of a chattel for which there is no time limit in general circumstances. Also the actions founded on a simple contract are subject to a six years limitation period (I.5.). An important prescription is to be found in I.27.A Actions for recovery of propriety obtained through unlawful conduct; this prescription was amended by the Proceeds of Crimes Act 2002, Serious Crime Act 2007 and Serious and Organised Crime and Police Act 2005.

In U.S. each State adopted statutes of limitations that set the time limit after which a crime can no longer be subject for prosecution. The legislators of each State had a different view on the seriousness of the crime.

Thus, if murder has no statute of limitation in any State, crimes involving public money usually have, except Arizona and California where there is no statute of limitation for such crimes. In Colorado for instance bribery and abuse of public office has a statute of limitation of 3 years while any forgery has none. In Kentucky crimes that may be associated with corruption may be prosecuted at any time.

In U.S. the rules for averse possession also differ from State to State for instance the period is five to seven years in California and Utah and twenty one to thirty years in Louisiana and New Jersey.

We can see that there is a general tendency worldwide to close the door that the principles of prescription and limitation opened for corruption. Article 29 of UNCAC states:

> *"Each State Party shall, where appropriate, establish under its domestic law a long statute of limitations period in which to commence proceedings for any offence established in accordance with this Convention and establish a longer statute of limitations period or provide for the suspension of the statute of limitations where the alleged offender has evaded the administration of justice."*

The phenomenon of corruption has an elusive dimension and the corrupt actions are always committed with direct intent. The level of danger that corruption poses to society is extreme, on the same class with war or terrorism, to which it is intricately related. I consider that, under any jurisdiction, in cases of corruption, prescription and limitation should not be operational.

Because of the elusive element, the flow of prescription is suspended *de facto*. In order to be effective one of the conditions of limitation and prescription is that the term is not suspended by a cause prescribed by law. I believe there is a major difference between one who occupies a plot of land for thirty years and uses it uninterrupted in plain sight and, after the thirty years invokes acquisitive prescription and one who occupies a plot of land thru corrupt means, by forgery of documents for instance.

In the second case I consider that the rules for acquisitive prescription cannot be invoked and cannot operate. Although he may no longer be held accountable for the crime because of the statute of limitation of the crime, from the civil point of view, the course of the acquisitive prescription was suspended the entire period.

Depending on the circumstances of each case and the legal system, law in general, regulates the flow of prescription and demands that the flow is uninterrupted.

This rather complicated situation, with matters regarding criminal law if the corrupt action or the corrupt contract are defined as offences and with matters regarding civil law in respect of claims and the proceeds of corrupt activities, criminal or otherwise, being in conflict with each other, could have been easily avoided if UNCAC would have made prescription and limitation inoperable in cases of corruption, as they are in fact.

Under current legislation, in any legal system, corruption may still be cleared by prescription and limitation, a situation I consider to be generated by a flawed law.

## 3.12. Conclusions

At the end of this chapter we can see why the phenomenon of corruption is so hard to understand from a legal perspective and how much clarity a proper definition can bring on the subject matter.

I consider that a synopsis of what we learned so far about the phenomenon of corruption is necessary and it will save the reader the time to extract each important aspect.

First, let us recount the definition of corruption once more:

Corruption is an antisocial phenomenon which manifests itself in the form of an illegal or immoral unilateral act or agreement between two parties, aiming to break or to elude a law or a social norm, for a personal gain.

From the definition we can extract the following conclusions:

- Corruption is an antisocial phenomenon that goes against the rule of law and the basic principles of ethics and moral living.
- Corruption may manifest itself in the form of a corrupt act or a corrupt contract. Embezzlement, for instance, is a corrupt act, while bribery is a corrupt contract.
- The main purpose of a corrupt act or a corrupt contract is to break or to elude a law or a social norm. The subsequent purpose is to procure for the perpetrator or perpetrators a personal gain of a patrimonial value.
- Corruption is illegal because of its illegal object or unlawful or unmoral cause. Corrupt acts or corrupt contracts are included in the category of illegal acts and illegal contracts.
- In corrupt acts and corrupt contracts, the active subject may be any person; the only practical requirement is that the active subject has the physical and mental capacity to perform such acts or contracts. The passive subject or the victim of corruption may be any person, natural, legal or a community of persons.
- Corruption brings upon the active subject two types of responsibility, criminal responsibility and non-criminal responsibility, such as civil or administrative responsibility.
- The consequence of corruption is the unjust or illicit enrichment of the active subject.
- The corrupt acts and corrupt contracts are usually null or annullable in a court of law. However, corruption may be hidden under a legal act or contract.
- Corruption may benefit from the rules regarding acquisitive and extinctive prescription.

With this definition and the subsequent analysis, anyone, no matter from which legal system he or she belongs, can identify properly the phenomenon of corruption.

No matter how hard I've tried, I cannot think of a form or modality of the phenomenon of corruption that is not covered by the definition I'm suggesting here. In other words, I am unable to find an exception to the rule, which can only indicate that the rule is veracious.

In the next chapter we shall explore those corrupt acts and corrupt contracts that are a subject of incrimination in Criminal Law, their authors and their sanctions.

*I have built my organization upon fear.*

Al Capone

# 4. Crimes of corruption

Even in the most primitive forms of human organization, certain actions and behaviors were considered unacceptable by the members of the society. No matter how far we go in human history we can see that there were always rules and there were always punishments for those who broke the rules.

As the complexity of human relations matured, the punishments had begun to diversify; throughout entire history people tried to punish antisocial behavior with a degree of severity dictated by the amount of damage the antisocial act has brought to the society. So, in a sense, crimes and laws against crimes had existed throughout history and they've developed into what we call today the criminal law, the crime and the sanction.

The term 'criminal law' is used in two modes; first it may refer to the body of laws concerning the criminal, the crimes and their sanctions, second, it may indicate a branch of the legal science, one that studies the crime, the authors of the crimes and the sanctions.

The sources of Criminal Law in the United States of America's legal system are the Common Law, Statutory Law, and Administrative Law, in matters regarding internal affairs, and the Constitution of the U.S. in matters of International Law, which in Article I, Section 8, states that *"The Congress shall have Power ... to define and punish Piracies and Felonies committed on the High Seas, and Offenses against the Law of Nations."*[1]

In the legal system of the United Kingdom of Great Britain and Northern Ireland, the sources of criminal law can be found in Common Law, Statute Law, and the European Communities and International Law; this model is similar in other countries that are either former British colonies or they were heavily influenced by the English laws or doctrine, countries that are often referred to as common law countries.

---

[1] See the text on www.archives.gov/exibits/charters/constitution_transcript.html.

In continental law systems the main sources of criminal law are the criminal or penal codes. Of course, the legislators of the codes cannot foresee every action that might be considered criminal; therefor the codified criminal law is subject to revision. Some of the crimes are incriminated in special laws or government acts, so when we speak about codification we should notice that the notion is relative.

The definition of the crime differs from country to country, sometimes crime is precisely defined by the law, or we can find a general accepted definition developed in the legal doctrine. Sir William Blackstone defined crime as *"...an act committed or omitted, in violation of a public law either forbidding or commanding it."*[2]

The Napoleon's Penal Code did not define the crime therefore the French doctrine developed several definitions of the crime from the prescriptions of the Code. One of those definitions is *"...crime is an act ordered or prohibited in advance by the law, under the sanction of a penalty precisely prescribed, and which is not justified by the exercise of a right."*[3]

In modern definitions crime is *"an act (or sometimes a failure to act) that is deemed by statute or by the common law to be a public wrong and is therefore punishable by the state in criminal proceedings"*[4] or, if we look in French doctrine *"action or omission, strictly forbidden by the law, which is sanctioned with a penalty, in order to preserve the politic, social and economic order."* [5]

In all legal systems, the criminal is the person who committed the crime; again here we can find several terms, depending on his position in the legal process; the author of the crime may be called defendant, perpetrator, accused, offender, before a sentence has been issued or convict, prisoner, felon, after a penalty was established for his crime.

Sanctions for criminal behavior also differ from one legal system to another in respect to their severity. Moreover, for similar criminal acts, in continental law systems, the penalties are established depending on the specific circumstances of each case, a process called the individualization of the penalty.

---

[2] See William Blackstone, *Commentaries on the Laws of England,* (Philadelphia: J.B. Lippincott Company, 1893), vol. 2, pg. 335

[3] Jean-René Garraud, *Traité théorique et pratique du droit pénal français.* (Paris: Librairie de la Société du Recueil général des lois et des arrêts et du Journal du palais, 1898), pg. 169

[4] Elisabeth Martin, *Oxford Law Dictionary*, pg.128

[5] http://www.larousse.fr/dictionnaires/francais/infraction/43017?q=infraction#42920

In U.S. doctrine[6], the goals and purposes of the criminal justice system are to discourage and deter people from committing crimes, to protect society from dangerous and harmful people, to punish people who have committed crimes and to rehabilitate and reform people who have committed crimes. With minor differences the same goals and purposes are to be found in any legal system.

Corruption, as an antisocial phenomenon, comes in various forms; some of them are object of study for the criminal law, as a discipline of the legal sciences and an object of incrimination in Criminal and Penal Codes, Statutes, Laws or International Conventions depending on the legal system.

When we consider the position of corruption in relation with criminality we might be misled by a phrase in the preamble of UNCAC, *"Concerned also about the links between corruption and other forms of crime, in particular organized crime and economic crime, including moneylaundering..."*

It seems that the authors of UNCAC, again, felled victims to semantics; to clarify this aspect, we shall say that corruption is the gender while money laundering is the specie.[7] Certain illegal acts and contracts are incriminated by the criminal law and they are also manifestations of the phenomenon of corruption, which can be defined as a part of the criminal phenomenon.

Crimes of corruption are those crimes committed with the intention to obtain a personal benefit, unlike crimes of passion for instance which are committed on an impulse. The difference between crimes where the element of corruption is present and other form of crimes is that the former are always premeditated and they always are meant to procure a benefit or a profit for the perpetrator.

In the previous chapter we defined corruption, from a legal point of view, as an antisocial phenomenon which manifests itself in a form of an illegal or immoral unilateral act or agreement between two parties, aiming to break or to elude a law or a social norm, for a personal gain. This definition combined with the principle of legality from criminal law reveals how the link between corruption and criminal law is created. Thus, criminal law is the one that defines which acts or contracts

---

[6] See Thomas Gardner, Terry Andersen, *Criminal Law*, 11th ed., (Belmont: Wadsworth, Cengage Learning, 2012), pg.9
[7] See also Jeremy Bentham, *The Works of Jeremy Bentham*, 11 vol., ed. John Bowring, (Edinburgh: William Tait, 1838-1843), vol. 2, pg. 127

constitute a crime, and when a criminal act is committed in order to break a law, and by that, to obtain a benefit or a profit, we are in the presence of corruption. As a literary convention, the term used to describe those criminal actions where the phenomenon of corruption is present will be 'crimes of corruption'.

## 4.1. Elements of Criminal Law Theory

In England, efforts had been made by the Law Commission to codify the English Criminal Law, while in U.S. there is a similar tendency materialized in The Model Penal Code, a creation of the American Law Institute. There is also a movement for reform in other common law systems, such as The Commonwealth of Australia or New Zeeland, but the process is facing extreme difficulties and it is unlikely that the above mentioned countries will adopt any drastic reforms any time soon.

Continental law systems benefited from a swift codification process, the French Penal Code of 1791 was adopted during the French Revolution, and it was based on the innovative ideas of Cesare Beccaria and Montesquieu. Subsequently, the Napoleon's Penal Code of 1810 influenced the Criminal Codes in Germany, Austria and Italy, and thus, with the inherent dissimilarities, a unitary doctrine of criminal law was created in the continental Europe.

Despite the differences between continental and common law systems, differences that are more even evident in procedural law, criminal laws share the same basic principles. A common principle present in all criminal law systems is *"Nullum crimen, nulla poena sine praevia lege poenali"*[8], which means that a human action cannot be considered a crime unless is defined as so by the criminal law. This principle is stated by article 111-3 in the French Penal Code, section 1 of the German Criminal Code or article 1 of the Italian Penal Code, to mention the most famous ones, but it may be useful to notice that it can be found in more exotic codes, e.g. in the Article 1 of the Penal Code of Somalia or Article 2 from Lao People's Democratic Republic Penal Code. In true, we can call the legality principle a universal principle of the criminal law.

---

[8] See Jerome Hall, *Nulla poena sine lege* in The Yale Law Journal Vol. 47, No. 2 (Dec., 1937), pp. 165-193

The crime as a philosophic concept has been broken into its constitutive elements by the doctrine, which differs from country to country and from legal system to legal system, but the differences are caused mostly by language or semantics and not by principles of legal philosophy.

In common law doctrine, *"all crimes had two essential elements: (1) the physical act or omission and (2) a mental requirement known as criminal intent or purpose."*[9] These elements are referred to as *actus reus* and *mens rea*. Depending on the specificity of the crime, other two elements must be considered, causation and concurrence.

Every crime, in French doctrine[10], has four constitutive elements that determines the criminal responsibility: a legal element, a material element, a moral element and an element of injustice.

The German doctrine uses a tripartite structure of constitutive elements, *Tatbestand,* composed of *objektiver Tatbestand* (offence description or *actus reus*) plus *subjektiver Tatbestand (mens rea)*, Rechtswidrigkeit (the illegal element) and *Schuld* (guilt).[11]

Crimes are classified in two main categories, felonies and misdemeanors, depending on their gravity. Some criminal codes are using a third category the one of petty offences which poses a reduced degree of threat to society, yet they must be sanctioned, therefore a penalty is applied but usually it not involves imprisonment.

The sanctions for felonies covers a range from capital punishment which is still legal in 49% of the world and actually used in 20%, to a term of imprisonment, the mildest form being house arrest. Misdemeanors are punished with a fine or in some cases they can be sanctioned with a short term of imprisonment or some other forms of administrative sanctions such as performing a service in the benefit of the community.

In general, crimes have been classified as belonging to one of the following main categories, crimes against the State, crimes against propriety, and crimes against persons. The order in which they will be presented in this chapter is dictated by the level of social danger they pose, which is not the usual order from the criminal codes, where crimes against the person are often addressed first.

---

[9] Gardner & Anderson, *Criminal Law*, pg.52
[10] Garraud, *Traité théorique et pratique du droit pénal français*, (Paris: Librairie de la Société du Recueil général des lois et des arrêts et du Journal du palais, 1898), pg. 217
[11] Michael Bohlander, *Principles of German Criminal Law*, (Portland: Hart Publishing, 2009), pg. 16

After explaining few of the general principles of the criminal law, in the following subchapters we shall explore the main categories of crimes as they are presented in both criminal law and legal doctrine, in order to establish a pattern that will help in identifying if the phenomenon of corruption is present or not. At the end of each subchapter we shall examine two case studies, chosen from the most famous ones, cases that will be placed in opposition, one where the phenomenon of corruption is clearly present and one where this antisocial phenomenon is absent.

## 4.2. Crimes of Corruption against the State

Generally speaking, the legal object of the crimes against the State is to define and to establish a sanction for those actions that pose a threat to the organization and the functionality of the State and its attributes. Crimes against the State take various forms, and sometimes same actions are defined differently by the criminal codes, but their essence remains the same. The main forms are treason, espionage, sabotage, sedition and last, but probably the most dangerous one is terrorism.

The material object of the crimes against the State may be the person of the sovereign in cases of treason, or it can be an important installation in cases of sabotage, for instance. Law usually defines the material object in the definition of the crime. In cases when the crime consists in communicating secrets to the enemy, we still have a material object of the crime even tough communication has been made orally.

The author (or the active subject) of a crime against the State can be any person. In certain cases the law establishes a special quality requirement, for instance Article 411-1 of the CP states that certain acts constitute treason if they are committed by a French national or soldier, and those acts are considered espionage if they are committed by other persons; definitions differ from legal system to legal system.

In crimes against State corruption manifest itself in both forms, as an act of a singular individual or as a corrupt contract. Contemporary definitions of corruption show a tendency to attribute a special quality to the author of a corrupt act, and often we can find phrases like a person in power, a person entrusted, and a public official.

For a person to perform a crime against the State a special social position is not a *sine qua non* requirement; any person can perform such acts. Here we are dealing with the confusion between a subjective special quality required for a person to perform such act, versus an objective special quality.

To commit an act of espionage one does not have to be hired by one of the organizations from the intelligence community; all is needed is the access to sensitive information. So, in crimes of corruption against the State, the general requirement regarding the author of the crime is that the respective person has the physical and intellectual capacity to perform such act.

When we are in the presence of a corrupt contract, selling of sensitive information for example, we must remember that a contract involves two parties, in this case a corruptor and a corruptee. The corruptor is the person who initiates the contract while the corruptee is the person who accepts and enters in the corrupt contract. The corruptor may ask a person from the intelligence community to sell information or a member of the intelligence community may initiate a contact and offer to sell information.

The passive subject or the victim of the crimes against the State may be the person of the sovereign, in case of treason, or it may not exist as a person but still exists as an entity, the State, in case of espionage for instance.

The *actus reus* in crimes against the State is an action or inaction that threatens the stability, integrity and functionality of the State and thus puts the citizens of the State in danger. The *mens rea* element was defined as *"...evil intent, criminal purpose, and knowledge of the wrongfulness of conduct."*[12] The authors of the Model Penal Code settled for a quadripartite classification of the forms of criminal intent, thus criminal responsibility intervenes when the act is committed purposely, knowingly, recklessly, negligently.[13] Crimes of corruption against the State cannot be committed out of recklessness or negligence because the criminal seeks a profit, a personal benefit.

In UK, a person was guilty of treason, as it was first defined by The Treason Act 1351 *"When a Man doth compassed or imagined the death of the King...."*[14], but the definition was extend by a series of acts such as Treason Acts of 1495, 1702,1708, 1814, Forfeiture Act 1870.

---

[12] Gardner & Anderson, *Criminal Law*, pg. 55
[13] See Joel Samaha, *Criminal Law*, 10th ed., ( Belmont: Wadsworth, Cengage Learning ,2011), pg.112
[14] See the full text in Norman language on http://www.legislation.gov.uk/aep/Edw3Stat5/25/2

In U.S., treason is the only crime defined in the Constitution as *"Article III Section 3 Treason against the United States, shall consist only in levying War against them, or in adhering to their Enemies, giving them Aid and Comfort"*.

The German Strafgesetzbuch, in section 81 and 82 defines high treason against the Federation and against a member State as: *"Whosoever undertakes, by force or through threat of force, 1. to undermine the continued existence of the Federal Republic of Germany; or 2. to change the constitutional order based on the Basic Law of the Federal Republic of Germany, shall be liable to imprisonment for life or for not less than ten years."* There are also incriminated milder forms of treasonous acts in Section 94 - Treason or Section 98 - Treasonous activity as an agent.

The CP, as mentioned earlier, states that *"The acts defined by articles 411-2 to 411-11 constitute treason where they are committed by a French national or a soldier in the service of France, and constitute espionage where they are committed by any other person"*. Those acts consists in handing over the national territory, the armed forces or equipment to a foreign power, providing intelligence to a foreign power, sabotage and supplying false information.

Strictly speaking, the crime of treason is quite rare, for instance no one was convicted in U.S. after the WWII.[15] The terms treason or traitor are often used in the media as synonyms for crimes that are, from a legal standpoint, acts of espionage. However, in the Cold War, the persons exposed by Aldrich Ames[16] for working with the western intelligence agencies, were convicted and executed in Soviet Union on charges of treason, beside those of espionage.

An act of treason may be considered as a crime of corruption if the author seeks and receive a material benefit; when treason is motivated by ideology, such acts are not crimes of corruption, because the author genuinely believes he is acting for a good cause.

Espionage is another type of crime against the State that in most cases is committed in order to obtain a personal gain. There are several forms of espionage such as military espionage, economic or industrial espionage and it may worth to mention that those types of actions are

---

[15] See M. Scheb and J. M. Scheb, *Criminal law*, (Belmont: Wadsworth, Cengage Learning, 2012), pg. 359
[16] See subchapter 4.2.1. Case study Aldrich Ames

not always performed by States intelligence agencies; private companies or individuals are often involved in actions to gather information about their competitors.

A side of this phenomenon is undoubtedly linked to our curios human nature but the main purpose of such acts is to obtain an advantage over the opponent. If the act of espionage is committed in order to sell the information to a third interested party, such crime is clearly a crime of corruption; if the crime is committed for other purpose and the element of personal material gain is absent, we cannot speak of corruption.[17]

Espionage is incriminated by several sections in the StGB; Section 95 defines the crime of disclosure of State secrets with intent to cause damage, Section 96 introduces the crime of treasonous espionage and spying on State secrets. We can see that the differentiation of the two crimes, treason and espionage, is quite difficult, the concepts here are intertwined.

In U.S. crimes of espionage are defined and incriminated in the Espionage Act of 1917, while in UK, the offences related to spying are defined in Official Secrets Act of 1911, 1920 and 1989.

Sedition is a crime against the State defined as "... *advocating the violent overthrow of the government*"[18] or "*the incitement of insurrection or revolution*"[19] . States and governments sometimes collapse from interior following poor management over the State affairs, but in numerous situations such collapse is caused by an exterior power. Revolutions often start with the 'help' of another State which has an interest in changing the form of the government of another State, e.g. the role of Germany in the Russian October Revolution or the role played by France in the Iranian Revolution. If a crime of sedition is committed by a person who received personal benefits from a foreign power or to whom it was promised an important position upon the success of the revolutionary movement, we can clearly state that such acts are crimes of corruption.

Sedition is incriminated by the Sedition Act of 1918 in U.S.; in UK however, criminal libel and sedition were abolished by the provisions of the Coroners and Justice Act in 2009. It has been considered that these types of crimes interfere with the right of free speech or the freedom of

---

[17] See subchapter 4.2.2. Case Study Edward Snowden
[18] Samaha, *Criminal Law*, pg. 456
[19] Scheb, *Criminal law*, pg. 361

the press. The CP contains several provisions, in Chapter II - Other offences against the institutions of the republic or the integrity of the national territory, which can be considered to incriminate seditious acts.

Sabotage is another crime against the State that is executed in the form of destruction of the infrastructure of the State in order to diminish its defense capabilities. Crimes of sabotage had a high frequency rate in the WWII and were performed either by military or by civilian resistance from all the states involved in the hostilities. Unlike espionage, the majority of cases of sabotage are not crimes of corruption. The saboteur usually does not seek to obtain a profit from the destruction he causes. Even if he receives a material reward in some form for his acts or he has logistical help from other belligerent power, his motives are of an ideological nature.

The U.S. Criminal Code defines sabotage as acts or attempts to injure, destroy, contaminate or infect any war material, war premises, or war utilities.[20] In the German StGB sabotage is incriminated in various forms under sections 87 and 88, 109e, 303b.

In recent years sabotage gained a new dimension, following the development of the cyberspace. It has become a growing threat since more of the state's infrastructure is controlled from a digital environment. Not only military installations can be a target for cyber-sabotage or cyber-espionage but also any civilian installations can be made unusable with relative ease.

Sabotage is not a crime of corruption unless is done in order to obtain a profit; in its most common form the element of corruption is absent.

The international legal community failed to agree on a compressive definition for terrorism while in academia we can find more than a hundred, each having its own merits and flaws. For the purposes of this thesis we shall say that acts of terrorism are criminal acts against the State, performed randomly against innocent persons and propriety.

In UK acts of terrorism are incriminated in the Prevention of Terrorism Act (Northern Ireland), 1974–89, Terrorism Act 2000, Anti-terrorism, Crime and Security Act 2001, Prevention of Terrorism Act 2005, Terrorism Act 2006, Counter-Terrorism Bill 2008.

In U.S. Omnibus Counterterrorism Act of 1995, Uniting and Strengthening America by Providing Appropriate Tools for Intercepting

---

[20] Samaha, pg. 457

and Obstructing Terrorism Act (USA PATRIOT Act) of 2001, Homeland Security Act of 2002, are the main source of law on this subject.

By his actions the perpetrator of a terrorist act aims to determine a certain course of action from a government, which will fulfill his purposes. Until recent years, terrorism was ideological motivated, crimes committed by ETA (Euskadi Ta Askatasuna), the Basque nationalist organization, or by the Red Brigades, an Italian Marxist-Leninist organization, were acts against the central power. Here, the concepts of ideology and that of corruption are mutually exclusive.

A particular aspect must be highlighted when we consider terrorist acts driven by religion. In these cases we can say that we are in the presence of corruption. Religious terrorists, at least in theory, do not seek a personal gain; they will not benefit directly from their action. Yet, they are promised fabulous rewards in another plane of existence. Here we are more in a presence of a contract of corruption; performance for reward. Moreover, before committing the act, the terrorist enjoy a lavish lifestyle, his family is given gifts, money, other benefits. There is also a corruptor, a person that has his own interests that will be fulfilled by the act of terror.

However, terrorist acts may be committed in the absence of corruption. It is important to note that there are no 'good' terrorists and 'bad' terrorists; any act of terror is a crime against humanity for which there cannot be a sane political, ideological or religious excuse.

### 4.2.1. Case study - Aldrich Hazen Ames

Aldrich Hazen Ames (born May 26, 1941) in River Falls, Wisconsin, U.S. is a former Central Intelligence Agency officer, who was convicted for espionage for the Soviet Union and Russia. Mr. Ames and his wife Maria del Rosario Casas Ames, were arrested by the F.B.I. on February 21, 1994, on charges of conspiracy to commit espionage on behalf of Russia and the former Soviet Union. He worked for the CIA for 31 years, in the Directorate of Operations, a division responsible for carrying out clandestine operations. Between April 1985, and continued to the time of the arrest, Mr. Ames sold classified documents to the Soviet Embassy, causing the exposure of several agents and double agents.[21] According to NY Times "...*K.G.B. and its successor agencies in*

---

[21] See An Assessment of the Aldrich H. Ames Espionage Case and Its Implications for U.S. Intelligence Senate Select Committee on Intelligence, 01 November 1994, on
http://fas.org/irp/congress/1994_rpt/ssci_ames.htm

*Russia paid him more than $2.5 million, in exchange for which he compromised more than a hundred Western intelligence operations and in effect sent at least 10 men to their death by identifying them as agents of the West.*"[22] Mr. Ames was formally charged by the United States Department of Justice with spying, charges for which he pleaded guilty on April 28 and for which he received a sentence of life imprisonment.

In Mr. Ames case we are in the presence of a corrupt contract. He begun to sell information to the Soviets in April 1985 in what he thought would be an easy con game to make some extra money. The information he first sold to the KGB for $ 50000 he believed to be of no value, and he later claimed that he intended just a onetime deal. However, since the Soviets were ready to pay anything for such a valuable source, it was not long before he exposed several top C.I.A. sources, causing their death.

For his activities of espionage he was paid with more than $2.5 million; in nearly a decade he compromised hundreds of operations and caused the death of at least ten high ranking persons from the Communist Block that were working for the C.I.A. and other Western intelligence services.

When we consider who the corruptor is and who is the corruptee, we might become easily confused. Since Mr. Ames was the one who initiated the contact, the one who made the offer, he should be considered the corruptor. But we certainly cannot say that Mr. Ames corrupted the officials of the Soviet Embassy to sell them classified documents of the outmost importance for...them. In other words we can't say that Mr. Ames corrupted the KGB.

Here we are in the presence of an implicit offer. Any intelligence service is willing to buy sensitive information, is part of their activity, and Mr. Ames was perfectly aware of this offer. By selling the information he accepted the offer. In this case and any other case similar, the corruptor is the foreign power who acquires the information while the corruptee is the person who sells them. As a rule, the party who pays the money or gives other benefits is the corruptor.

### 4.2.2. Case study - Edward Snowden

Edward 'Ed' Joseph Snowden was born on 21 June 1983 and he worked as a computer professional in the intelligence community. From 2006 to 2009 Mr. Snowden was a system administrator for the Central Intelligence Agency. In 2009 he had begun working as a contractor for Dell inside National Security Agency. The last three months of his

---

[22] www.nytimes.com/1995/01/27/us/how-the-fbi-finally-caught-aldrich-ames.html

career in the American intelligence community he worked for the consulting firm Booz Allen Hamilton.

Most of the disclosures refer to the modalities by which CIA and NSA and their British counterparts obtained data on users of phones and internet communications. The fact that the U.S. used surveillance techniques on its allies has created a difficult diplomatic situation.

Mr. Snowden disclosures didn't achieve much; the intelligence agencies will develop new surveillance programs and techniques, the public has the tendency to forget easily, and the criminal elements are already using coded messaging or language to avoid detection. Beside a huge media and diplomatic scandal and some minor changes in legislation, Mr. Snowden's action did nothing to change the overall situation.

Former officials of NSA had accused that Snowden's leaks helped terror groups to better avoid detection. [23]

Here we are using Mr. Snowden's case as an example of a crime against the State where corruption is absent. From the data we have Mr. Snowden can be considered a whistle blower on certain practices in the intelligence community that may be considered wrong or immoral. There are few question marks in this case. Somehow, Mr. Snowden ended up in Russia after knocking on the gate of China, Hong Kong, two of the former enemies from the Cold War. It is hard to understand why Mr. Snowden did not sought refuge in one of the countries that were targeted by the NSA or CIA.

When we analyze such cases, a certain degree of caution should be exercised, especially when we are looking at the world of espionage and secret services where there is no black and white, just various shades of grey. In lack of any adverse evidence we shall conclude that corruption is absent in Mr. Snowden's case.

## 4.3. Crimes of Corruption against Propriety

Article 17 of the Universal Declaration of Human Rights states that:
> *"(1) Everyone has the right to own property alone as well as in association with others.*
>
> *(2) No one shall be arbitrarily deprived of his property."*

Indeed, the right of propriety is one of the fundamental human rights and criminal law incriminates those acts that affect the right of

---

[23] http://www.washingtontimes.com/news/2014/sep/4/islamic-state-using-edward-snowden-leaks-to-evade-/?utm_source=RSS_Feed&utm_medium=RSS accessed on 9/6/2014.

propriety. Thus, the legal object of the crimes against propriety is to protect the legal relations regarding the right of propriety.

The material object in crimes against propriety is another source of differences of opinion in criminal law doctrine. Continental law adopted a generalist approach and the material object of crimes against propriety may be anything that holds a patrimonial value. Common law based systems opted for a specialized approach, defining precisely what can be the material object of a certain crime.

The author (or the active subject) of a crime against propriety may be any person. The text of incrimination usually prescribes if a certain quality is required for the active subject. Criminal responsibility intervenes if the person has legal capacity; usually crimes against propriety committed by minors are not punished with imprisonment. The passive subject or the victim may be any person. It is important to mention that the form by which the material object is held by the victim is of no relevance. From the point of view of criminal law it is no distinction between an owned propriety and a leased propriety.

The *actus reus* in crimes against propriety are those actions that bring harm to the victim's right of propriety. The *mens rea* is manifested in the form of direct intent or, in other words, the author acts purposely or knowingly when he commits the crime.

When we are dealing with crimes that have propriety as a material object and we want to determine if the phenomenon of corruptions is present, the analysis is harder than in the other cases, because they share a common element, the material object.

A crime of corruption is an intentional breaking of the law in order to obtain a profit, a benefit. A crime against propriety aims to procure something of a patrimonial value for the perpetrator. The two concepts overlap each other here. Only the analysis of each case can determine if corruption is present or not in crimes against propriety.

Stealing food, in any circumstances, is not corruption, is in most cases a matter of necessity, of survival, in probably a very difficult personal situation. Stealing one million dollars from the employing company's accounts is clearly an act of corruption, putting aside for a moment the specific circumstances. But is hard to define *a priori* what kind of material object and of what patrimonial value determines if it is a crime of corruption or not.

In common law systems, theft or larceny was defined[24] as the felonious taking and carrying away of the personal goods of another, and was classified as simple if *"unaccompanied with any other atrocious circumstances"*[25] and mixed or compound in *"...either one or both of the aggravations of a taking from one's house or person"*.[26] Other forms of theft, false pretenses, embezzlement, and receiving stolen property were incriminated by the British Parliament enactments in the 18th century.[27] In modern law, the definitions of various types of theft are to be found in Theft Act 1968 in U.K. or in Title 18 of the U.S. Code Chapter 31 - Embezzlement and Theft.

In continental law systems, the notion of theft is a fraudulent appropriation of things belonging to another.[28] In the Penal Codes there are various forms of theft, depending on the specific circumstances.

Although it may be counterintuitive, the simpler forms of theft are crimes against the right of propriety where corruption is absent. Stealing may come from a necessity, even if the material object is something that is not essential for survival, like food for instance.

Here we are dealing with the active subject's perception of what is a necessity and not with an objective necessity. In modern society, various items have become a necessity, a mobile phone, a portable computer, a car, not to mention money, of course. The needs for communication or social interactions have become basic human needs just like food, shelter and clothing and this types of items facilitates the satisfaction of those needs. When this type of antisocial behavior becomes a profession, theft becomes a crime of corruption, it is no longer performed to satisfy a necessity, but in order to obtain a profit.

Embezzlement can be regarded as a form of theft but also as a form of fraud. The author of the crime of embezzlement is a person entrusted to take care of propriety; in this case, a special quality from the active subject is required unlike in other forms of theft or fraud, which may be committed by any person. Embezzlement is a crime of corruption because the criminal action is directed against a law or a social norm, in

---

[24] See Blackstone, Book IV, pg. 229
[25] Ibid.
[26] Ibid., pg. 239
[27] Scheb, pg. 196
[28] See French Code Penal - Chapter I Theft Articles 311-1 or the German Strafgesetzbuch - Chapter Nineteen , Section 242 Theft

order to obtain a profit, while in other crimes against the propriety the action is directed against the property itself.

Many cases of embezzlement in the private sector are unreported; the employer evaluates the cost of a trial against the damage and if the cost is higher he chooses not to report the crime. Moreover, if he is involved in illegal practices, such as tax evasion, bribery, short weights and so on, he will not report the crime because a criminal investigation might reveal the nature of his business.

In U.S. embezzlement is a statutory offence so the definition differs from State to State and in U.S. Code is defined in Chapter 31 - Embezzlement and Theft; in UK embezzlement is now regarded as a form of fraud and incriminated under Fraud Act 2006.

Embezzlement and abuse of trust in incriminated in the StGB under Section 266, while the CP under Articles 314-1 to 314-4 incriminates the fraudulent breach of trust.

Robbery is an aggravated form of theft[29] that implies an element of violence against a person and it is not a crime of corruption, unless the author of the crime has another purpose from which he obtains a profit. The situation is similar in cases of burglary, in normal circumstances these acts are not crimes of corruption. Again, if these acts are committed with other purposes in mind, or in other words if the author commits these acts in order to obtain a profit from other source that the material object of the crime of burglary or robbery, we can also call these acts crimes of corruption.

Robbery and burglary were common law crimes, today they are statutory crimes. These offences are incriminated under Theft Act 1968 in UK while in U.S. each State has its own statutes. In the StGB robbery is incriminated under Section 249-251 and burglary under Section 123, 124. The CP incriminates as aggravated forms of theft, under Article 311-4 4°, 6°, Article 311-5-10.

Blackmail and extortion are crimes in which the victim is forced to do or to give something against her will. Undoubtedly they are crimes of corruption and it is hard to imagine situations when these types of acts are committed without a corrupt purpose. Those two crimes share similar elements and sometimes they can be easily confused. Specific circumstances of each case, as well as the law of the place, will determine the exact offence.

---

[29] See Scheb, pg. 201

These types of crimes are classified as crimes against propriety because the primary material object of the crime is the propriety of the victim and not its person, which is the secondary material object. This view is shared by both common law and continental law systems.

The greater social danger of such crimes exists when those acts are performed in an organized criminal form. Blackmail and extortion are an important source of income for gangs and mafia type criminal structures and the fact that most of them go undetected and unreported makes them very attractive. The fear factor induced in the victims, acts as an inhibitor in reporting these crimes to the authorities. Another aspect worthy to be mentioned is that in cases of blackmail the victim also has a motive to hide the crime, the motive of the blackmail may be a criminal or an immoral act of the victim.

In common law systems they are now statutory offences, their incrimination is to be found in several statutes like Theft Act of 1968, Larceny Act of 1916, Public Order Act of 1986 or Criminal Damage Act of 1971 in UK or in Title 18, Part I, Chapter 41, § 873 of the U.S. Code and in States law. In the StGB robbery and blackmail are incriminated by the sections 249 to 255 and in CP, extortion and blackmail are to be found in Article 312-1to 312-11.

Shoplifting is another offence where corruption seems to be absent, yet even this type of crime, sometimes considered a petty offence, may be a crime of corruption if it is performed by professional thieves. In some cases, shoplifting may have its cause in a psychological condition, also known as kleptomania or theft addiction, case in which, if such medical disorder exists, we cannot speak of a crime of corruption.

In its organized form, shoplifting involves elaborate schemes to distract the shop personnel, to avoid the security cameras and other security measures. Sometimes is performed by teams of criminals, each playing a well-defined role and, horizontally, creates other forms of criminality in selling and distribution of stolen goods.

Apparently these types of crimes pose a lesser danger to society, the element of violence is absent, the volume and value of stolen merchandise is quite small and the shops are usually insured against this type of crimes. The networks are relatively easy to dismantle by the law enforcement and the investigation, prosecuting, judging and sentencing of this type of criminal acts do not raises any significant problems for the justice system. The real social danger appears when this type of criminality becomes endemic. Moreover, it can evolve in to more advanced forms as organized crime.

Trafficking of stolen goods is another form of criminal activity that can be associated with corruption. The author clearly has the knowledge that his acts are illegal but he purposely break the law in order to obtain a profit. It also involves a form of organization, a network; the trafficker of stolen goods is a link between the professional thieve and the seller, which sometimes may be unaware that the goods are stolen. When the networks are well organized this type of criminality is very hard to detect, therefore they create a significant damage to the economy until this kind of networks are dismantled.

. In UK a variety of acts that involves stolen goods are incriminated under Theft Act 1968 while in U.S. trafficking in stolen goods is defined by the statutes of each State.[30] The CP incriminates trafficking of stolen goods and associated offences under Chapter I Of Receiving Articles 321-1 to 321-5 and the StGB the handling of stolen goods under Sections 259, 260, 260a.

Destruction and arson are crimes where corruption is usually absent. But when these types of crimes are committed to obtain a profit, we are in the presence of corruption. For instance, these acts may be committed by units of the organized crime as intimidation or to threat small business owners in order to extort them or to impose or to protect illegal monopoles.

The level of social danger posed by this type of criminality is high, because the effects are uncontrollable and beside the passive subject who is targeted, other proprieties and people may be affected in the criminal action. Also, these types of crimes may be performed in order to collect the insurance for the object destroyed which, undoubtedly, makes them crimes of corruption.

In United States v. Marc E. Thompson, the defendant was sentenced to 190 years imprisonment for burning his house, and his 90 years old mother with it, in order to collect the insurance money and in the People of the State Of New York, v. Julio Gonzalez, the defendant, Julio Gonzalez, was sentenced to 25 years to life on 174 counts of murder for setting on fire the Happy Land Social Club, after an argument with his girlfriend Lydia Feliciano. These two cases may serve as an example for

---

[30] See Gardner & Anderson, pg. 415

a crime of corruption and a crime of passion, yet, the principal offence in both is arson.

In U.S. they are statutory crimes and in UK they are incriminated under the Criminal Damage Act 1971. In the StGB, arson is incriminated under Section 306 a-d and destruction under sections 303, 3-4 and 305. In the CP arson is considered a modality of destruction which is incriminated in several forms under Chapter II Destruction, damage and defacement, Articles 322-1 to 322-17.

Forgery and counterfeiting are crimes of corruption by which the author aims to make a profit by selling or exchanging false products as genuine. The material object of these crimes may vary from clothing items to money, basically anything can be replicated, duplicated or tampered with.

Sometimes, our modern bureaucratic system raises barriers that can be evaded by a simple forgery; although by no means justifiable, these actions may have a solid reason. For instance, forging the documents of a relative in need of an operation in order to be admitted to hospital is not corruption. The crime still exists, no doubt, but was not committed in order to obtain profit.

In UK this types of crimes are incriminated by the Forgery and Counterfeiting Act 1981, the term counterfeiting referring to the offence of making a counterfeit of a currency note or of a protected coin, while the terms forgery refers to offence of making a false instrument such as documents, stamps, post marks and other devices that store information. In U.S.,[31] counterfeiting of currency is a federal offense while the incrimination for counterfeiting other products may be found in the criminal code of a State or in federal statutes like Title 18 U.S.C.A. § 1341, § 1343 and others.

The StGB in section 100a incriminates under Treasonous forgery acts that causes danger or serious prejudices to the external security of the Federal Republic of Germany; under Section 267 Forgery incriminates forging of records, data, other documents, and in Chapter Eight Counterfeiting Of Money and Official Stamps, sections 146 - 152b extends the incrimination not only for money but also for stamps, credit cards, cheques and securities.

---

[31] Ibid., pg. 410

The CP, in Title IV Undermining Public Trust, incriminates forgery under Articles 441-1 to 441-12 and counterfeiting under Articles 442-1 to 442-15.

Bribery is the crime that is the most associated with the term corruption. What is specific to bribery is that is solely a crime of corruption; for other crimes presented in this chapter we can find other motives than profit, but in cases of bribery there is no other motive. For this reason there is a lot of confusion between the two terms, sometimes they are used as synonyms not only in the media but also in academic and legal writings.

In cases of bribery we are in the presence of a corrupt contract. Even if both parties are satisfied with each other's performance, we cannot speak of a victimless crime; in this case the society in general is hurt.

There are forms of bribery when the corruptor pays the bribe in order to obtain a counter performance from the corruptee out of his own free will, but there are also situations were a bribe is solicited by the public official; in other words the public official imposes a bribe as a condition to perform his duties.

What we define today as bribery was a long established custom in all societies, and it has been seen as a gesture of respect and gratitude towards a person in power. These types of archaic mentalities are dangerous because they contravene to the principles of democracy and the rule of law.

Gifts are also a form of bribery when are given to a person to perform his duty, and despite the fact that they usually represent a small money value, they add up to impressive figures if they are numerous in time and in frequency. Moreover, these corrupt habits spread easily inside the organization and to others, and if they are not condemned and discouraged by the society they can only lead to endemic corruption.

The term 'kickback' refers to a form of bribery, where a percentage from a legitimate business transaction is returned to the corruptee, or kicked back. This form of bribery is specific to the public sector and the public officials and usually requires from the public official to sign or to agree to a transaction in exchange for a percentage from the profits.

Although bribery was incriminated since the most incipient forms of criminal law, the phenomenon of globalization gave to this type of crimes an international dimension, unknown before in human history. As a consequence to the social danger posed by these crimes to the global economy, several legal instruments have been created by the international organizations.

Here we shall mention the United Nations Convention against Corruption, which requires from member States to incriminate the bribing of national public officials and foreign public officials and officials of public international organizations[32], the Convention on the Fight against Corruption involving Officials of the European Communities or Officials of Member States of the European Union signed at Brussels on the 26th May 1997, or the Inter-American Convention Against Corruption of 1996.

The OECD Convention on Combating Bribery of Foreign Public Officials in International Business Transactions, adopted in 1997, requires from signatory States to *"...take such measures as may be necessary to establish that it is a criminal offence under its law...to offer, promise or give any undue pecuniary or other advantage...to a foreign public official..."* [33]

Following the ratification of the mentioned international conventions, the UK Parliament enacted The Bribery Act of 2010 which replaced Public Bodies Corrupt Practices Act 1889, the Prevention of Corruption Act 1906 and the Prevention of Corruption Act 1916.

The German StGB incriminates several forms of bribery, in Sections 108b and 108e the bribing of voters and delegates, Section 299 Taking and giving bribes in commercial practice, Section 331 Taking bribes, Section 332 Taking bribes meant as an incentive to violating one's official duties, Section 333 Giving bribes.

The CP incriminates bribery under Article 435-3,4, Articles 432-12,13 Unlawful taking of interest, Articles 433-1,2.

There is no better example to illustrate the principle expressed earlier that corruption generates more corruption, than the crimes of money laundering. In order to make use of the money obtained thru illegal means, the criminal must find a way to bring that money into legal money circuit and thus, crimes of money laundering appear. It must be emphasized that the material object of these crimes consists in money or other valuables that are proceeds of previous criminal activities.

---

[32] See art. 15 and art.16 of United Nations Convention against Corruption adopted by the General Assembly resolution 58/4 of 31 October 2003

[33] http://www.oecd.org/daf/anti-bribery/ConvCombatBribery_ENG.pdf, accessed on 1/19/2015;

In 1989, the G7 established the Financial Action Task Force on Money Laundering (FATF), an intergovernmental organization with the purpose to develop policies to combat money laundering and, after 2001, to combat terrorist financing. The policies developed by FATF can be found in Forty Recommendations on money laundering and the 9 Special Recommendations on Terrorism Financing.[34] Each State developed its own system of incrimination, for instance the CP incriminates several forms of money laundering in Chapter IV Money Laundering Articles 324-1 to 324-9, the gravity of the sanction being higher for circumstances in which the crime is performed in organized forms while the German StGB defines money laundering under Section 261 Money laundering; hiding unlawfully obtained financial benefits. Continental law doesn't make a distinction if the money is obtained from a felony or a misdemeanor in relation with the existence of the crime of money laundering.

In UK there are several acts that contain provisions regarding money laundering such as Proceeds of Crime Act 2002, Serious Organised Crime and Police Act 2005, Money Laundering Regulations 2007, Terrorism Act 2000 and Anti-terrorism, Crime and Security Act 2001. The legislation is more severe, the incrimination extends to any handling or involvement with any proceeds of any crime.

In U.S., Money Laundering Control Act of 1986 incriminates financial transactions with proceeds that were generated from certain specific crimes. Other acts on this subject-matter are The Annunzio - Wylie Anti - Money Laundering Act of 1992, Money Laundering Suppression Act of1994, Money Laundering and Financial Crimes Strategy Act of 1998, Patriot Act of 2001 or the Racketeer Influenced and Corrupt Organizations Act (RICO) of 1970.

Money laundering is strictly a crime of corruption, the perpetrators intentionally or in other words with direct intent, break the law in order to obtain a profit.

Fraud is a class of crimes of corruption on its own. Depending of the subject, active or passive, the material object, the list of modalities of fraud seems to stretch to infinite. The active subject may be a natural person, a legal person or a public official. The victim, or the passive subject, is usually the public, but fraud also can be performed against private property, making the victim a private individual.

---

[34] See http://www.fatf-gafi.org/documents/ accessed on 1/14/2015.

In regards to the material object of the crimes of fraud, it's usually money, but again it may also be anything that holds a patrimonial value. Fraud may be a civil wrong, or a tort at it is known in common law systems or it may be a criminal offence. Undoubtedly, fraud is a crime of corruption when it is incriminated by the criminal law, and most of its forms are, because it is manifested in the form of a deceptive act or contract made with the purpose to obtain an immoral or illegal benefit.

Tax fraud is a crime against public propriety but it not always occurs as a consequence of corrupt activities. In most cases of tax fraud, the money is made thru legitimate businesses and not thru a criminal activity. Tax fraud can come in simple forms such as failure to report a profit or can develop into elaborate schemes involving off-shore companies, fictitious transactions, false accountings, and so on.[35]

There is a natural tendency for all the tax payers, natural or legal persons, to find ways to pay as lower taxes as possible. The situations when the tax payer uses legal means to avoid taxes are usually referred to as legal tax evasion. From a moral stand point the answer to the question if such acts are corruption or not, may be open for debate. From the point of view of the criminal law, if we recall the principle of legality, such acts do not constitute a crime therefor they are not crimes of corruption either. If the tax payer resorts to illegal means to avoid payment, it is a form of corruption.

Beside the specific legal instruments of the criminal law, such as criminal statutes and criminal or penal codes, the incrimination for certain illegal practices may be found in commercial, financial, fiscal or accounting laws or codes. For instance, in Germany, false declaration of taxes is incriminated under the German Tax Code, *die Abgabenordnung*, or in France, foreign bank account reporting is incriminated under French General Tax Code.

Nevertheless, the criminal law is the main area of the law where fraudulent behavior are incriminated; thus in the StGB, several forms of fraud are incriminated under Section 263 Fraud, Section 263a Computer fraud, Section 264, Subsidy fraud, Section 264a Capital investment fraud, Section 265Insurance fraud, etc. The CP incriminates fraudulent obtaining under Articles 313-1 to 313-4 and offences similar to fraudulent obtaining Articles 313-5 to 313-6-1, improper demands or exemptions in relation to taxes Article 432-10.

---

[35] Scheb pg. 244

In UK several forms of fraud are incriminated under Fraud Act 2006, while in U.S. the most common forms of fraud are to be found in the Title 18, Part I, Chapter 47 of the U.S. Code.

Fraud, checks and credit card fraud, mail fraud are criminal acts associated with corruption. The purpose of such acts is to obtain money by illegal means. The author is perfectly aware that he is breaking the law, yet the lure of the gain, doubled by the idea that he won't be caught, are stronger then common sense.

The internet has created a new business environment and, besides the enormous benefits, has created also a new criminal environment. Crimes against propriety, especial intellectual propriety are the bulk of cybercrimes, but we shall not forget espionage or sex crimes, like child pornography.

Most of the crimes committed on the virtual environment are crimes committed in order to obtain a profit but not always corruption is present. For instance, downloading movies from torrent sites for personal use is not a crime of corruption, and there is an ongoing debate if those acts should even be considered a crime, but selling those downloads as counterfeited DVD-s is undoubtedly a crime of corruption which bring a harm to the propriety rights of the person (legal or natural) who owns the movie.

### 4.3.1. Case study - Bernie Madoff

Bernard Lawrence 'Bernie' Madoff (born April 29, 1938) was the founder and chairman of the Wall Street firm Bernard L. Madoff Investment Securities LLC and the author of the largest Ponzi scheme in history, for which he was sentenced to 150 years imprisonment.[36]

A Ponzi scheme is based on people's greed; the common sense is obstructed by the idea that a quick and substantial profit can be made. Sometimes people do know that is a fraud, a scheme, yet they are still willing to participate, hoping to exit with the pray before the scheme collapses.

Basically, a Ponzi scheme attracts investors with promises of huge, fast, returns; the returns are paid from the new investors' money and the scheme works as long as the ratio between new investments and

---

[36] Sarna, David E. Y. *History of Greed. Financial Fraud from Tulip Mania to Bernie Madoff*, ( Hoboken, John Wiley & Sons, Inc., 2010), Samaha, *Criminal Law*, 10th ed., pg. 379, Gardner T. J., Anderson T. M., *Criminal Law*, 11th ed. ,2012, pg. 400

returns is a positive one. Eventually the ratio becomes negative and the scheme collapses; the bigger the return, the faster the scheme collapses.

In Mr. Madoff's case, the return was 10 to 13 percent which may not look so suspicious, it is the reason why his scheme lasted so long, from early 90's to the time of his arrest on December 11, 2008. Probably his scheme would have had lasted longer, but the financial crisis of 2008 caused massive withdraws, which accelerated the collapse.

Mr. Madoff founded his company in 1960 as a penny stock trader and grew to be the largest market maker at the NASDAQ and the sixth-largest market maker on Wall Street. In a nearly half of century career, he became a legend of Wall Street, a well-respected member of the community and a philanthropist.

At the time of the collapse Mr. Madoff told his investors they had 65.8 billion in their accounts while he told his sons that the fraud amounted 50 billion.[37] The total amount of losses differs from source to source, and is probably unknown to Mr. Madoff himself. Keeping in mind the fact that several organization and many individuals lost their entire fortune, the prejudice is simply impossible to calculate.

In Mr. Madoff's case we are in the presence of multiple crimes of corruption against propriety, such as fraud, money laundering and theft. In March 2009 Mr. Madoff was charged with 11 felonies, among those securities and investment advisor fraud, money laundering, theft from an employee benefit plan. Mr. Madoff pleaded guilty to all the charges on March 12, 2009 and was sentenced to 150 years in federal prison on June 29, 2009.

Frauds of such magnitudes, no matter how elaborate or well hidden under an appearance of legitimate businesses are not possible without the passivity of the authorities. Here corruption finds a lush ground to expand, underpaid watchers are easy to bribe or they can be detoured from investigations by using trafficking in influence. Sometimes fraudulent schemes attract high profile figures as associates, thus gaining credibility from their reputation.

One more aspect deserves to be emphasized here; beside Mr. Madoff, his family and couple of senior staff members of his company, none of the other participants were indicted. To believe that other people from financial control institutions, banks, political environment or intelligence community were aware of at least some if not all the illegalities committed over such an extended period, it's a matter of common sense.

---

[37] Ibid., pg. 147

### 4.3.2. Case study - Enric Duran

To find a case study for crime against propriety where the phenomenon of corruption is absent was a particular difficult task and that is because they share a common material element. Despite the fact that the loses in Mr. Duran case seem to be more of a petty offence by comparison with Mr. Madoff case, here we are concerned with the legal aspects more that the economics and accounting issues. Enric Duran Giralt was born on 23 April 1976 in the province of Catalonia, Spain.

Between 2006 and 2008 Mr. Duran took 68 personal and commercial loans from several banks without intending to pay the loans back, and, allegedly, he used the money, amounting nearly a half a million euro, to finance several anti-capitalist movements.

Mr. Duran's case is somehow similar to Mr. Snowden's case presented in the previous subchapter. Mr. Duran actions are driven from an anti-capitalist ideology that accuses banks of wrongful appropriation.

Mr. Duran had at his disposal other forms of protest against the banking system; all the accusations he made were not brought to a court of law first, either in the Spain's justice system or before European Court of Justice or European Court of Human Rights. Even if we accept the fact that Mr. Duran hadn't benefited in any way from the money he took, a crime against propriety has been clearly committed. To play a bit with Mr. Duran's logic, the money he took from the banks are, at least in part, the money of the deponents he is trying to protect.

Again, like in Mr. Snowden's case, with the reserve that the analysis was based only on the evidence made public, we can conclude that we are not in the presence of a crime of corruption.

## 4.4. Crimes of Corruption against Persons

Article 3 of the Universal Convention of Human Rights declares that *"everyone has the right to life, liberty and security of person."* Criminal law, thru its instruments, comes to protect the person and the attributes related to a human person, its physical integrity, liberty, freedom or fundamental rights. Therefore, the legal object of crimes against persons is to incriminate and to sanction those actions or inactions that harm the human person. The material object of the crimes against person is the human life and the human body.

The *actus reus* in crimes against persons are actions or inactions directed against the human body that have as result the death of a person or causes so much harm that the victim is permanently affected, not only physically but also emotionally. All forms of guilt are possible.

The author or the active subject of crimes against persons may be any person. The law however may introduce a special requirement for a certain crime. The passive subject or the victim of the crimes against persons may be any person.

In common law countries criminal acts against persons are divided in murder, manslaughter, and negligent homicide. This type of division is to be found also in continental law systems and it is related to the form of intention used to commit the crime and the result, the death of the person.

The questions to be asked are if and when crimes against persons become crimes of corruption. Again, we must look at the definition of corruption to eliminate confusions. Corruption is an act (or contract) that breaks a law for personal gain. When we analyze crimes against persons we can see cases where corruption is evident, yet is hard to pinpoint its position.

Depending on the result, criminal law distinguishes between lethal offences against persons, having as a result the death of the victim and here we have several forms called murder, manslaughter, criminal negligence, or non-lethal crimes against persons, where the end result of the crime is not the death of the victim, but a severe harm to a person's body that causes a permanent or a long lasting disability.

Murder of another human was a crime punished in the most incipient forms of social organization; the Code of Ur-Nammu, 2100 - 2050 BC, prescribed that *"if a man commits a murder, that man must be killed"* , the Old Testament considers the murder of Abel as the first crime in human history, the laws of ancient Greece's legislators, Draco, Solon and Lycurgus as well as the Law of the Twelve Tables of Rome punished murder with the outmost severity.

Sometimes murder is committed in order to obtain a benefit. The author of such crime does not seek the elimination of the victim; he seeks another objective and the murder of the victim is just a mean to an end. The victim may be any person but usually it is in a position that interferes with the murderer's goal. The victim may be a public official[38] but it may also be a person without any official quality, for instance a

---

[38] See 4.4.1. Case Study Giovani Falcone;

rich relative that is murdered in order to claim the inheritance, or a spouse is killed in order to collect the insurance.

There is a subtle difference in regards to the matter of contract killing between common law and continental law systems. In common law systems, the contract to commit an indictable offence is not enforceable in court of law. In continental law systems, a contract cannot have an illegal purpose (it is one of the validity conditions for a contract to exist), such an agreement is not viewed as a contract.

Sir William Blackstone defined felonious homicide as "... *the highest crime against the law of nature that man is capable of committing*"[39] and considered it to be of three kinds, justifiable, excusable and felonious.

In US's modern statutes, the forms of homicide have been classified based on the degree of the offender's culpability[40] , in first and second degree murder, voluntary manslaughter, reckless homicide, and criminally negligent homicide.

Crimes of corruption are crimes committed with direct intent; therefore involuntary manslaughter, reckless homicide, or vehicular homicide cannot be crimes of corruption. When we consider criminally negligent homicide, negligence itself may have its root in a corrupt purpose, for instance, a manager does not provide for his employee the safety equipment required by law to perform a certain job, in order to maximize his profits.

In UK, murder is a common law offence; it is not defined in any statute[41] , although the term is used in several acts such as the Abolition of Death Penalty Act 1965 or Criminal Justice Act 2003. UK' legislation regarding murder is undergoing a reforming process that will hopefully bring more clarity in the subject. An important statute to our subject is the Offences against the Person Act 1861, which incriminates under article 4 the act of conspiring or soliciting to commit murder.

Section 211(2) of the StGB incriminates murder committed out of greed or in order to facilitate or to cover up another offence as a crime committed in aggravating circumstances, for which the penalty is life imprisonment.

The CP defines murder in Article 221-1 and, in Article 221-3 defines murder committed with premeditation as assassination; moreover, in

---

[39] See Blackstone, pg.176
[40] See Scheb pg. 132
[41] See Catherine Elliott and Frances Quinn, *Criminal Law*, 3rd ed. (Harlow: Pearson Education Limited, 2000), pg. 45

Article 221-5-1, the act of *"Making another person offers or promises, or offering him gifts, presents or benefits of any kind to induce him to commit an assassination or a poisoning is punished...by ten years' imprisonment and by a fine of €150 000."* This text is important to be mentioned because it unambiguously establishes a penalty for the corruptor, which is usually regarded as a participant to the crime, not as a criminal himself.

Assault, battery and other forms of physical and psychological violence are crimes against persons where corruption is absent. However, violent acts against persons may be used in organized forms of criminality such as gangs or mafia in order to establish a dominant social position. In those cases, violence is committed in order to obtain a profit; therefor it can be called corruption.

In common law, assault and battery are two separate offences;[42] today's statutes also incriminate both as distinctive offences. In UK they are defined in Criminal Justice Act 1998, Offences against Persons Act 1861[43], while in U.S. they are incriminated under the Title 18 of the Federal Criminal Code and in States statutes.

The CP incriminates acts of violence under Articles 222-7 to 222-16-1 and threats under Articles 222-17 to 222-18-2; the StGB covers this subject under Section 223-224, 226, 231.

Kidnapping and abduction are, undoubtedly, another class of crimes of corruption, because they involve intentionally breaking the laws that protect a person's freedom in order to obtain a profit. There are however exceptions, when a parent 'kidnaps' his child that was given to the other parent following a divorce or a child that was placed in someone else's custody. In these situations we are dealing with an act of rebellion against a court decision which the author considers to be unjust.

Also, kidnaping or abduction may be performed out of revenge, making them a crime of passion or a crime of hate. Whenever the author of these types of crimes seeks a ransom or a reward or any other result that might be turned into a material benefit, the act is a crime of corruption.

Kidnaping was a common law crime, now incriminated under Child Abduction Act 1984 in UK, and in U.S. each State has its own legislation on the subject matter. The CP, under Articles 224-1 to 224-5-2 Abduction

---

[42] Scheb pg. 158
[43] Elliott and Quinn, pg. 102

and Illegal Restraint and the German StGB specifically incriminates under Section 239a Abduction for the purpose of blackmail, the corrupt form of abduction.

Human trafficking was defined[44] as a modern form of slavery. The purposes of human trafficking are sexual exploitation and forced labor; therefore we can safely call such acts, crimes of corruption. The large majority of the victims are women and children, and without the help of the State authorities they are unable to liberate themselves.

The main issue with human trafficking is that most of these crimes happen undetected and unreported. Another problem is the victims themselves, who accept to be exploited in hope for a better life. Moreover, sometimes the conditions under which these persons live and work, regarded as inhumane by normal standards, are far better than the hell they left back home, so they don't even consider themselves slaves and consider the abuser to be their benefactor.

The main legal instruments in the international arena designed to combat human trafficking are the Universal Declaration of Human Rights and the United Nations Convention against Transnational Organized Crime and the Protocol to Prevent, Suppress and Punish Trafficking in Persons especially Women and Children.

Several forms of human trafficking are incriminated in Sexual Offences Act 2003 and Asylum and Immigration (Treatment of Claimants, etc.) Act 2004 and in U.S. we have the U.S. Code, Title 22, Chapter 78 - Trafficking Victims Protection, PROTECT Act of 2003 and the Mann Act of 1910.

Article 18 of the Council of Europe Convention on Action against Trafficking in Human Beings 2005 requires from the States of the European Union to "...*adopt such legislative and other measures as may be necessary to establish as criminal offences*..."the "... *recruitment, transportation, transfer, harbouring or receipt of persons, by means of the threat or use of force or other forms of coercion, of abduction, of fraud, of deception, of the abuse of power or of a position of vulnerability or of the giving or receiving of payments or benefits to achieve the consent of a person having control over another person, for the purpose of exploitation*"(Article 4).

Thus, in the CP, is incriminated the trafficking in human beings Articles 225-4-1 to 225-4-9, the exploitation of begging Articles 225-12-5

---

[44] See United Nations Office on Drugs and Crime's Global Report on Trafficking in Persons pg.6

to 225-12-7 and the working and living conditions which infringe human dignity Articles 225-13 to 225-15-1. The StGB incriminates human trafficking under Sections 232 and 233 and child trafficking under Section 236.

Sex crimes are those crimes that incriminate acts of sexual nature which are considered by the society to be unacceptable. Several acts of sexual nature may fall into this category, such as rape and statutory rape, sexual abuse, incest, or sexual harassment, prostitution, pimping and procuring.

Rape is a form of a violent crime that is more of a crime of passion, than a crime of corruption. However, there are circumstances when women suffer multiple rapes as well as other abuses to force them into a 'career' in prostitution, and those situations fall within our definition of corruption. These crimes are rarely reported, the victims are too scared to report or even talk about such crimes, and, unfortunately very little protection is offered to them, even in developed countries.

The victim of rape may be any person; until recent years[45] the general view was that only women may be victims of rape, but the fact that males are also subjects to these crimes is now accepted.[46]

Rape was one of the common law crimes, Sir Blackstone defined rape as "...*the carnal knowledge of a woman forcibly and against her will*".[47] In modern times rape is a statutory offence; in UK rape is defined and incriminated by Sexual Offences Act 1956[48] , while in U.S. each State has its own rape laws.

The StGB incriminates rape under Section 177 Sexual assault by use of force or threats; rape and the French Code Penal under Articles 222-23-26 with the note that in French criminal law, rape may be part of other crime such as Torture and acts of barbarity Article 222-1, 3.

Prostitution is an activity which is regarded differently worldwide. In some legal systems it is considered a crime and is severely punished, in other systems the practice is legislated or tolerated. Leaving the moral aspects beside for a moment, we must distinguish between the practice of prostitution out of one's free will and forced prostitution when the person if forced into such practices.

---

[45] Elliott and Quinn, pg. 117-118
[46] Scheb, pg. 167
[47] See Blackstone, pg. 209; Samaha, pg. 329
[48] See Michael Molan, *Sourcebook on Criminal Law*, (London: Cavendish Publishing, 2001), pg. 857

The element of free will is essential. A person is entitled to the use his own body and even if such acts are performed in order to obtain money, corruption is absent. If the money is a secondary objective and the author aims to obtain some other profit, in those cases corruption is present.

Regarding forced prostitution we can say that the prostitute is a victim, determined to perform such acts thru acts of physical and psychological violence. Other criminal activities related to prostitution such as pimping and procuring, creating and managing prostitution networks, sexual exploitation are clearly crimes of corruption.

The main international legal instruments designed to protect persons against forced prostitution are The United Nations Convention for the Suppression of the Traffic in Persons and the Exploitation of the Prostitution of Others, which has not been yet ratified and the United Nations Convention against Transnational Organized Crime (UNTOC) and the Protocol to Prevent, Suppress and Punish Trafficking in Persons, especially Women and Children.

In U.S., prostitution is illegal exception the State of Nevada where it is regulated. All aspects regarding prostitution are incriminated under States laws and thus there are several degrees of severity in punishing such acts.

In UK prostitution is legal but certain aspects about this activity are incriminated. The Sexual Offences Act 2003 incriminates soliciting, causing or inciting prostitution for gain, controlling prostitution for gain, paying for sexual services of a prostitute subjected to force, trafficking humans for sexual exploitation, and the Policing and Crime Act 2009 incriminates paying for sexual services of a prostitute subjected to force and amends the offence of loitering for purposes of prostitution of the Street Offences Act 1959.

In France prostitution in the time of Napoleon was legal, but gradually become illegal by outlawing brothels and today France is moving towards the Nordic Model, which considers prostitution a system of exploitation and was introduced in Sweden, Iceland and Norway.[49] The French Code Penal incriminates procuring and assimilated offences under articles 225-5 to 225-10-1, and recourse to minors' prostitution under articles 225-12-1 to 225-12-4.

---

[49] See Taina Bien-Aime, *France Takes First Steps Towards Abolition of Prostitution* on
http://www.huffingtonpost.com/ taina-bienaime/france-prostitution-laws_b_4775608.html

In Germany prostitution is legal and regulated under the Act Regulating the Legal Situation of Prostitutes (Prostitution Act), which came into force on 1 January 2002. The StGB incriminates certain criminal activities; under Section 180 the causing minors to engage in sexual activity, Section 180a the exploitation of prostitutes, Section 182 the abuse of juveniles, or under Section 184e the unlawful prostitution.

Drug trafficking is a significant part of the criminal phenomenon, both in terms of money and in the number of victims and causalities. It is also a strong generator of corruption and other forms of criminality and requires enormous human and financial efforts to be kept under control.

The drug dealer or the seller is perfectly aware that he is breaking the law in order to make a profit, and intentionally does so, which fits our definition of a crime of corruption. Drug dealing is a corrupt contract but there are several aspects that need to be explained.

First, there is a corrupt contract of sale between the producer of the drug and the drug dealer, or the person who resells the drug to the consumer. Between the two there is also a long chain of intermediaries that handles the transport, the export, the import or the storage of the drugs. It is clear that all the persons involved up to this stage, the producer, the intermediaries and the final seller break the law with direct intent in order to obtain a profit.

Second, we also have a buy-sell contract between the final seller, the drug dealer and the consumer of the drug, and here the situation is more complicated. The question to be asked is if the consumer of the drug is equally guilty of a crime of corruption.

In most States consumption of illegal drugs is considered a felony so the buyer knows that he is breaking a law. On the other hand he is also a victim of a dependency, of the addiction that drugs bring. He is not breaking the law in order to obtain a profit, like the drug dealer, he is breaking the law in order to satisfy a need. Therefore, in my opinion, even in cases where it is incriminated by the criminal law, drug consumption is not a crime of corruption.

Acknowledging the danger posed by drugs, the United Nations, trough the United Nations Office on Drugs and Crimes adopted three international conventions.[50] The Single Convention on Narcotic Drugs,

---

[50] The full text of the conventions at http://www.unodc.org/doD/Int_Drug_Control_Conventions /Ebook/The_International_Drug_Control_ Conventions E.pdfcuments/commissions/CN , accessed on

1961, amended by the 1972 Protocol, requires for member States to *"...to limit exclusively to medical and scientific purposes the production, manufacture, export, import, distribution of, trade in, use and possession of drugs."* The Convention on Psychotropic Substances of 1971 in Article 22 requires from member States to *"...treat as a punishable offence when committed intentionally, any action contrary to a law or regulation adopted in pursuance of its obligations under this Convention, and shall ensure that serious offences shall be liable to adequate punishment, particularly by imprisonment or other penalty of deprivation of liberty."* The convention provides measurements are to be taken *"...that abusers undergo measures of treatment, education, aftercare, rehabilitation and social reintegration...."* And last, the Convention against Illicit Traffic in Narcotic Drugs and Psychotropic Substances, under Article 3 specifically requires from the member State to establish as criminal offences the production, cultivation, possession or purchase, etc. of narcotic drugs or psychotropic substances.

#### 4.4.1. Case study - Giovani Falcone

Giovanni Falcone (18 May 1939 – 23 May 1992) was an Italian magistrate who dedicated his life to the fight against Sicilian mafia. Falcone defined himself as *"a servant of the State in terra infidelium"*.[51]

He was killed by a road bomb detonated by Giovanni Brusca on 23 May 1992 on the orders of Salvatore 'Toto' Riina.

Today the term mafia is used to describe a form of criminal organization, based on common scope, usually illegal, having an internal system of rules and conducted by a pyramidal hierarchy. In time, the assassination methods and tools of the Sicilian Mafia had evolved from artisan made rifles to automatic assault weapons and high tech explosives.

In cases similar to Mr. Falcone's, is not just the law that stands between the criminal activities of a certain group, but also the person who is incorruptible and willing to apply the law. In other words the impediment is not a law but a person.

Therefore, in order to achieve their goal the criminal elements need to eliminate a person physically. Thus, crimes of corruption against persons are born. This type of crimes appears when we have an utterly corrupt justice system, when honest men are the exception.

---

1/21/2015
[51] Giovani Falcone, *Cose de la Cosa Nostra*, (Milano: RCS Libri, 1998)

The physical elimination of a magistrate seems logical for the criminal elements only when there is a certainty that the successor will be less threatening. It is a calculated risk here. If the core of the magistrates is incorruptible it would be unprofitable to assassinate any of them. In a way, the corruption in the magistrate core is the generator of these assassinations.

In a more sophisticated form, an undesirable magistrate, thru trafficking of influence, is advanced or moved in a higher position, from which he cannot hurt directly the criminal group. Usually, the criminal groups seek to find weaknesses in a person that they can exploit by blackmail or that can compromise a person in the public eye.

Human vices, alcoholism, the use of prostitutes, drugs, a bribe taken in the early career or any other 'skeleton in the closet' can be used by criminal elements in their favor. Once one magistrate accepts a bribe he becomes controllable, it is a method often used by the secret services, and criminal groups like mafia have no reservations to use such methods.

There are situations when the leader of a branch of State administration is a corrupt individual; in those cases he will seek to promote in the organization other corrupt characters. In States with endemic corruption in administration, to become corrupt is the only way to advance in career, and criminal elements are more than happy to provide support for an ambitious person as long he or she is willing to serve their interests.

The perfect example is the declaration of Frank Copolla when he answered the question *"What Is Mafia?"* he replied *"Your Honor, three magistrates want to become General prosecutor. One is intelligent, the second has the support of the government parties, and the third is an idiot, but he is the one who get the job. This is the Mafia..."*[52]

Assassination of an incorruptible public servant comes only as a last resort. The first step is to bribe the person in power that disrupts the activities of the organization. A second stage involves threats, intimidation, blackmail or other forms of physical or psychological pressure. In a third stage, strangely enough, mafia uses political influence to promote the incorruptible persons to quiet or well remunerated positions in the central administration, position from which no harm can be caused to the organization.

Another lesson is to be learned from Mr. Falcone's death. Not only in Sicily, but on entire Italy a numerous number of public officials were assassinated by what we generally call the Mafia. This situation

---

[52] See Falcone, pg. 21

continued until a public movement against those types of crimes emerged and the society as a whole opposed this organizations.[53]

### 4.4.2. Case study - Oscar Pistorius

Oscar Leonard Carl Pistorius, born 22 November 1986, is a South African athlete that caught world attention by competing in 2012 summer Olympics. Nicknamed 'Blade runner', Mr. Pistorius legs were amputated when he was 11 months old, motive for which he runs on two blades like springs prosthetic legs. After competing in several disability sports events, he was granted permission to compete in the summer Olympics were he had a decent performance.

On 14 February 2013 Mr. Pistorius shot dead his girlfriend Ms. Reeva Steenkamp, which he mistook for a burglar. On 21 October 2014 he was convicted by the High Court of South Africa in Pretoria to a penalty of five years imprisonment for culpable homicide. However, the Supreme Court of Appeal in Bloemfontein overturned the sentence and convicted Mr. Pistorius of murder and the case was returned to the previous court for resentencing.

The case caught media's attention and the trial was covered by all the news agencies around the world. It's a tragic story, no matter how we look at it, as a negligent homicide or as a murder based on *dolus eventualis*.

In Mr. Pistorius case, we can conclude that corruption is absent. The crime was either a crime of passion as the prosecutors tried to demonstrate or an unfortunate accident, which was the defendant's claim. In either case, the crime was not committed in order to obtain a profit.

## 4.5. Other Forms of Crimes of Corruption

Until now, in this chapter we've examined those crimes that are clearly incriminated by the criminal law, crimes that belong in three major groups, crimes against the State, crimes against propriety and crimes against persons.

This tripartite classification was inherited from the first generation of penal codes and is based on the material object of each crime. Because criminal law evolved, modern criminal codes contain more laborious

---

[53] See Schneider and Schneider, *Reversible Destiny. Mafia, Antimafia, and the Struggle for Palermo*, ( University of California Press), pg. 160

classifications, but in general, we can say that any crime belongs in one of the three mentioned classes.

The emergence of new legal relations had as consequence the genesis of new types of antisocial behavior that were later incriminated by the criminal law. In common law systems this issue was easily resolved by enacting a new statute; in continental law things are a bit more complicated. The legislative procedures to modify a criminal code are complicated in any country and they usually take a long period of time.

In the following subchapters we shall take into consideration several categories of crimes that became object of incrimination in recent years. First we shall explore the white collar crimes as a part of the phenomenon of corruption. Crimes against environment and crimes in sports became subject of incrimination only in the last few decades. Political crimes and criminal regimes are also a subject of interest because of their enormous cost in human lives. Last, we shall consider the crimes of traffic in influence, another grey area were corruption lurks.

## 4.5.1. The mythical white collar crimes

In a book about corruption, white color crimes should occupy a special place, a standalone designated chapter, yet here we analyze white collar criminality as a subtitle in a subchapter.

'White collar criminality' is a term that was introduced by Edwin Sutherland[54] and was largely adopted by the media and academia alike, but it has no relevance from the point of view of modern criminal law.

Almost any legal system in the world adopted the principle of equality before the law; the Universal Declaration of Human Rights states:

"*Article 1.*

*All human beings are born free and equal in dignity and rights. They are endowed with reason and conscience and should act towards one another in a spirit of brotherhood.*

*Article 2.*

*Everyone is entitled to all the rights and freedoms set forth in this Declaration, without distinction of any kind, such as race, colour, sex, language, religion, political or other opinion, national or social origin, property, birth or other status. Furthermore, no distinction shall be made on the basis of the political,*

---

[54] Benson M.L. and Simpson S.S, *White Collar Crime An Opportunity Perspective* (New York: Routledge, 2009) pg.5

*jurisdictional or international status of the country or territory to which a person belongs, whether it be independent, trust, non-self-governing or under any other limitation of sovereignty.*
*Article 7.*
*All are equal before the law and are entitled without any discrimination to equal protection of the law. All are entitled to equal protection against any discrimination in violation of this Declaration and against any incitement to such discrimination.*
*Article 10.*
*Everyone is entitled in full equality to a fair and public hearing by an independent and impartial tribunal, in the determination of his rights and obligations and of any criminal charge against him."*[55]

The Universal Declaration of Human Rights, was adopted by the UN General Assembly on 10 December 1948, nearly a decade after Sutherland developed the concept of white collar crime. The text of the UDHR should have ended any discussion about white collar crime, at least in the science of Criminal Law; it is hard to understand why the term is even used in modern academic books.

For Sutherland, the white collar criminal is a *"person of high socio-economic status"*.[56] In short, Sutherland's theory is that white collar criminality is learned just as any other criminal activity and a man becomes criminal thru a process called differential association. He wrote: *"The inventive geniuses for the lower class criminals are generally professional criminals, while the inventive geniuses for many kinds of white-collar crime are generally lawyers."*[57]

In the article published in the American Sociological Review, Sutherland noticed how the two classes are treated differently by the legal system, *"...white-collar criminals are relatively immune because of the class bias of the courts and the power of their class to influence the implementation and administration of the law. This class bias affects not merely present-day courts but to a much greater degree affected the earlier courts which established the precedents and rules of procedure of the present-day courts."*[58]

The economic status of a person is now irrelevant in any court of law in the world; therefore the classification of criminals in persons of low economic status and persons of high economic status bares no relevance

---

[55] http://www.un.org/en/documents/udhr/
[56] Edwin H. Sutherland, *White-Collar Criminality*, American Sociological Review, Vol. 5, No. 1 (Feb., 1940), pp. 1-12
[57] Ibid.
[58] Ibid.

today. The situation which Sutherland described was a deficiency or perhaps a series of deficiencies in the American justice system.

The term had such an impact it is still in use today. The FBI defines white collar crime as *"...those illegal acts which are characterized by deceit, concealment, or violation of trust and which are not dependent upon the application or threat of physical force or violence."*[59] The fact that in the FBI's definition *"...there is no mention of the type of occupation or the socioeconomic position of the 'white-collar' offender"*[60] was subject of criticism. In my opinion this 'deficiency' makes the definition accurate from a legal perspective.

My objection to the use of the term white collar - crime, criminal, criminality, is that it creates the impression that the criminal phenomenon is somehow different in the upper class, which is utterly wrong.

Any form of the so called white collar crimes are in fact very well defined in statutes and criminal codes. Fraud, bribery, embezzlement, forgery and counterfeiting, are crimes of corruption because their aim is to procure a benefit for the perpetrator by breaking or eluding a law.

Last, sociological oriented theories regarding corruption and the so called white collar criminality are useless because of the hidden dimension of the phenomena in question. There is no sociological method to determine the dimension of bribery for instance, which is only one facet of the phenomenon of corruption. The World Bank's estimation that world-wide bribery amounts to US $1 trillion dollars[61], is just an estimation, anyone can claim the figure is ten times higher or lower and there is no scientific method to prove him wrong.

Even if we can accept the fact that by the time Sutherland developed his theory a *de facto* category of white collar crimes might have existed, now they belong in legal history, or better yet in legal mythology.

## 4.5.2. Crimes against the environment

The negative effects of human activities on the environment have become better known in the last half of the 20th century, and,

---

[59] See Cynthia Barnett, *The Measurement of White-Collar Crime Using Uniform Crime Reporting (UCR) Data,* on https://www.fbi.gov/stats-services/about-us/cjis/ucr/nibrs/nibrs_wcc.pdf
[60] Ibid.
[61]http://web.worldbank.org/WBSITE/EXTERNAL/NEWS/0,,contentMDK:20190187~menuPK:34457~pagePK:34370~piPK:34424~theSitePK:4607,00.html

subsequently, a strong environmental movement was born. Gradually, each environmental issue has been addressed in International Conventions and Agreements and the signatory States have implemented the measures to protect the environment in their internal legislation. Today, environmental law has grown to become a vast discipline; virtually any human activity is covered by environmental law.

Crimes against the environment take several forms such as illegal trade of wildlife, dumping and illicit trade in hazardous waste, toxic and nuclear substances, trafficking in ozone depleting substances, illegal fishing and illegal lodging.

Wildlife, because it's rarity, was used as raw material for luxury items or pseudo-medical treatments. Following the ban on exploiting such resources, without addressing the core issue, and that is the culture that generates the demand, a black market for any rare wildlife item emerged.

Modern society produces enormous amounts of waste that needs to be disposed of, therefore industrial means are necessary. Only that disposing of the waste costs as much or even more than the costs of production. Thus, the industry of waste disposal became the playing ground not only for unscrupulous characters, but also for organized crime.[62] Toxic and nuclear wastes are the most dangerous types of waste because it takes nature a very long time to neutralize them. The costs of managing such waste is high, therefore it's convenient and highly profitable to dispose of them in any secluded places. Thus they pollute the water sources, poison the lands, and expose humans and wildlife to radiation or toxic elements.

Population growth led to the overexploitation of what were once abounded resources such as fish and timber. Here not only rarity brings profits, but also quantity, and legal limits imposed to ensure sustainability are often surpassed.

Academia and media rushed, in my opinion, to introduce new terms, green crimes, green criminology, eco criminology; beside the obvious contradiction in terms, in fact we are dealing with the age old problem of corruption. Crimes against the environment are strictly crimes of corruption because the author is aware that he is breaking the law and by doing so, he intends to obtain a profit.

---

[62] For a detailed account on the relation between organized crime and crimes against environment see Donald R. Liddick, *Crimes Against Nature* (Santa Barbara: Praeger, 2011)

Severe legislation to protect the environment exists in most countries, and the only answer to the question why such legal instruments don't produce the desired effects is, no doubt, corruption.

In U.S. criminal acts against environment are defined in Clean Air and Clean Water Acts, Endangered Species Act, Toxic Substances Control Act, and so on. The Directive 2008/99/EC of the European Parliament and of the Council of the European Union of 19 November 2008 on the protection of the environment through criminal law, in Article 3 defines a series of acts that bring harm to the environment that should be incriminated as offences by the member States of the European Union.

In UK most of the environmental offences are incriminated under several acts such as the Environmental Protection Act 1990 (as amended) or the Water Resources Act 1991. The StGB incriminates criminal acts against the environment under Chapter 29, section 324 to 330d. In the CP, crimes against environment are incriminated in general as a modality of the crimes of destruction under Article 322-5, 6 and because Article 410-1 defines the natural surroundings and environment as one of the fundamental interests of the nation, under Article 421-2 it incriminates certain acts against environment as terrorism.

### 4.5.3. Crimes of corruption in sports

Sport had become in the last part of the 20th century a multibillion dollars industry; therefor it also attracted and generated a significant part of the phenomenon of corruption. Corruption in sports however is not a modern phenomenon; accounts of fixed games were given by Aristotle or Homer. When we speak about corruption in sport we must notice that the phenomenon is manifested in two forms, either by enhancing the athlete's performance by illegal means or by not defending the sporting chance fairly, seeking an positive result from laying a bet.

Doping was a mean to give an athlete an advantage over the opponents by chemically increasing his physical capabilities. One by one, each sporting discipline had its share of doping scandals; athletics, weightlifting and cycling are the leading negative examples.

In 2008 Olympic Games,[63] four horses were disqualified from the individual show jumping final, following positive tests for capsaicin, a substance extracted from chilly papers, which enhances horse's performances. The immorality of doping an innocent animal exceeds, in my opinion, the immorality of the act of doping performed by an athlete on himself.

We can only expect that in the future, new doping methods and techniques will be developed. The goal is nothing less than to obtain an untraceable substance or method that will give an athlete that 5% advantage over the other competitors, which is more than enough to guarantee a victory. Detection methods, unfortunately, will always be a step behind, and thus, entire world of sports is at risk to be thrown in to anarchy, with financial and social consequences impossible to predict.

Another aspect worth emphasizing is the corrupt character of the medical professionals that participate in such practices. The athlete does not have the medical knowledge to make use of drugs to enhance his abilities; we are not talking here about self-injection with steroids. Medical expertise is needed for a doping program that will give peak athletic performance in the competition. Thus, corrupt doctors that find it easy to procure performance enhancing drugs, to make use of the state of the art medical laboratories in order to develop doping methods and programs are parties in a corrupt contract with the athlete.

In most States, doping is not incriminated *per se*; it falls under the laws that prohibit the use of certain substances or drugs, for instance the U.S. Controlled Substances Act 1970 as amended by the Crime Control Act of 1990 makes it an offence the possession of steroids without prescription.

In 1999 the International Olympic Committee convened the World Conference on Doping in Lausanne, Switzerland, having as a result the establishing of the World Anti-Doping Agency, an independent international agency that fights for a doping-free sporting environment. The main document implemented by the Agency is the World Anti-Doping Code, a *"...document that harmonizes anti-doping policies, rules and regulations within sport organizations and among public authorities around the world."*

More than 660 sport organizations have accepted the WADA Code including the International Olympic Committee (IOC), the International Paralympic Committee (IPC), all Olympic Sport International

---

[63] See "Olympic horses fail drugs tests" on
http://news.bbc.co.uk/sport2/hi/olympics/equestrian/7574220.stm;

Federations (IFs) and all IOC-recognized IFs, National Olympic and Paralympic Committees, National Anti-Doping Organizations.[64] WADA is publishing the annual List of Prohibited Substances and Methods, banning the use of non-approved substances, anabolic agents, hormones, growth factors, diuretics and masking agents, stimulants and narcotics, and prohibiting the use of several methods such as manipulation of blood and blood components, chemical and physical manipulation, gene doping.

The International Convention against Doping in Sport adopted by the 33rd UNESCO General Conference on October 19, 2005, is the first international legal instrument against doping in sport, having as purpose *"to promote the prevention of and the fight against doping in sport, with a view to its elimination."*[65] The Convention requires from member States to take appropriate measures (legislation, regulation, policies or administrative practices) according to the principles of the WADA Code.

Match fixing is a form of bribery, therefore a crime of corruption. It involves bribing athletes or staff in exchange for a sporting performance lower that the true capabilities. The corruptor does not seek to obtain an improbable result, but a certain one. It is very hard to bribe the world champion, no matter the sporting discipline; it is easier to bribe the challenger to lose in a certain manner or at a certain score. Thus match fixing becomes hard to prove, because the result is expected, but by knowing the exact result in advance, the corruptor obtain a guaranteed profit from gambling on that result.

Another form of match fixing is generated by the competition's system itself. There are situations when wining is contrary to the athlete's or team's interest; a defeat may assure an easier path, more accessible opponents in the next events or simply there is no interest in winning and the efforts are spared. In this type of situations we cannot speak about 'a crime' but there is an element of moral corruption that affects the competition.

Other forms of crimes of corruption in sport includes tax frauds, illegal fees, bribery and kickbacks, which have been discussed already in the previous subchapters. One significant impediment in combating corruption in sports is the fact that sport has developed its own set of

---

[64] https://www.wada-ama.org/en/what-we-do/the-code
[65] Art. 1

rules, governing bodies, and tribunals; in fact it's a legal system within a legal system.

### 4.5.4. Political crimes

Last century was a dark one in human history. Following the death of 10 million soldiers and more than 7 million civilians in The Great War, two dangerous doctrines emerged: national-socialism in Germany and communism in Russia. The end of the World War II marked the ending of only one of those doctrines, national-socialism, and the political and military leaders of Nazi Germany were deferred to justice in a series of trials, the most important ones were held at Nuremberg. Following those trials, the Holocaust of the Jewish minority was made known to the general public, together with a series of genocides against Slavic and Roma people, homosexuals and other minorities. Most of the perpetrators of those crimes were sentenced to death but there are few[66] who escaped judgment.

Communism, unfortunately, thrived for another half of century, bringing human kind close to self-destruction, and causing the death of more than 150 million people.[67] The crimes against their own population in communist regimes have become known to the public only after the fall of the Iron Curtin in 1989 and the dissolution of the Soviet Union 1991.

But communism was not an ideology that was always imposed by force; many scholars from different fields failed in its trap; its principles of equality constitute the main lure. In fact, the elites of the communist regimes are the first who break the principles of equality. The party elite live a different life than the rest of the population, in that respect, as a political doctrine, communism is the epiphany of corruption.

In the case of criminal regimes, regardless the political orientation, we are in the presence of a corrupt social contract. The corruptor, the political regime uses a variety of manipulation techniques in order to assure public support. The corruptee in these cases is the entire society. Large masses of people allow themselves to be manipulated and indoctrinated, sometimes against the most elementary common sense.

---

[66] According to the Annual Status Report on the Worldwide Investigation and Prosecution of Nazi War Criminals of the Simon Wiesenthal Center, eight persons were still alive in 2013
[67] R. J. Rummel, *Death by government*, (New Brunswick, NJ: Transaction Publishers, 1994).

There is also a charismatic leader, often referred to as a dictator in the free world, around who public support is rallied. It is extremely important to understand that the dictator is not the only one responsible for the crimes; after all he is just one person. It is the regime that stands behind him, formed by few thousand individuals, lacking the most elementary morals, which gained absolute and discretionary powers, and make use of terror, murder, genocide in order to remain in power.

Technically, such political crimes are covered by the State's legislation; those criminal actions have an appearance of legality. Anyone labeled as an enemy of the State was subject to prosecution, and sentenced to long term imprisonment or death. Inhumane prisons, concentration and labor camps, famine, reeducation institutions, meant that any term of imprisonment was in fact a death sentence.

The level of social danger posed by criminal regimes is the maximum conceivable. It is the responsibility of the international community to intervene and to put an end to criminal regimes no matter the circumstances.

I consider that the principle of non-interference in internal affairs of the States cannot be extended to cover the murder of innocent civilians based on race, religion or political opinion. The U.N. Resolution No. 36/103 states that "*1.No State or group of States has the right to intervene or interfere in any form or for any reason whatsoever in the internal and external affairs of other States.*"[68] I believe that this principle needs a revision in the sense that it should be restricted to the legal internal and external affairs of other States, and by legal I mean those affairs that do not interfere with the U.N. Universal Declaration of Human Rights. The international community has not only the right, but the obligation to intervene by any means necessary to put an end to a criminal regime, no matter the costs, as soon as possible, because the longer it endures, the higher the body count is. A regime that kills its own citizens, no matter the reasons, loses any right to exist.

## 4.5.5. Traffic in influence

Traffic in influence, also called trading in influence or influence peddling was, and perhaps still is, a controversial issue that deserves a short

---

[68] See the full text on http://www.un-documents.net/a36r103.htm, accessed on 1/20/2015

analysis. The article 18 of the UNCAC requires from member States to adopt legislative measures to incriminate the traffic in influence. According to the definition in the article 18, trafficking in influence is:

*"(a)The promise, offering or giving to a public official or any other person, directly or indirectly, of an undue advantage in order that the public official or the person abuse his or her real or supposed influence with a view to obtaining from an administration or public authority of the State Party an undue advantage for the original instigator of the act or for any other person;*

*(b) The solicitation or acceptance by a public official or any other person, directly or indirectly, of an undue advantage for himself or herself or for another person in order that the public official or the person abuse his or her real or supposed influence with a view to obtaining from an administration or public authority of the State Party an undue advantage."*

Traffic in influence is a corrupt contract by which the corruptor promises or gives to a person an undue advantage in exchange for that person's performance of a corrupt act of obtaining an undue advantage from a third party. In other words, traffic of influence is a corrupt contract, linked thru the counter performance to a corrupt act.

The main problem with trafficking in influence is that is similar to lobbying, which is a legal activity in several countries, although a matter of controversy in itself. Lobbying is a method of influencing government's or legislators decisions in the benefit of an interested party.

Raising the authority's awareness on a certain issue is based on the right to freedom of speech and by no means is related to the phenomenon of corruption. For instance, requesting the allocation of more resources for cancer research is a moral and ethical act and lobbying is an effective method to obtain funding.

Lobbying for the interests of a single person or group or enterprise, and here I shall refrain to give any example, raises the ethical dilemma if the satisfaction given to the interested party doesn't contravene to the public interest. Determining the State's authorities to take a decision in favor of a group or a person against the interests of the public good or even against the legitimate interests of another group or person is, in my opinion, a form of corruption.

Traffic in influence may come in several variations usually referred to as favoritism and nepotism. Favoritism is a preferential treatment based on a personal relation; it is not considered an offence, and sometimes it may have a positive side. A person with certain qualities may need encouragement or support in order to perform better in the workplace.

The down side is that may give an undue advantage and it may affect negatively the organization's overall performance.

Nepotism is a controversial issue and it usually means hiring a family member or a relative in a certain position. Hiring a family member can have its rewards; for long, trade secrets have been passed down from generation to generation, ensuring the continuance of the family business and protecting and expanding the family's patrimony. When we are speaking about hiring a relative in a private enterprise, the owner is entitled to pass his legacy to his successors or any person he chooses, but when this happens in the public administration it is, undoubtedly, is a form of corruption. A public official is not the owner of the public office he holds, he is an employee, paid from the public money, and therefor he does not have a right of disposition. These milder forms of trafficking in influence are not incriminated; they are usually sanctioned by ethics and good practices codes.

In U.S. the issue of lobbying was addressed under the Lobbying and Disclosure Act of 1995, which brings a degree of transparency in the sector. Lobbying in UK was regulated by the Transparency of Lobbying, Non-Party Campaigning and Trade Union Administration Act 2014 but the offering, promising or giving of advantages is not criminalized yet.

In France, lobbying was a legal practice under the law regarding freedom of association from 1901 and it's going under a difficult legislative process, because of the thin demarcation line[69] between traffic in influence and lobby. The French criminal law incriminates the offence of trafficking in influence under Article 433-1, Article 433-2, and Article 432-11, texts that implemented the article 18 of the UNCAC. In Germany, lobbying is regulated by the rules of the Bundestag, and the criminalization of trafficking in influence is about to begin following the ratification of UNCAC on 12 Nov 2014.

## 4.6. Defenses for crimes of corruption

Criminal law, in all legal systems, prescribes for those situations when, although a crime has been committed, the person who committed it cannot be held responsible. Defenses are classified in general defenses,

[69] See http://www.lepetitjuriste.fr/droit-des-affaires/droit-penal-des-affaires/existe-il-une-limite-entre-le-trafic-dinfluence-et-le-lobbying, accessed on 2/1/2015

which can be valid for any crime and specific defenses, applicable only for a particular crime.[70] Here we are only concerned with general defenses especially those that may be used in cases of crimes of corruption, for instance self-defense or absence of intent to commit a crime cannot be considered as defenses for crimes of corruption. In theory, general defenses are valid in all criminal cases. Crimes of corruption are crimes committed to obtain a profit; therefor, by definition, any defense that involves lack of criminal intent is excluded.

Infancy is a defense based on the fact that the defendant does not have the age necessary to be held liable for his actions. Crimes of corruption are crimes committed with direct intent so the author knows what he is doing; unless the law prescribes an absolute age requirement for criminal capacity, infancy cannot be invoked as an excuse. Common law held that children under seven have no criminal capacity and children between seven and fourteen are presumed not to have capacity.[71] In U.S. the matter of the age of criminal responsibility is settled in statutes while in UK the question of age in criminal accountability is a matter for debate.[72] In German Strafgesetzbuch, Section 19, children under the age of fourteen cannot be held criminally accountable. The French Code Penal doesn't set an age limit, but a requirement of understanding of the act.

Insanity, in the broad sense, may be a genuine valid defense in crimes of corruption, for instance crimes against propriety may be caused by kleptomania, crimes against the State by psychosis and crimes against persons by psychopathy. The problem with the insanity defense is that is very hard to establish a definite conclusion, medical opinions on many diseases and disorders are contradictory, even more, moments of lucidity or temporary insanity at the moment of the crime, are, in my opinion, impossible to prove. However, if the court acknowledges the existence of such condition, there is no criminal liability for the defendant.

In U.S., and UK[73] the insanity defense is based on the M'Naghten rules, but because modern science provides a better understanding of mental disorders, it is likely that the process of reform will take in consideration new elements in defining insanity defense.

---

[70] Elliott and Quinn, pg. 239
[71] Samaha, pg. 190
[72] Elliott and Quinn, pg. 240
[73] See Gardner & Anderson, pg. 113, Elliott and Quinn pg. 243

The CP, under article 122-1 states that *"A person is not criminally liable who, when the act was committed, was suffering from a psychological or neuropsychological disorder which destroyed his discernment or his ability to control his actions."* Section 20 of the StGB states that a person *"incapable of appreciating the unlawfulness of their actions or of acting in accordance with any such appreciation due to a pathological mental disorder, a profound consciousness disorder, debility or any other serious mental abnormality, shall be deemed to act without guilt."*

Necessity and duress may be the only solid defenses in cases of corruption; for instance, in crimes against persons involving a form of organized crime, members of gangs or mafia like criminal organizations may be forced by the leaders to commit criminal acts, or in crimes against propriety involving elaborate schemes, the principal perpetrator may use threats in order to make other persons to commit criminal acts in his benefit.

Article 122-2 of the CP states that *"A person is not criminally liable who acted under the influence of a force or constraint which he could not resist."* And Article 122-7 A person is not criminally liable if confronted with a present or imminent danger to himself, another person or property, he performs an act necessary to ensure the safety of the person or property, except where the means used are disproportionate to the seriousness of the threat. The StGB defines necessity and duress under Section 34 and Section 35.

Mistake of law may be a defense in some cases of corruption; the modern business environment is governed by a staggering amount of laws, rules and regulations and it is conceivable that some acts that may be seen as some forms of frauds to be mistakes.

The StGB under Section 17 Mistake of law, states that *"If at the time of the commission of the offence the offender lacks the awareness that he is acting unlawfully, he shall be deemed to have acted without guilt if the mistake was unavoidable."* The FCP states that Article 122-3 *"A person is not criminally liable who establishes that he believed he could legitimately perform the action because of a mistake of law that he was not in a position to avoid."*

Diplomatic immunity is a controversial issue from a moral perspective because it allows for the members of diplomatic missions not to be prosecuted; under the cover of diplomatic immunity, crimes of corruption especially crimes against propriety may be carried out without any fear of prosecution. It is true that the author may face criminal charges in his own country but in countries with a high level of corruption in the justice and political system it is highly unlikely to expect a fair verdict.

## 4.7. Conclusions

In this chapter and in the previous one, we defined corruption as an antisocial phenomenon manifested in the form of illegal or immoral acts or contracts aiming to break or to elude a law or a social norm in order to procure a personal benefit.

Criminal law is the branch of the law that defines certain unilateral acts or contracts as crimes. Crimes of corruption are those unilateral acts or contracts, defined as felonies or misdemeanors by the criminal law, which are committed with the principal purpose of obtaining a profit.

As an antisocial phenomenon, corruption is the most dangerous one because it is a generator of other antisocial phenomena such as war, terrorism, genocides, destruction of the environment and economic crisis. Corruption is a part or a subdivision of the criminal phenomenon and crimes of corruption are a modality of other crimes.

In this chapter we used the legislation of four legal systems, two from the common law systems family, the United Kingdom and the United States and two from the continental law systems, France and Germany. The general view is that the differences between legal systems, even those belonging to the same family, are irreconcilable. In this chapter I tried to prove the contrary; when it comes down to the essence, to the basic principles, the science of criminal law is similar almost everywhere in the world.

Corruption was associated with bribery for a long time; the two terms are often used as synonyms. In legal texts treating corruption, gradually, other terms were introduced, embezzlement, money laundering, fraud, yet, no matter how many terms we add, we are unable to cover corruption in its integrality. Virtually any type of crime can be committed with the purpose of obtaining a profit. Crimes that traditionally are regarded as they have nothing to do with corruption, such as violence or rape, arson and destruction, treason and sabotage, may be very well committed for a corrupt purpose, in order to obtain a gain or a profit.

Several offences incriminated by the criminal law are strictly crimes of corruption, or, in other words, these offences are committed only with a corrupt purpose. In this category we can find those offences that are traditionally regarded as corruption, such as bribery, fraud, embezzlement.

Corruption is not incriminated *per se* in any jurisdiction; it is considered as an aggravating circumstance[74]. Crimes of corruption should be sanctioned with the outmost severity because the level of social danger they pose to society is maxim. A contract killer is far more dangerous for society than one who kills out of passion.

Criminal law incriminates antisocial behaviors only after they begin to manifest in the society with a force and frequency that threatens the social stability; some actions or behaviors that common sense defines as corrupt, may pass unsanctioned until new legislation is introduced in the legal system.

For the criminal, the sole motive is the profit, the gain; the crime is just a mean to an end. The materialization of his primordial objective is conditioned by the realization of the secondary objective.

Crimes of corruption are always premeditated. It is inconceivable that a criminal commits a crime of corruption by accident or out of anger, hate, love or any other emotion. The criminal has a clear purpose and he knows what he is doing. The other forms of guilt, negligence and recklessness are excluded in cases of corruption.

The authors or the active subjects of the crimes of corruption may be any persons. All that is needed is the physical and mental capacity to perform such crimes. The rules regarding legal capacity will determine if the sanction is applicable in that particular case or not.

The victim or the passive subject of crimes of corruption may be any natural person, legal person or community of persons. Under no circumstances crimes of corruption may be considered victimless crimes. When no person suffers a prejudice from a crime of corruption, although it will be really hard to find an example, we may accept it as theoretically possible, society and the rule of law should be considered as victims.

---

[74] See 18 U.S. Code § 3592 (c), (7) Procurement of offense by payment and (8) Pecuniary gain

The analysis of the cases presented in this chapter shows how a certain crime may be a crime of corruption or not. As a disclaimer, the analysis was based on the information that is publicly available. The three types of offences presented, espionage, murder and financial fraud were chosen because of their notoriety. For each offence two cases are used as examples, in the first corruption is clearly present, while in the second corruption is absent. The same line of reasoning may be applied for other offences.

I believe that we can use a simple method to identify if corruption is present or not. If an illegal act is committed in order to obtain a material benefit, a profit, a gain, then corruption is present. If the same act is committed for any other purpose, then corruption is absent.

In the last chapter we shall explore four major contemporary issues related to corruption and the efforts to fight it.

*Beware of false knowledge;*
*it is more dangerous than ignorance.*

George Bernard Shaw

# 5. Contemporary issues

The phenomenon of corruption is omnipresent in our life; in almost any news bulletin we can see one of its forms from war and terrorism to petty bribes.

The fight against corruption is also reflected by the media. We can see politicians questioned about their management of the public affairs, financiers arrested for misusing the funds entrusted to them, sports gods falling into disgrace. The general feeling after watching these events is that there is a fight against corruption but it is an anarchical one, which lacks any methodology, planning and strategy. This situation is understandable for developing countries but it is inexcusable for advanced democracies.

In this chapter we shall examine several contemporary issues regarding the phenomenon of corruption which, if addressed, will turn the tide and bring back corruption to manageable levels.

The first issue we shall address is the quantification of corruption, what are the true dimensions of the phenomenon and its consequences. In my opinion this is the biggest problem that the fight against corruption must address.

The second issue that needs to be taken in consideration seriously is education. Corruption has been with us for so long that we are no longer able to see its catastrophic effects. Every person must be educated that corruption kills, the final end of corruption is the death of innocent people.

The third issue that needs to be examined is the justice system. There are two reasons for which corruption endures in a society. First, the justice system is incapable to remove it, situation which can be corrected by addressing those objective and subjective reasons that stand behind the lack of performance. Second, the justice system is unwilling to eliminate corruption, due to endemic corruption inside the justice system itself. This situation is harder to correct and requires far more resources than the previous scenario. The cleansing process must start with the justice system itself, and this is a laborious process.

Last, the law itself needs a revision. Maybe it is the time for the legal science to abandon the dogmatism, the antiquated procedures and the narrow views and make use of the tools that science and technology provided for the modern man.

Corruption is an antisocial phenomenon that occurs naturally in a society or in an organization founded on laws. The eradication of corruption is a desirable goal, it should be the final purpose of the fight against corruption, but is it a realistic objective?


## 5.1. Quantifying corruption

Globalization gave corruption an international dimension; the economic effects are no longer felt only by a single State or organization, those effects are putting pressure on the entire global economy.

Acknowledging the dangers posed by corruption at a global scale, the United Nations begun a process to implement a set of legal instruments and measures to combat the phenomenon through international cooperation.

The United Nation Convention against Transnational Organized Crime was adopted by a resolution of the United Nations General Assembly on 15 November 2000 and it was followed by the United Nations Convention against Corruption, adopted by the United Nations General Assembly on 31 October 2003 by Resolution 58/4.

According to the Preamble of the UNCAC, corruption poses a threat to the stability of societies, undermines *"...the institutions and values of democracy, ethical values and justice"* and jeopardizes *"...sustainable development and the rule of law"*.

The purposes of UNCAC are to promote measures to prevent and combat corruption, to promote and support international cooperation and to promote integrity, accountability and proper management of public affairs and public propriety.

On a critical note we shall wonder why the purposes of the convention were limited to public propriety and affairs; is the corruption in the private sector less threatening? Isn't there a strong connection between

216

the two? Is it realistic to assume that we can eliminate corruption in the public sector, while ignoring corruption in private sector?

It is true that articles 12 and 13 contain provisions for the private sector and civil society, but still the balance is tilted in favor of the public sector and public officials. In all respects acts of corruption should be treated equally, regardless of the persons involved, domain of economic activity or country.

The UNCAC is not a perfect legal instrument but still is a perfectible one; article 69 provides the opportunity for States Parties to propose amendments after five years from entry into force.

The fight against corruption is well reflected in the media; corrupt dealings involving public and private persons, spectacular arrests of persons in power, large captures of illegal drugs and so on. What we don't see is a clear strategy, a plan, some goals that we intent to achieve in a certain timeframe.

In order to be successful, any responsible government has to develop a strategy to combat corruption. Such strategy must allocate proper resources in areas where they are needed, and hence, the need for quantification becomes self-evident.

And here we have the first major problem that needs to be solved if we intend to defeat corruption. The best tool available so far to quantify the phenomenon of corruption are the indexes and rankings provided by non-governmental organizations.

Transparency International is probably the flag ship of the fleet of non-profit, non-governmental organizations dedicated to fight corruption. It was established in 1993 and now has branches in more than 100 countries. The scope of TI is to "... *raise awareness of the devastating effects of corruption, and work with governments, businesses and international organizations to develop effective programs to tackle it.*"

TI is well known for its reports such as Corruption Perception Index and Bribe Payers Index, documents that are used by private enterprises, governments, and mass-media. The efforts made by the men and women involved with this organization in particular or other similar organisms in general are to be commended and admired; they deserve not only our gratitude but also our entire support.

The 2015 CPI was calculated by aggregating data from 13 different sources that have to meet certain criteria set by TI, respectively to quantify perceptions of corruption in the public sector, to be based on a valid methodology, to be credible and regular and to allow the possibility to make distinctions between countries. Consequently the data is standardized to a scale of 0-100 and an average is calculated and the degree of error is determined.

According to TI's Short Methodology Note *"...the CPI aggregates data from a number of different sources that provide perceptions of business people and country experts of the level of corruption in the public sector."* In other words, the CPI is based on the opinions of business people, experts, and general public.

By examining the sources that TI uses we learn that the experts consulted by the Bertelsmann Foundation are asked to assess if public officeholders are abusing their position and if the abusers are prosecuted and penalized. The Freedom House experts are called to evaluate bureaucracy and laws. Global Insight's experts are asked to assess corruption's effects on businesses. African Development Bank experts are asked to assess transparency, accountability and corruption in the Public Sector for the African Countries while Political and Economic Risk Consultancy is focused on Asian Countries.

World Justice Project asks experts and respondents from the general population about the use of public office for private gain in a variety of sectors health system, regulatory agencies, the police and the courts, and Political Risk Services assess corruption within the political system.

The result of the aggregation of these data is the Corruption Perception Index, that gives a score for each country, Denmark, the least corrupt country in the world scores 92 while Somalia scores 8 out of 100. Does this mean that if one lives in one of the top countries he or she is not affected by corruption? Of course not, no other assertion could be further from the truth. So what this index is telling us after all? Beside the fact that country X is more corrupt than country Y, with some disputable results, ... not much.

But let us examine some of the issues raised by the index. First, we learn that the CPI is based on *"perceptions"*. Quantifications made on *"perceptions"* are not quantifications from an objective, scientific point of view. Moreover, perceptions are affected by the subjectivity of the observer, one's vision of his own country or his own people might not be shared by peoples from other countries.

218

Second, we learn that the index is based on the opinions of the business people, and here we should exercise some caution. Every entrepreneur is motivated by profit. Managers are bound by their employment contracts to their employers to generate profit. Sometimes corruption is good for business especially in countries with a large bureaucracy; 'a little grease on the wheels' may translate into better performances for managers and more profits for entrepreneurs and investors.

In recent years, new legal instruments were implemented in every developed economy, that are incriminating corrupt business practices conducted overseas under the same sanctions as they are applied at home.[1]

So, the question to be asked here is how many of the business people that were actually involved in corrupt affairs are willing to admit it? Sociological research methods cannot provide estimations, nor can compensate for errors in this specific case.

One of the assumptions that every sociological survey makes is the fact that most respondents will answer truthfully to the questions. In this particular case, it will not be in the interest of a business person to admit involvement in corrupt practices, for the sake of a sociological survey. This goes against any person's common sense.

Third, we learn that the index is based on the opinion of experts from the countries in question, and here we can identify another major problem.

An expert in a certain field is defined as a person whose knowledge on a particular area exceeds the knowledge of the general public. The opinions of an expert are presented in the form of an expert report. The report usually begins with the question that the expert is called to answer. The expert evaluates evidence, proofs, and facts and presents his expert opinion in the conclusions of his report. An expert report is considered in any legal system a scientific proof.

In this particular subject we may be entitled to ask what kind of evidence and scientific facts an expert evaluates in his assessments. Another question to be asked here is how can a person become an expert in corruption? There aren't any Bernie Madoff University for Finances or Al Capone College for Organized Crime.

---

[1] See the OECD Convention on Combating Bribery of Foreign Public Officials in International Business Transactions

The truth is that those people consulted by TI are experts in different fields, law, finances, accounting, statistics, and they claim to have an extended knowledge on the phenomenon of corruption. While their expertise in their own field might be beyond questioning, we have no reason to doubt that, the extent of their expertise on a phenomenon that lacked a clear definition or a general theory is debatable.

One might claim an expertise on the corruption in the high finance and it might be true if that person worked in this particular area but I sincerely doubt that he or she has any expertise on trafficking of human beings, for instance. One might claim an expertise in drug trafficking, but again I doubt that he may also claim an expertise in, let's say crimes against environment.

It is safe to assume that members of the intelligence community will have and extended knowledge about a certain subject, but still, their knowledge is not exhaustive, it will only be extended by the knowledge acquired in the specific area were they carry out their activity.

Following the same line of reasoning, an expert from one of the legal professions will have his extra knowledge limited to his domain. A medical expert might know a thing of two about corruption in the healthcare system but is hard to assume that he has any knowledge about corruption in the banking industry; he lacks the expertise to make an assessment, he is no longer an expert in this field.

Moreover, the expert's knowledge is limited by his own environment and restricted to his personal experiences. Since he has no scientific method to quantify the phenomenon, even in his area of expertise, how is an expert opinion any different than an educated guess?

The absolute scientific data on the subject-matter can be found only in ministries of justice statistics, and that is how many people have been prosecuted, trialed and sentenced for crimes related to corruption. To estimate the level of corruption in a country, beside the number of people that are proven to be corrupt beyond doubt in a court of law, one must add the number of people that manage to escape or to elude the justice system. And the value of this factor is unknown in the equation.

Last, the CPI is based on the perceptions of the general public. If it is true that corruption affects us all, it involves only a segment of a country's population. Another segment of the population is completely ignorant about the phenomenon of corruption, especially about its size.

How large is this segment of population that is unaware or uninformed about corruption, no one can tell.

The bulk of the population is not involved in corrupt activities, thus, they cannot have a personal experience, a firsthand knowledge on the subject to relate to. Their opinion on whether their country is corrupt or not is based solely on secondary sources of information that can be either friends, relatives, family members that were involved in corrupt activities as active subjects or as victims, or on information acquired from media. And this is not an objective perspective.

Moreover, among the general public there are also corrupt individuals. It is likely that those involved in corrupt activities will deny the existence of corruption, no matter how anonymously the surveys are, out of the fear of being exposed and face the consequences.

The classical sociological methods used to gather data about corruption are producing false results. Organizations like Transparency International have done an excellent job in raising public awareness about a major social problem and, as pointed out in the opening, they truly deserve our gratitude and respect for their work. But the attempt to quantify corruption proved the limitations of sociological research methods; it is imperative to find a new way to quantify the phenomenon of corruption in order to fight it.

General country ratings may be deceiving from another point of view. A good score may create a false sense of security. Governments may be tempted to transfer resources that are allocated to the fight against corruption for other purposes. One of the characteristics of corruption is its rapid growth; a good position may be lost fast and tremendous efforts are needed to regain it. At the other end, a low score will create a sense of helplessness not only for the government but for the entire society.

The conclusion is scary; we do not know how corrupt we are. Therefore I think that it is imperative to find a proper scientific method to quantify corruption.

## 5.2. Education

The most effective weapon against corruption is education. Unfortunately, it is also the most neglected and perhaps this is no coincidence. For a very long time knowledge has been perceived as something dangerous, something that should be controlled and restricted. Throughout history, the rulers tried, and too often succeeded, to control their subjects thru fear, superstition and ignorance.

Fear is a powerful emotion that once served a precise role in our evolution; the survival of our specie depended on our fear of predator animals, toxic plants or poisonous insects. Once our intellect developed, and we climbed on top of the food chain, strangely enough, we used fear to keep order among the members of our society.

Frightened persons or groups of persons are paralyzed and incapable to stand against abusive authorities; only fear explains how millions obey and submit to the will of few. Thru manipulation and indoctrination millions of people are kept in a constant state of fear that makes them submissive and obedient.

If the fear of the authority was not enough, the rulers used superstition to induce fear in their subjects. The concept of an eternal punishment was a powerful inhibitor which once may have served a moral purpose but now it has become obsolete.

Ignorance is one of corruption's best friends. In totalitarian regimes the quality of the education system is intentionally degraded, the freedom of speech is among the first human rights that are lost and censors impose their own version of the truth, the one that serves their purposes. In these circumstances corruption thrives in the high echelons of power, and the people is incapable to react.

The information revolution that we are lucky enough to witness changed humanity forever because it allows an almost unrestricted access to information. One can educate himself in any domain for free or he has access to buy the best books or materials on any given subject. There is, however, a danger, in acquiring an incomplete or a perverted education; this type of deficiencies cannot be corrected by censorship, it should be corrected by offering an alternative based on the objective scientific truth.

Today we are tormenting our children in schools with complex mathematical equations and we teach them little about the laws. Every young person should be aware that there are institutions designed to protect them against abuses they may suffer at school and at home.

Fear is often induced in young minds, an act which I consider to be criminal. An educational system based on fear is meant to produce new generations of slaves and soldiers to serve and to defend a corrupt ruling class.

In most countries the high school curriculum contains courses on civic education, nevertheless, in my opinion, this is insufficient. A high school graduate should be aware of his rights and duties as a citizen. After graduating high school, most young men and women enter in the labor market completely unaware about the laws that control their environment. Often they become victims of corruption or enter in corrupt affairs simply because they are incapable of telling the difference between legal and illegal.

Legal education should be continued in university. Any human activity is regulated by law, so it would be useful to know which laws are relevant in one's domain of activity. For instance, a student of music will have little interest in law, yet, after graduation, he will have to educate himself about intellectual propriety laws, copyrights, royalties, contracts and so on. An engineer will find useful the knowledge of environmental law and the prescriptions regarding malpractice are extremely important for a doctor. No matter which profession we chose for ourselves, we will enter in legal relations sooner or later.

Understanding the law that regulates each domain by those who are involved will cause a decrease of the phenomenon of corruption; educated people will be hard to extort or to be convinced to pay bribes. A person aware of his rights will have no fear to expose corruption to competent authorities, as long as the authorities are able and willing to offer him protection.

Often, people become part in affairs of corruption without fully understanding the consequences of their actions. A person educated about the sanctions for crimes of corruption might have a second thought before committing such crimes. Crimes of corruption are always premeditated therefore a person has the time to evaluate his course of action or to seek advice or help.

A significant part of the phenomenon of corruption is generated by business persons and entrepreneurs. Driven by the desire to obtain a profit, entrepreneurs often result to corrupt means to facilitate a deal, to obtain a contract or to overcome bureaucratic obstacles.

Thru corruption, the hurdles created by bureaucracy may be easily avoided, and this can be profitable for business. In fact the two are closely related: bureaucracy is a creation of corruption. The obstacles that an entrepreneur has to face are intentionally created by the corrupt bureaucrats in order to determine him to indulge in corrupt business practices.

An honest business environment, based on the principles of market economy is far more rewarding than a system where bribery and traffic in influence make the rules. An entrepreneur might be tempted to think that he can pass the costs of corruption down the line to his customers and he will lose nothing if he pays a bribe. But no entrepreneur is self-sufficient, sooner or later he will become a customer, and the costs of other acts of corruptions will be paid by him as well. In the long run, nobody benefits from corruption, not even the corrupt themselves.

The products of corruption are, in a certain amount, useless. The money hidden in former fiscal paradises can now be traced and recovered; today there are no more safe havens for dirty money. What is the point to store money, jewelry or expensive works of art if one cannot use the wealth acquired freely? Even the corrupted can be educated that is far more rewarding to live a life in freedom than inside a golden cage.

Thru education any corrupted person can be reintegrated in the society and their experiences may be useful in understanding the mechanisms of corruption and to educate others that corruption is not a path worth taking. Thru education, open discussions, transparency, exchange of information, the deficiencies of a corrupt business environment can be corrected. But the most important result of a proper education will be the eradication of fear from our lives and that will cut any root of corruption and destroy any of its germs.

## 5.3. Corruption in the justice system

The justice system is one of the first victims of corruption, yet it is also the main culprit that allows for corruption to develop. I have affirmed before that in a country with an efficient justice system, corruption cannot develop. It does not mean that it will be absent, after all it is a phenomenon that occurs naturally, but it will never develop into the endemic phase.

In the first line of defense against criminality we can find the law enforcement bodies. The first problem that can be identified here is that their role begins *post factum*; these bodies can rarely intervene in a crime or stop it before it happens. When a custom officer stops a shipment of drugs, the offence of drug trafficking has already been committed, even if by this action other crimes related to the drugs will not happen.

We often see in the media large captures of drug shipments; what we don't see are the shipments that got thru. We see their ill effects on the streets and in other crimes related to drug dealing, a reality that cannot be denied; one can find illegal drugs in any large city in the world with relative ease.

When we wonder how these drugs end up on our streets there are only two logical explanations. First, there is a deficiency in custom control; due to the large traffic of goods, custom officers cannot verify every single shipment of goods, and drugs, in most cases, are hidden inside or among goods that are legal to trade. This might be a logical explanation but by no means can it be an excuse. Second, there is of course the corruption of custom officers that allows for illegal shipments to pass thru the net.

In any case, the worst policy that can be applied here is that of tolerance; we should either legalize drugs and control distribution, sale and consumption, or we should strictly ban drugs and see that the law is enforced among sellers and buyers with the outmost severity.

The existence of other forms of criminality such as human, wildlife, and illegal substances trafficking is generated at least in part by the corruption in the bodies and organisms entrusted with border protection and control.

Inside the State, there are organisms and bodies that control the economic life. Crimes of corruption like fraud, bribery, extortion, embezzlements that occur naturally in any economy, are expanding to endemic levels when the State's control mechanisms malfunction. A fraud of billions of dollars cannot exist without deficiencies in the financial and fiscal bodies entrusted with the control of the business environment. We can find objective deficiencies, mainly the improper allocation of the human resource necessary to control the business environment but there is also subjective deficiency, the corruption in the core of those controlling organisms.

The second line of defense that society has against the criminal phenomenon is to be found in the courts of law. Again, objective deficiencies in the system allows for criminals to walk free. But there are also subjective deficiencies sometimes generated by incompetence, sometimes by corruption.

There are two systems to conduct a trial: the adversarial system that is used in the common law systems and the inquisitorial system, used in continental law countries. Each system has his strong points but the problem here is that neither system is perfect; we have seen criminals walking free out of a court of law in both systems. The adversarial system and the inquisitorial system are medieval inventions and they are equally obsolete.

The laws of a country are of little importance if the judges are incapable or unwilling to clean their own society of these tares. A judge cannot invoke the deficiencies of his legal system; his duty is to perform in the existing legal framework. I do not know of a legal system in the world that does not incriminate theft, bribery, fraud, incriminations that are sufficient to cover most of the crimes of corruption.

Traditionally the power of the judge was absolute; the patriarch, the king, the emperor, they all played the role of the judge. The role of the lawmaker and law enforcer gave an enormous power to a single person, therefore, since antiquity, society developed models in which those powers are separated and shared in collective bodies.

Professional judges appeared when the number of cases was too large to manage by a single person, and the ruler delegated his power to other individuals. It is interesting to notice that the king's right to judge was of divine origin, and the rights of the professional judges were invested in them by the king's authority.

The person of the judge is surrounded by an aura of mystique; the robe, the wig and the hammer are symbols of power that do not belong in the space age. A judge is a person like any other, he or she do not poses any superpower, and there is no divine endorsement of the judgement. Because the judge is only human, he is susceptible to mistake or to corruption. The mistake or the unrighteous decision can be corrected by the courts of appeal or recourse or by the high courts. I cases where the judge is corrupt, the corrections in higher courts may be harder to apply.

The position of an honest judge in a corrupt system is a very difficult one. He is fighting on two fronts, from the bench, trying to see that the criminals are brought to justice and outside the court, trying to resist to a system that seeks to eliminate him, sometimes literally.

If the fight against corruption is more than a mere declaration of intent it is imperative that the process of cleaning starts with the justice system. And this is perhaps the hardest task. Judges and members of the legal profession are united by an *esprit de corps*, and in time they form personal relations that are stronger than the working relations in other professions.

A member of the legal profession, for personal reasons, might find it hard to prosecute or to judge a colleague, situation in which he must recuse himself. He must allow for other magistrates to see that justice is done. Here the sense of loyalty may be misplaced, the magistrate has taken an oath to serve justice not his colleagues; he is not bind in any way to protect or to cover the corrupt ones.

One last deficiency in the justice system that is important to be mentioned here is the fact that the system of privileges that a corrupt person enjoys is perpetuated in his punishment. The only form of punishment is the complete loss of special status and the 'degradation' to the rank of normal citizen. From this point the process of recovery for the corrupt person may begin.


## 5.4. Simplify the law

One of the reasons advanced societies collapsed, is the inefficiency of the justice system. Clogged with poorly written laws, the justice system becomes incapable of stopping corruption from growing.

In history, we have several examples when advanced States collapsed due to corruption. The new form of State administration enacted simpler laws, laws that can be understood and obeyed with ease. Perhaps it would be wise for the modern society not to experience a total collapse and decide to simplify the law while it is not too late.

The fight against corruption in the absence of a major legal reform will have little success. Let us not forget that the laws of today got us in this situation. It is simply not realistic to believe that in the same legal framework corruption can be contained, just by changing a few laws, or even worst, by enacting new ones.

In the European Union a wonderful opportunity has been missed; the European Constitution proved to be a major failure. What is stunning is the fact that the Treaty establishing a Constitution for Europe was rejected by referendum in France and in Netherlands, two of the countries that founded the European Economic Community in 1958.

The European Constitution[2] was a complex document, a hybrid between a Constitution and an International Treaty. Is hard to understand why the authors of the European Constitution did not learned from the American model which proved to be a success.

The role of the Constitution is to establish the fundamental rights and duties of the citizens and to create institutions that protect the respective rights and impose the respective duties. It is not for a Constitution to regulate policies, financial matters, labor and so on; beside The Charter of Fundamental Rights of the Union, the Union's justice system and the major institutions, not much more was needed.

The Constitution should have been completed by a Constitutional Code, a Criminal Code, a Civil Code and a Commercial Code and the result would have been a solid unitary legal system in the entire union. There is a lesson to be learned from the sad story of the European Constitution: politicians do not make good laws.

The superiority of a codified legal system is evident. This fact was acknowledged by the countries from the common law family and a movement for reform was initiated. In UK, Law Commissions Act 1965 created the Law Commission of England and Wales and the Scottish Law Commission. The aim of the Commissions is to ensure that the law is: fair, modern, simple, effective. After 50 years of reforms the number of codes in force is zero.

The United States Code[3] was published by the Office of the Law Revision Counsel of the U.S. House of Representatives, but this document is not a code of laws, as the term is understood by the continental lawyer; it is a compilation of statutes.

It is clear that in common law systems there is a strong resistance against major legal reforms. And there is a solid argument here. A swift codification process will make any judge, prosecutor or lawyer incompetent under the new law. The solution might be to actually write the codes and allow time before entry in force for the members of the legal professions to become acquainted with the new system.

Codification does not mean the binding of all existing statutes under a single cover; it is supposed to create a new, more effective, legal

---

[2] http://europa.eu/eu-law/decision- making/treaties/pdf/treaty_establishing_a_ constitution_for_ europe/
[3] http://uscode.house.gov/about_code.xhtml#.xhtml

system. The common law systems are based on the institution of precedent therefore it is very difficult to abandon the jurisprudence carefully constructed over several centuries.

In continental law systems the codes are hard to modify thru the regular legislative process. Therefore, legislators enact special laws to regulate a certain issue. The consequence is that conflicts of laws occur sooner or later and, in time, the codes become obsolete.

In the European Union a hybrid of the two systems was created, the decisions of the European Court of Justice and the European Court of Human Rights are applicable in similar cases. Beside the benefits of the two systems, some of the deficiencies were also inherited, making the justice process incredibly long and difficult. Another great opportunity to create a modern justice system was missed.

On top of all we have the international law that adds more and more documents, most of them necessary and animated by good intention as it is the case with the UNCAC, but also confusing, incomplete and poorly written.

Legal relations in modern society are the most complex that had existed in human history. It is obvious that we cannot return to the Code of Hammurabi, the Laws of Moses or the Law of the Twelve Tables in search for simplicity, but a lot of the legal ballast that our society carries can be laid to rest.

A better vision on our legal system may come from the academic environment. Where else can one find the most illuminated legal scholars and the most passionate drive to change the world for the better? I think it will be a good idea to stimulate competitions between universities to create new model codes, or laws, or legal procedures. The result, I'm sure will be impressive. Started as an intellectual exercise, such legal models may be a solid base for the laws and the legal systems of tomorrow.

But our purpose here is not to propose a new legal system or to correct the existing deficiencies. We must understand that the laws and the legal systems as they are now will not be able to eliminate corruption from our society.

The simplification of our laws will provide immense benefits. The speed of the judicial process will be significantly increased. The number of cases will decrease; no one goes to court when he knows that the law is clearly against him. The economic costs of the justice system will also diminish, allowing for those resources to be used for other purposes. Last, the most important consequence is that simpler laws will hit hard the phenomenon of corruption, especially in those facets that are hidden or masked under an appearance of legality.

## Final Conclusions

At the beginning of this project I believed that the eradication of the phenomenon of corruption from our society was possible; at the end I am convinced of the contrary.

The eradication of corruption at this level of social development is a non-realistic objective; we are not ready for such ambitious goal. The fight against corruption in the best case scenario will last decades and in the worst case will span over several generations.

I believe this to be a realistic view and not a defeatist one. By no means I intent to suggest that we should declare ourselves overpowered and lay down our weapons. On the contrary, we should multiply our efforts, by evaluating correctly the magnitude of the problem, by establishing a clear strategy and implementing legal reforms. Then and only then we can say that the fight against corruption has begun and hopefully this antisocial phenomenon will be eradicated.

I consider that the fight against corruption is not taken seriously. We do not have a clear strategy to combat corruption, there is no roadmap, we don't know where we want to go and what we want to achieve. We don't know how corrupt we are, therefore no one can say with certainty what kind of resources are needed to fight corruption. Almost nothing is done in educating people about the consequences of corruption, especially those materialized in millions of deaths, war, famine, terrorism, genocides.

A strategy to combat corruption should establish short, medium and long term objectives. Finding a way to quantify corruption in order to know what kinds of resources are necessary to fight it should be the first step. Without a proper quantification, the fight against corruption will be inefficient, even in the situation when excess resources are allocated, which is rarely the case.

The elimination of corruption from the justice system should be the first of the short terms objective. I have said it several times in this book that without the corruption in the justice system, this antisocial phenomenon cannot expand in the endemic phase.

One thing must be clearly understood, though; it is not for the justice system to act as a selective controller for corruption. As citizens, we are paying the wages for the policeman, prosecutor and judge to find, to indict and to apply a punishment if found guilty for those who broke the law. We are not paying taxes for a selective justice.

When we see a corrupt character finally brought before a court of law, we should also see the long line of servants in the justice system that failed to do their job. It is unacceptable that after a major case of corruption there is no accountability for those who allowed it to happen.

There are only two logical possibilities here; first, those allowing corrupt acts or contracts to happen are incompetents, then they should be given other jobs, and second, they are corrupt also, situation in which they should be removed from the system.

With the corruption from the justice system eliminated, medium term objective can be set and pursued. Legal reforms, organizational and structural reforms in the sectors affected by corruption, the creation of new institutions are among medium term objectives. If the elimination of corruption from the justice system costs next to nothing, the medium term objective involves vast resources in human power and money to be fulfilled.

Education is among the long term objective; it takes an awful long time to educate people, even when the results are in their best interest. Again, the achievement of the long term objectives will require enormous resources. But also, in this stage we will see the benefits of the previous steps beginning to show. This should be enough motivation to keep moving in the same direction.

I believe that corruption is the most complex antisocial phenomenon that humanity ever experienced. Throughout this book I've tried to explain that the phenomenon of corruption is far more complex than previously thought.

All the crimes in the statutes and criminal codes may be crimes of corruption. Any person can commit a corrupt act or can enter in a corrupt contract. The costs of corruption are far beyond any estimation; in fact I consider them to be impossible to calculate.

Blinded by sociological rankings, the western world is considering itself immune and safe from the ill effects of corruption. Since there is no scientific method to quantify corruption, all that is known with certainty is that the northern countries are more honest than the southern ones and that the western world is less corrupt that the oriental and eastern parts. We fail to see the obvious, the fact that the entire world is corrupt, from world leaders planning the next war in order to protect the billions they stole to fishermen turned pirates in the corner of Africa.

As a last thought, an exercise in imagination, we should ask ourselves how life would be in a world without corruption.

If corruption will be eradicated, we will achieve the long desired world peace since corruption is the spark that ignites the flames of war. In a world without war there will be no need for armies, except perhaps a small security armed force for unforeseen events. All the resources wasted for armament, war itself and cleaning up after the hostilities had ceased can be put to a better use in the interest of humanity.

With war out of the picture, underdeveloped countries will have the chance to build a functional economy and provide food, medical care and education for their citizens. Free trade will develop and the benefits of scientific and technological advancements will be enjoyed by all. Prosperity will reach those pockets of the world that today suffer from famine, droughts, endemic diseases; it will give those unfortunates a reason to live and not a reason to die.

Environment protection and sustainable development should be a real object of concern for all nations. The phenomenon of corruption is the primordial cause of crimes against environment. In a world without corruption, crimes against environment will be kept under control and their effects will be managed with ease. Nature has the power to regenerate itself if allowed and helped. The eradication of corruption will restore the populations of wildlife that had not been extinct by now. The levels of pollution in air and water will decrease, allowing a clean, healthy living, for all.

A corruption free society will be a happy society. Some of the major problems we are facing today will be eliminated naturally. Terrorism, genocides, ethnic cleansing, will disappear; even if corrupt leaders will accede to power from time to time, they will never find the human resource ready to follow them in criminal adventures.

The eradication of corruption will be a costly process involving a tremendous amount of money and the efforts of millions of people, in a timeframe of generations, but the benefits will be beyond anything we can imagine.

THE END

# Bibliography

## Books

Aristotle. *The Complete Works of Aristotle: The Revised Oxford Translation*. Edited by J. Barnes. Bollingen Series. Princeton, NJ: Princeton University Press, 1983.

Aquinas, St. Thomas. *Summa Theologica*. Literally translated by Fathers of the English Dominican Province. Second and revised edition. London: Burns Oates and Washbourne, 1920.

Augustine, St. *City of God* Translated by Henry Bettenson. London: Penguin Classics, 1984.

Augustine St. *The Confessions of St Augustine*. Translated by John K. Ryan. New York: Image Books, 1960.

Augustine St. *On the Free Choice of the Will*. Indianapolis: Hackett Publishing Co., 1993.

Bar, Karl Ludwig von. *A History of Continental Criminal Law*. Translated by Thomas S. Bell. Boston: Little, Brown &Co, 1916.

Bentham, Jeremy. *The Works of Jeremy Bentham*. Editor John Bowring. 11 vols. Edinburgh: William Tait, 1838-1843.

Benson M.L. and Simpson S.S. *White Collar Crime. An Opportunity Perspective*. New York: Routledge, 2009.

Blackstone, William. *Commentaries on the Laws of England*. Philadelphia: J.B. Lippincott Company, 1893.

Bohlander, Michael. *Principles of German Criminal Law*. Portland: Hart Publishing, 2009.

Bracton, Henry de. *De Legibus et Consuetudinibus Angliae*. 4 vols. Edited by G. E. Woodbine, translated by S. E. Thorne. London: Publications of the Selden Society, 1968–77.

Brissaud, Jean. *A History of French Public Law*. Boston: Little, Brown &Co., 1912.

Bruns, Carolus Georgius, Theodor Mommsen, Otto Gradenwitz. *Fontes Iuris Romani Antiqui*. Tübingen, Friburgi in Brisgavia: In Libraria Academia I.C.B. Mohrii (P. Siebeck), 1909.

Buckland, W.W. *A textbook on Roman law from Augustus to Justinian* Cambridge: Cambridge University Press, 1921.

Butler, Charles. *Memoir of the life of Henry-Francis D'Aguesseau.* London: John Murray, 1830.

Carawan, Edwin. *Rhetoric and the Law of Draco*. Oxford: Clarendon Press, 1998.

Carpzovii, Benedicti. *Practicae Novae Imperialis Saxonicae Rerum Criminalium*. Christiani Kirchneri, 1669.

Cicero. *The Orations of Marcus Tullius Cicero*. Translated by C.D. Yonge. London: G. Bell and Sons, 1913-21.

Coke, Edwardo. *The Institutes of Laws of England*. London: W. Clarke &Sons, 1817.

Coke, Edwardo. *Selected Writings and Speeches of Sir Edward Coke*, Edited by Steve Sheppard. Indianapolis: Liberty Fund, 2003.

Collier, J. G. *Conflict of laws*. Cambridge: Cambridge University Press, 2001

Cooke, John. *Law of tort*. Ninth edition. Harlow: Pearson Education Limited, 2009.

Crawford, M. H. *Roman Statutes* London: Institute Of Classical Studies, School Of Advanced Study, University Of London, 1996.

Crawford, Harriet. *Sumer and the Sumerians*. Cambridge: Cambridge University Press 1991, 2004

Diogenes Laertius. *The Lives and Opinions of Eminent Philosophers*. Translated by C.D. Yonge. London: Henry G. Bohn, 1853.

Dwyer, Philip G. and Peter McPhee. *The French Revolution and Napoleon. A sourcebook*. London: Routledge, 2002.

Einhard, *Life of Charlemagne*, Translated by Samuel Epes Turner. New York: Harper & Brothers, 1880.

Elliott, Catherine and Frances Quinn. Criminal Law, 3rd ed. Harlow: Pearson Education Limited, 2000.

Foot, Philippa. *Virtues and Vices and Other Essays in Moral, Philosophy.* Berkeley: University of California Press, 1978.

Falcone, Giovani. *Cose de la Cosa Nostra.* Milano: RCS Libri, 1998.

Gagarin, Michael. *Writing Greek law.* Cambridge: Cambridge University Press, 2008.

Gardner, Thomas, Terry Andersen. *Criminal Law.* Eleventh edition. Belmont: Wadsworth, Cengage Learning, 2012.

Garraud, Jean-René. *Traité théorique et pratique du droit pénal français.* Paris: Librairie de la Société du Recueil général des lois et des arrêts et du Journal du palais, 1898.

Gildenhard, Ingo. *Against Verres.* Cambridge: Open Book Publishers CIC Ltd., 2011.

Giustiniani Luigi, Rev. *Papal Rome as it is.* Baltimore: Publications Rooms 1843.

Glanville, Ranulf de. *A translation of Glanville.* Translated by John Beams. Washington: John Byrne & Co,1900.

Greene, Joshua D. M*oral Tribes, Emotion, Reason, and the Gap between Us and Them.* New York: The Penguin Press, 2013.

Hegel, Georg Wilhelm Friedrich. *Philosophy of Right*, Translated by T. M. Knox. Oxford : Oxford University Press, 1978.

Henderson, Ernest F. *Select historical documents of the Middle Ages.* London: Charles Bell and Sons, 1903.

Hume, David. *The Philosophical Works of David Hume.* In four volumes. Edinburgh: Printed For Adam Black And William Tait And Charles Tait,1826.

Johns, C. H. W. *Babylonian and Assyrian Laws, Contracts and Letters.* New York: Charles Scribner's Sons, 1904.

Johnston David, Reinhard Zimmermann, Editors. *Unjustified Enrichment: Key Issues in Comparative Perspective.* Cambridge: Cambridge University Press, 2004.

Kant, Immanuel. *Lecture on Ethics*, Edited by Peter Heath and J. B. Schneewind. Translated by Peter Heath. Cambridge: Cambridge University Press, 1997.

Kant, Immanuel. *Religion within the Bounds of Bare Reason.* Translated by Werner S. Pluhar. Introduction by Stephen Palmquist. Indianapolis/Cambridge: Hackett Publishing Company, 2009.

Kenny, Anthony. A New History of Western Philosophy. Volume I Ancient Philodophy. Volume II Medieval Philosophy. Volume III The Rise Of Modern Philosophy. Volume IV Philosophy in the Modern Word. New York: Oxford University Press, 2006 .

Langbein, John H. *Prosecuting Crime in the Renaissance: England, Germany, France*, Cambridge: Harvard University Press, 1974.

Levy, Neil. *Neuroethics Challenges for the 21st Century.* Cambridge: Cambridge University Press, 2007.

Liddick, Donald R. *Crimes against Nature.* Santa Barbara: Praeger, 2011.

Livy. *Rome and Italy Books VI–X. The History of Rome from its Foundation.* Translated and annotated by Betty Radice. London: Penguin Books, 1982.

Le Goff, Jacques. *Your money or your life.* Translated by Patricia Ranum. New York: Zone books, 1990.

Luther, Martin. *Works Of Martin Luther*, in two volumes. Albany: Books For The Ages, 1997.

Mann Richard A. and Barry S. Roberts. Smith & Roberson's Business Law. Fifteenth Edition. Stanford: Cengage Learning, 2012.

Markesinis, Sir Basil, Hannes Unberath and Angus Johnston. *The German Law of Contract. A Comparative Treatise.* Oxford: Hart Publishing, 2006.

Markesinis, Sir Basil and Hannes Unberath. *The German Law of Torts A Comparative Treatise.* Fourth edition. Oxford: Hart Publishing, 2002.

Molan, Michael. *Sourcebook on Criminal Law.* London: Cavendish Publishing, 2001.

Montesquieu. *The complete works of M. de Montesquieu*. Translated form French. London: T. Evans & W. Davis, 1977.

Mousourakis, George. *A legal history of Rome*. New York: Routledge, 2007.

Nietzsche, Friedrich. *On the Genealogy of Morals. Ecce Homo*. Translated by Walter Kaufmann and R. J. Hollingdale. New York: Random House, 1967.

Nietzsche, Friedrich. *Human, All Too Human*. Translated by R. J. Hollingdale. Cambridge: Cambridge University Press 1986, 1996.

Nietzsche, Friedrich. *The Gay Science*. Edited by Bernard Williams. Translated by Josefine Nauckhoff. Cambridge: Cambridge University Press, 2001.

Nietzsche, Friedrich. *The will to power*. Translated by Walter Kaufmann and R. J. Hollingdale. Edited by Walter Kaufmann. New York: Vintage Books, Random House,1967.

Ortolan. *The history of Roman law*. Translated by Iltudus T. Prichard, David Nasmit. London: Butterworths, 1871.

Oughton, David and Davis Martin. *Sourcebook on Contract Law*. Second edition. London: Cavendish Publishing, 2000.

Planiol, Marcel. *La Tres Ancienne Coutume de Bretagne*. Rennes: J. Plihon et L. Herve, Libraires-Editeurs, 1896.

Planiol, Marcel. *Traite Elementaire de Droit Civil*. Paris: Librarie Cotillon, 1902.

Plato. *Complete Works*. Edited by John M. Cooper and D. S. Hutchinson. Indianapolis: Hackett Publishing Company, 1997.

Plutarch. *Plutarch's Lives*. The Translation called Dryden's. Corrected from the Greek and Revised by A.H. Clough, in 5 volumes. Boston: Little Brown and Co., 1906.

Pollock, Sir Frederick and Frederic William Maitland. *The History of English Law before the Time of Edward I*. Reprint of 2nd edition, with a Select Bibliography and Notes by Professor S.F. Milsom. Indianapolis: Liberty Fund, 2010.

Pothier Robert Joseph. *Treatise on Obligations*. Newbern: Martin & Ogden, 1802.

Pothier, Robert Joseph. *Obligations considered in a Moral and Legal View*, 2 volumes. Newbern: Martin & Ogden, 1802.

Roth, Martha T. *Law Collections from Mesopotamia and Asia Minor*. Second edition. Georgia: Society of Biblical Literature Scholars Press, 1997.

Rousseau, Jean-Jacques. *The Social Contract and The First and Second Discourses*, Edited by Susan Dunn. New Haven: Yale University Press, 2002.

Rummel, R. J. *Death by government*. New Brunswick, NJ: Transaction Publishers, 1994.

Russell, Bertrand. *A History of Western Philosophy, And Its Connection with Political and Social Circumstances from the Earliest Times to the Present Day*. New York: Simon and Schuster, 1945.

Russell, Bertrand. *Education and the Social Order*. New York: Routledge, 2009.

Samaha, Joel. *Criminal Law*. Tenth edition. Belmont: Wadsworth, Cengage Learning, 2011.

Samuel, Geoffrey. *Law of Obligations and Legal Remedies*, Second edition. London: Cavendish Publishing, 2001.

Sarna, David E. Y. *History of Greed. Financial Fraud from Tulip Mania to Bernie Madoff*. Hoboken: John Wiley & Sons, Inc., 2010.

Scheb J. M. and J. M. Scheb. *Criminal law*. Sixth edition. Belmont: Wadsworth, Cengage Learning, 2012.

Schneider Peter and Jane Schneider. *Reversible Destiny. Mafia, Antimafia, and the Struggle for Palermo*. University of California Press, 2003.

Senior, Ian. Corruption – the World's Big C. Cases, Causes, Consequences, Cures. London: The Institute of Economic Affairs, 2006.

Somerset, Anne. *The Affair of the Poisons: Murder, Infanticide, and Satanism at the Court of Louis XIV* , St. Martin's Press, 2003.

Stephenson, Andrew. *A History of Roman Law*. Boston: Little, Brown and Co., 1912.

Staël de, Germaine. *Considerations on the Principal Events of the French Revolution*. Edited and translated by Aurelian Craiutu. Indianapolis: Liberty Fund, 2008.

Stein, Peter. *Roman Law in European History*. Cambridge: Cambridge University Press, 2004.

Stephen, James Fitzjames. *A history of Criminal Law of England*. London: McMillan & Co. 1883.

Stephenson, Andrew. *A History of Roman Law*. Boston: Little & Brown Company, 1912

Strachan-Davidson, James Leigh. *Problems of the Roman Criminal Law*. Oxford: Claredon Press, 1912.

Tellegen-Couperus, Olga. *Short History of Roman Law*. London: Routledge, 1993.

Thomsett, Michael C. *Heresy in the Roman Catholic church*. Jefferson: McFarland & Company, Inc., Publishers, 2011.

Voltaire, *The Works of Voltaire. A Contemporary Version*. 21 vols. Critique and Biography by John Morley. Translated by William F. Fleming New York: E.R. DuMont, 1901.

Vormbaum, Thomas. *A Modern History of German Criminal Law*. Edited by Michael Bohlander. Translated by Margaret Hiley. Berlin: Springer-Verlag, 2014.

Wright, David P. *Inventing God's law: how the covenant code of the Bible used and revised the laws of Hammurabi*. New York: Oxford University Press, 2009.

Williston, Samuel. *The law of contracts*. New York: Baker, Voorhis & Co., 1920.

Yoffee, Norman. *Myths of the Archaic State*. Cambridge: Cambridge University Press, 2004.

Zimmermann, Reinhard. *The Law of Obligations*. Roman Foundations of the Civilian Tradition.

John Maxcy Zane. *The Story of Law*. Second edition. Introduction by
   James M. Beck. New Foreword, Annotations, and Bibliographies
   by Charles J. Reid, Jr. Indianapolis: Liberty Fund, 1998.

*Articles*

Pound, Roscoe. *Liberty of Contract*, in Yale Law Journal, Volume 18.

Hall, Jerome. *Nulla poena sine lege* in The Yale Law Journal Vol. 47, No.
   2

*An Assessment of the Aldrich H. Ames Espionage Case and Its*
   *Implications for U.S. Intelligence Senate Select Committee on*
   *Intelligence*, 01 November 1994, on
   http://fas.org/irp/congress/1994_rpt/ssci_ames.htm

Johnston, David. *How the F.B.I. Finally Caught Aldrich Ames* on
   www.nytimes.com/1995/01/27/us/how-the-fbi-finally-caught-
   aldrich-ames.html

http://www.oecd.org/daf/anti-bribery/ConvCombatBribery_ENG.pdf,
   accessed on 1/19/2015

Taina Bien-Aime, *France Takes First Steps Towards Abolition of*
   *Prostitution* on http://www.huffingtonpost.com/ taina-
   bienaime/france-prostitution-laws_b_4775608.html

Edwin H. Sutherland, *White-Collar Criminality*, American Sociological
   Review, Vol. 5, No. 1 (Feb., 1940)

Cynthia Barnett, *The Measurement of White-Collar Crime Using*
   *Uniform Crime Reporting (UCR) Data*, on
   https://www.fbi.gov/stats-services/about-us/cjis/ucr/nibrs/nibrs_
   wcc.pdf

*Olympic horses fail drugs tests* on http://news.bbc.co.uk
   /sport2/hi/olympics/equestrian/7574220.stm;

*Dictionaries*

Bunnin Nicholas and Jiyuan Yu, editors. *Blackwell, Dictionary of*
   *Western Philosophy*. Blackwell Publishing, 2004.
Collin, P.H. *Dictionary of Law*, Forth edition. London: Bloomsbury
   Publishing.
Garner, Bryan A. editor. Black's Law Dictionary, Eight edition. 2004

Liddell, Henry George and Robert Scott, *A Greek English Lexicon*, (Oxford: Claredon Press, 1996.

Martin, Elisabeth. *A Dictionary of Law,* Fifth edition. Oxford: Oxford University Press, 2003.

## Web Resources

http://archive.org

www.archives.gov

www.bailii.org

http://conventions.coe.int

www.constitution.org

http://www.courts.state.ny.us

http://droitromain.upmf-grenoble.fr

http://www.fatf-gafi.org

http://fas.org

https://www.fbi.gov

www.genome.gov

http://www.humanistic texts.org

www.kchanson.com

http://ledroitcriminel.free.fr

http://www.legislation.gov.uk

http://www.lexinter.net

http://oll.libertyfund.org

www.papalencyclicals.net

http://www.newadvent.org

http://www.oecd.org

www.sec.gov

http://www.transparency.org

http://www.un-documents.net

http://www.unodc.org

http://uscode.house.go

https://www.wada-ama.org

http://www.washingtontimes.com

http://web.worldbank.org

# TABLE OF STATUTES

## *Ancient*

Code of Urukagina ca. 2350 BC
Code of Ur-Nammu ca. 2050 BC
Code of Hammurabi ca.1754 BC
Gortyn Code', ca. 5ᵗʰ century BC
Draco Ordinances, ca. 620 BC
Lycurgus Laws, ca. 700 BC
Solon Laws, ca. 594 BC
Leges Duodecim Tabularum 450 BC
Lex Poetelia De Ambitu 358 BC
Lex Licinia de Modo Agrorum 367 BC
Lex Thoria Agraria of 107 BC
Lex Genucia de Feneratione 342 BC
Lex Aemilia Balbia 182 BC
Lex Cornelia Baebia 181 BC
Lex Cornelia Fulvia 159 BC
Lex Maria 119 BC.
Lex Calpurnia 149 BC
Lex Gabinia Tabellaria 139 BC,
Lex Cassia Tabellaria 137 BC
Lex Papiria Tabellaria 131 BC
Lex Caelia Tabellaria 107 BC
De Corruptione Iudicis 74 BC
Lex Acilia Calpurnia 67 BC
Lex Tullia de Ambitu 63 BC
Rogatio Aufidia de Ambitu 61 BC
Rogatio Aufidia de Ambitu 61 BC
Lex Pompeia de Ambitu 52 BC
Lex Julia de Maritandus Omnibus 4 AD
Lex Julia de Adulteris Coercendis of 18 BC
Lex Papia Poppaea 9 AD
Lex Julia De Ambitu 18 BC
Lex de response prudentium 426 AD
Codex Gregorianus 291-294 AD
Codex Hermogenianus 293–94 AD
Codex Theodosianus 438 AD
Corpus Juris Civils 534 AD

## Medieval

La Loi Salique, ca. 500
Lex Romana Burgundionum, 500-506
Lex Romana Wisigothorum or Breviarium Alarici Regis, 506
Lex Romana Ostrogothorum or Edictum Theodorici Regis, 511-515
Capitulary de Charlemagne, 802
Ordinance of William the Conqueror, 1072
Dictatus papae, 1075
Bulla Aurea, 1213
Unam Sanctam, 1302
Bambergensis, 1507
Constitutio Criminalis Carolina, 1532
Act of Supremacy, 1534
Constitutio Criminalis Carolina, 1532
La coutume de Bretagne, ca.1320
Treason Act 1351, 1495, 1702, 1708, 1814
Exurge Domine, 1520
Ordonnance criminelle de 1670
Magna Charta, 1215
Codex Juris Bavarici criminalis, 1751
Constitutio criminalis Theresiana, 1769
Déclaration des Droits de l'Homme et du Citoyen de 1789
Code Pénal, 1791
Code des Délits et des Peines Du 3 brumaire, an 4 Contenant les Lois relatives à l'instruction des affaires criminelles, 1783
Loi Le Chapelier, 1791
Quum Memoranda, 1809
Code Des Délits Et Des Peines De 1810
Strafgesetzbuch für das Königreich Bayern, 1813

## Modern

### Codes of laws

Bürgerlichen Gesetzbuches, 1896
Code pénal, 1994
Code de procédure pénale, 1959
Code civil, 2015
Code de procédure civile, 2007
Strafgesetzbuch für das Deutsche Reich, 1871
Strafgesetzbuch, 2013
U.S. Code

**Statutes**

Abolition of Death Penalty Act, 1965
Act Regulating the Legal Situation of Prostitutes, 2002
Asylum and Immigration (Treatment of Claimants, etc.) Act, 2004
Anti-terrorism, Crime and Security Act, 2001
Annunzio - Wylie Anti - Money Laundering Act, 1992
Ballot Act, 1872
Bribery Act, 2010
Child Abduction Act, 1984
Coroners and Justice Act, 2009
Corrupt Practices and Prevention Act, 1854
Corrupt and Illegal Practices Prevention Act,1883
Counter-Terrorism Bill, 2008
Crime Control Act, 1990
Criminal Justice Act 1998, 2003
Criminal Damage Act, 1971
Espionage Act, 1917
Environmental Protection Act, 1990
Endangered Species Act
Fraud Act, 2006
Forgery and Counterfeiting Act, 1981
Homeland Security Act, 2002
Larceny Act of 1916
Lobbying and Disclosure Act, 1995
Mann Act, 1910
Money Laundering Regulations, 2007
Money Laundering Control Act, 1986
Money Laundering Suppression Act, 1994
Money Laundering and Financial Crimes Strategy Act, 1998
Parliamentary Elections Corrupt Practices Act, 1885
Policing and Crime Act, 2009
Prevention of Terrorism Act (Northern Ireland), 1974-89
Prevention of Terrorism Act, 2005
Proceeds of Crime Act, 2002
PROTECT Act, 2003
Public Order Act, 1986
RICO, 1970
Official Secrets Act 1911, 1920, 1989
Offences against the Person Act, 1861
Omnibus Counterterrorism Act, 1995
Sedition Act, 1918
Serious Organised Crime and Police Act 2005
Sexual Offences Act 1956, 2003
Street Offences Act 1959
Terrorism Act 2000, 2006
Theft Act, 1968
Toxic Substances Control Act, 1976

Transparency of Lobbying, Non-Party Campaigning and Trade Union Administration Act, 2014
USA PATRIOT Act, 2001
Controlled Substances Act, 1970
Water Resources Act, 1991

## International Conventions

Convention for the Surrender of Criminals Between the United States and France and Associated Documents, 1843

Convention to Suppress the Slave Trade and Slavery, 1925

Convention Concerning Forced or Compulsory Labour (28 Jun 30) as Modified by the Final Articles Revision Convention, 1946

United Nations Charter, 1945

UNESCO - Constitution of the United Nations Educational, Scientific and Cultural Organisation, 1945

Universal Declaration of Human Rights proclaimed by the United Nations General Assembly in Paris, 1948

Convention for the Suppression of the Traffic in Persons and of the Exploitation of the Prostitution of Others, 1950

The Single Convention on Narcotic Drugs, 1961, amended by the Protocol Convention on Psychotropic Substances, 1972

Convention against Illicit Traffic in Narcotic Drugs and Psychotropic Substances, 1988

Inter-American Convention Against Corruption of 1996

OECD Convention on Combating Bribery of Foreign Public Officials in International Business Transactions, 1997

Convention on the Fight against Corruption involving Officials of the European Communities or Officials of Member States of the European Union signed at Brussels, 1997

United Nations Convention against Transnational Organized Crime and the Protocol to Prevent, Suppress and Punish Trafficking in Persons especially Women and Children adopted by General Assembly resolution 55/25, 2000

United Nations Convention against Corruption adopted by the General Assembly by resolution 58/4, 2003

International Convention against Doping in Sport adopted by the 33rd UNESCO General Conference on October 19, 2005

Council of Europe Convention on Action against Trafficking in Human Beings, 2005

The Directive 2008/99/EC of the European Parliament and of the Council of the European Union of 19 November 2008

# TABLE OF CASES

Salem witchcraft trials 1692 -1693, 1878

Anna Göldi case of 1782

Barbara Zdunk case of 1811

Helen Duncan case of 1944

Lipkin Gorman v Karpnale Ltd., 1991

People of the State Of New York, v. Julio Gonzalez, 1995

Banque Financière de la Cité v. Parc (Battersea) Ltd., 1999

United States v. Marc E. Thompson, 2008

United States v. Bernard L. Madoff, 2009

Georgia Malone & Co. v. Rieder, 2012

Director of Public Prosecutions, Gauteng v Pistorius, 2015

Julien Patureau contre Boudier, 1892

# Abbreviations

BGB - Bürgerlichen Gesetzbuches

CC - Code civil

CCC - Constitutio Criminalis Carolina

CCF - Code Civil des Français

CPC - Code de procédure civile

CP - Code pénal

CPP - Code de procédure pénale

CPI - Corruption Perception Index

StGB - Strafgesetzbuch

TI - Transparency International

UDHR - Universal Declaration of Human Rights

UNCAC - United Nations Convention against Corruption

UNTOC - United Nations Convention against Transnational Organized Crime

# Index

act, 14, 23, 33, 36, 37, 40, 49, 50, 55, 56, 69, 74, 76, 83, 85, 86, 93, 113, 115, 122, 126, 130, 131, 134, 139, 140, 144, 145, 146, 147, 148, 149, 150, 153, 155, 156, 157, 158, 159, 160, 161, 162, 163, 164, 165, 167, 168, 171, 172, 173, 178, 179, 180, 181, 183, 185, 186, 187, 188, 189, 190, 194, 196, 197, 198, 202, 207, 209, 210, 218, 223, 227, 228, 230, 231

actio, 20

action, 23, 24, 46, 75, 82, 103, 104, 106, 109, 110, 122, 135, 137, 143, 144, 145, 148, 149, 152, 153, 156, 157, 159, 161, 162, 164, 165, 166, 167, 168, 171, 172, 175, 177, 180, 182, 185, 190, 192, 195, 198, 214, 231, 243

*actus reus*, 53, 86, 183, 185, 193, 207

adultery, 9, 10, 13, 23, 30, 40, 45, 46, 56, 58, 74, 75, 77, 81

*ambitu*, 55

anticorruption, 14, 33

antisocial, 2, 53, 114, 139, 140, 141, 142, 143, 156, 178, 179, 181, 184, 194, 217

Aquinas, 4, 37, 82, 83, 84, 85, 86, 98, 249

Aristotle, 4, 12, 13, 15, 16, 65, 67, 70, 72, 73, 74, 75, 76, 77, 81, 82, 83, 103, 105, 121, 222, 249

atheism, 36, 52, 88, 101

Augustine, 4, 34, 43, 78, 79, 80, 81, 82, 98, 249

avarice, 24, 36, 90, 94, 95, 111

Bernie Madoff, 6, 204, 240, 254

blackmail, 12, 196, 210, 215, 216

blasphemy, 37, 46, 53, 60, 87

bribery, 3, 10, 13, 18, 20, 23, 27, 50, 60, 63, 94, 113, 114, 131, 132, 136, 137, 139, 146, 153, 157, 158, 160, 161, 162, 163, 176, 178, 195, 199, 200, 201, 220, 224, 225, 244

capacity, 132, 149, 154, 159, 160, 161, 162, 170, 172, 178, 185, 193, 229

Church, 3, 4, 25, 26, 29, 34, 35, 36, 37, 38, 39, 40, 41, 42, 43, 44, 45, 47, 56, 78, 82, 86, 88, 101, 105, 106, 107, 116, 119

common law, 4, 38, 47, 59, 61, 105, 140, 147, 151, 152, 168, 173, 174, 179, 180, 182, 183, 194, 196, 202, 207, 208, 209,

210, 212, 217, 232, 244, 245, 246, 247

communism, 105, 118, 225, 226

contract, 28, 40, 66, 91, 93, 103, 141, 146, 147, 148, 150, 151, 152, 153, 154, 155, 157, 159, 160, 161, 162, 163, 165, 168, 169, 171, 172, 173, 176, 177, 178, 185, 190, 191, 199, 202, 207, 208, 213, 226, 227

*Corpus Juris Civils*, 22, 25, 45, 259

counterfeiting, 23, 27, 33, 49, 55, 161, 198, 199, 220

courts, 16, 19, 21, 31, 33, 52, 73, 93, 112, 150, 151, 152, 166, 167, 168, 170, 173, 219, 244

crime, 14, 23, 30, 31, 38, 39, 40, 46, 49, 50, 53, 60, 77, 79, 86, 89, 103, 107, 112, 121, 123, 124, 134, 135, 137, 144, 158, 162, 163, 165, 174, 176, 177, 179, 180, 181, 182, 183, 184, 185, 186, 187, 188, 189, 190, 192, 193, 195, 196, 197, 198, 199, 201, 202, 203, 204, 206, 207, 208, 209, 210, 211, 212, 213, 217, 218, 219, 220, 221, 224, 225, 229, 230, 243

crimes against environment, 2, 221, 222

doping, 223, 224

Draco, 13, 15, 77, 208, 250, 258

drug trafficking, 2, 141, 148, 243

embezzlement, 19, 20, 23, 27, 48, 49, 58, 63, 73, 96, 114, 132, 136, 137, 138, 157, 160, 194, 195, 220

envy, 14, 36, 87, 127

Epicurus, 12, 127

espionage, 54, 184, 185, 186, 187, 188, 189, 190, 191, 192, 203

ethics, 4, 12, 65, 83, 98, 101, 109, 116, 117, 119, 120, 121, 124, 126, 178, 229

evil, 18, 30, 33, 37, 39, 74, 75, 79, 80, 81, 83, 86, 88, 92, 98, 99, 100, 104, 106, 109, 115, 127, 152, 185

extortion, 13, 20, 27, 29, 49, 51, 58, 96, 132, 136, 163, 196, 197

Favoritism, 228

forgery, 23, 27, 33, 45, 46, 48, 55, 61, 63, 150, 176, 177, 198, 199, 220

fraud, 13, 15, 23, 54, 58, 85, 103, 138, 139, 149, 151, 173, 195, 202, 203, 204, 205, 211, 244

God, 10, 25, 29, 33, 36, 37, 38, 43, 58, 78, 80, 81, 82, 83, 85, 88, 98, 100, 101, 107, 249, 255

guilt, 9, 183, 230, 231

Hammurabi, 9, 10, 255, 258

Hegel, 4, 101, 102, 103, 104, 105, 251
heresy, 37, 42, 43, 46, 50, 53, 60, 82, 85, 88, 112
homicide, 13, 31, 33, 46, 50, 207, 208, 217
illegal, 7, 84, 122, 123, 133, 139, 140, 141, 142, 143, 144, 145, 146, 147, 148, 149, 150, 151, 152, 153, 154, 155, 156, 160, 163, 165, 168, 169, 172, 173, 178, 181, 183, 195, 197, 198, 201, 202, 203, 208, 213, 214, 215, 220, 221, 223, 225, 243
incest, 30, 31, 36, 40, 46, 58, 211
insanity, 159, 230
judges, 11, 28, 29, 31, 48, 60, 65, 68, 89, 95, 97, 102, 118, 138, 150, 172, 244
jurists, 11, 17, 18, 21, 22, 25, 32, 49, 56, 59
justice, 3, 11, 12, 13, 22, 23, 28, 29, 32, 33, 34, 44, 49, 50, 60, 62, 63, 66, 68, 70, 74, 75, 76, 77, 84, 85, 89, 93, 102, 105, 112, 134, 144, 176, 181, 197, 206, 215, 220, 225, 231, 235, 243, 244, 245
Kant, 4, 98, 99, 100, 101, 105, 123, 251
lèse-majesté, 33, 49
Lycurgus, 7, 14, 77, 208, 258
manslaughter, 50, 207, 208

moral, 3, 4, 7, 12, 21, 34, 44, 62, 65, 67, 70, 73, 79, 80, 90, 91, 99, 100, 101, 103, 104, 105, 107, 108, 109, 110, 113, 114, 116, 117, 119, 123, 126, 131, 132, 136, 144, 149, 150, 153, 154, 156, 166, 178, 183, 203, 212, 225, 228, 231
morals, 4, 12, 23, 30, 65, 78, 83, 92, 98, 106, 107, 110, 119, 120, 121, 125, 126, 146, 147, 152, 154, 226
murder, 8, 9, 10, 12, 13, 15, 20, 30, 32, 36, 39, 45, 48, 50, 57, 71, 75, 81, 103, 111, 176, 207, 208, 209, 226
Nepotism, 39, 228
Nietzsche, 105, 106, 107, 108, 109, 252, 253
nullity, 171, 172, 173
offence, 36, 49, 54, 57, 60, 61, 87, 131, 134, 136, 144, 160, 161, 162, 163, 164, 165, 166, 167, 168, 170, 176, 183, 195, 196, 197, 198, 200, 202, 206, 208, 209, 212, 213, 214, 223, 228, 229, 231, 243
patrimony, 35, 91, 105, 169, 170, 171, 228
Plato, 4, 12, 14, 15, 67, 68, 69, 70, 71, 72, 80, 81, 82, 125, 253
Plutarch, 11, 14, 253
Pope, 32, 34, 38, 39, 40, 41, 42, 43, 44, 52, 86

privileges, 1, 37, 51, 52, 63, 91, 97, 121, 127, 128

propriety, 10, 16, 18, 19, 24, 27, 35, 45, 55, 56, 91, 113, 144, 156, 174, 176, 184, 189, 193, 194, 195, 196, 202, 203, 205, 206, 217, 230, 231, 242

rape, 8, 9, 12, 13, 27, 30, 32, 33, 36, 40, 45, 46, 50, 55, 211, 212

religion, 8, 12, 25, 27, 30, 36, 38, 44, 49, 51, 52, 58, 60, 64, 66, 69, 77, 80, 97, 99, 100, 101, 105, 107, 116, 117, 119, 120, 189, 218, 226

rights, 3, 5, 19, 32, 39, 49, 51, 54, 59, 60, 93, 131, 134, 142, 144, 159, 161, 171, 193, 204, 206, 218, 219

robbery, 9, 10, 20, 30, 32, 33, 45, 46, 58, 71, 75, 196

sabotage, 184, 186, 188, 189

sacrilege, 53, 81

sedition, 31, 110, 184, 188

sin, 4, 36, 37, 39, 63, 79, 80, 83, 84, 85, 86, 100

Solon, 13, 15, 16, 18, 77, 79, 208

terrorism, 2, 142, 176, 184, 189, 201, 222, 235

terrorism,, 2, 142, 177, 189, 201

theft, 12, 18, 30, 33, 45, 46, 47, 56, 61, 71, 73, 75, 85, 156, 176, 194, 195, 197, 205, 244

treason, 19, 20, 28, 33, 45, 49, 51, 54, 57, 60, 71, 174, 184, 185, 186, 187

undue advantage, 134, 135, 136, 145, 157, 158, 163, 164, 227, 228

Urukagina, 9, 258

Usury, 18, 39, 85

War, 1, 46, 56, 57, 141, 186, 187, 192, 225

white color crimes, 218

witchcraft, 30, 37, 38, 46, 50, 53, 60

wrong, 16, 33, 53, 60, 66, 90, 103, 115, 120, 138, 139, 144, 180, 192, 202, 220

This page intentionally left blank